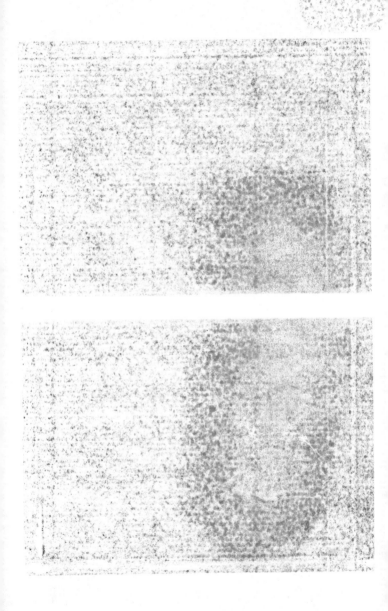

ENGLISH RECUSANT LITERATURE
1558–1640

Selected and Edited by
D. M. ROGERS

Volume 349

LEONARDUS LESSIUS
Rawleigh his Ghost
1631

LEONARDUS LESSIUS
Rawleigh his Ghost
1631

The Scolar Press
1977

ISBN o 85967 388 x

Published and printed in Great Britain by
The Scolar Press Limited, 59-61 East Parade,
Ilkley, Yorkshire and
39 Great Russell Street,
London WC1

NOTE

Reproduced (original size) from a copy in Cambridge University Library, by permission of the Syndics.

References: Allison and Rogers 460; STC 15523.

RAVVLEIGH

HIS

GHOST.

Or, A Feigned Apparition of *Syr VValter Rawleigh*, to a friend of his, for the tran-flating into English, the Booke of *Leonard Leffius* (that moft learned man) entituled, *De prouidentia Numinis*, *& Animi immorta-litate*: written againft *Atheifts*, and *Poli-titians* of thefe dayes.

Tranflated by A. B.

Quæ hæc fumma delicti, nolle illum agnofcere, quem ignorare non poffis? *C. prim. l. de Idolorum vanitate*.

Permiffu Superiorum. M. DC. XXXI.

THE
APPARITION

to his Friend.

EARE Friéd, whome I much prized, whiles my foule was inuefted with Flefh, & my Body enioyed the Ayre, which now thou breatheft. My Spirit is, at this tyme, permitted by the Almighty to appeare to thee, to intreat a Boone, or Fauour. Thou well knoweft, that the World (whofe dialect is euer deliuered in the blacke notes of Obloquy and Reproach,) hath at fundry

* 2   tymes,

tymes, caſt a fou!e, & moſt vniuſt aſperſion vpon Me, for my
preſumed deniall of a *Deity*. Frō
which abhominable and horrid
crime, I was euer moſt free. And
not any man now liuing, better
knoweth the ſame, thē thy ſelfe,
in whoſe preſence (if thou doeſt
remember) I was often accuſtomed highly to praiſe and eſteeme
the Booke of *Leſſius*, written in
proofe of the being of a *Deity*, &
entituled, *De prouidētia Numinis*.

Since then, that Treatiſe euen
fruſtrateth with ſhame and con-
fuſion, all the impugners of ſo illuſtrious and euident a Principle
(Charactered in our Soules by
Gods owne ſeale;) therefore my
humble, and earneſt requeſt is,
that thou wouldſt take the paines
to

The Apparition.

to translate the said Treatise into English; and let the Title beare my Name, that so the Readers, may acknowledge it, as done by my sollicitation. In the performance of which labour (besides the accomplishmét of my desire heerein) thou payest some small Tribute of that Homage to him who gaue thee & me our Being: *In ipso* enim *vivimus, mouemur, & sumus.* So wishing thee true felicity, and the world more charity in its Censures, I am in hast to leaue thee, since my Spirit is not suffered to stay any longer vpon earth ; but must returne with speedy wing, to the place from whence it came.

The Ghost of W. *Rawleigh.*

*3

THE

TRANSLATOVR

to the Reader.

OVRTEOVS Rea-
der, seing the iniquities of
these dayes are such, that
diuers men there are , of
so flagitious liues , in their conuersa-
tion and manners ; that they liue as
though there were neither God, Hea-
nen , Hell , or any Immortality of
the soule; *and it is to be feared, that*
diuers of thē, are in their secret iudg-
mēts so inwardly perswaded: Ther-
fore for the awakening of all such, so
monstrously peruerted and blynded, I
haue taken the paynes to translate
this ensuing Treatise, written by the
most learned Iesuite Leonard Les-
sius (*a man in these tymes of extra-*
                                                    er

*ordinary talents in learning) wherin
by many moſt irrefragable argumēts
is conuinced, and proued the* Being
of a Deity, *and,* the Immortality
of the Soule.

*I haue feigned the occaſion hereof
to be an Apparition of* Syr Walter
Rawleighs Ghoſt, *to a liuing fried,
of his, intreating of him to tranſlate
the ſame. My reaſon of vſinge this
Fiction is, becauſe it is well knowne,
that* Syr Walter, *was a mā of great
Naturall Parts, and yet was ſuſ-
pected of the moſt foule and execrable
crime of Atheiſme. How truly,
God and himſelfe only know; though
I muſt thinke the beſt of him, & the
rather in regard of that moſt excellent, and learned Deſcription of God,
which himſelfe ſetteth downe in the*

firſt

To the Reader.

first lines of his History or Cronicle.

Now, in regard of his eminency in the world when he was aliue. I am the more eafily perfwaded, that the very Name of him (by way of this feigned Apparition, and the like anfwerable Title of the Tranfiatio) may beget in many an earneft defire of perufing this Booke; and fo become the more profitable. I hope for taking this method, I cannot be iuftly blamed; for if I haue offended any, it muft be Syr Walter himfelfe. But him I haue not wronged, fince I do vindicate, & free him from the former blot, as prefuming him to be innocent of the fufpected Crime. And thus(good Reader) thou haft the reafon of this my proceding. And fo I remit thee to the Treatife it felfe.

A.B.

THE

TABLE

OF CHAPTERS.

The first Booke, of the Being of a God.

VVHO they were, that denied a *Deity*: and what were the Reasons perfua-
ding them thereto *Chap.* 1. *pag.* 2.

2. That there is one fupreme power, by whofe Prouidence all things are gouerned; is made e-
uident by many reasons.   *pag.* 11.

3. The firft Reafon is taken from the confeffió of all Countryes, and of all wife men. *pag.* 13.

4. The fecond Reafon drawne from the motion of the heauenly Orbes.   *pag* 19.

5. The 3 Reafon taken from that, that corpore-
all fubftances, and fuch as are fubiect to the eye and fight, cánot haue their being by Cháce, or Fortune.   *pag* 27.

6. The 4. Reafon, from the beauty of things, and the ftructure, and compofition of the parts, in refpect of the whole.   *pag.* 41.

7. The

THE TABLE.

7. The 5. Reason drawne from the structure and disposition of the Parts of the world, with reference to their ends. *pag.* 59.

8. The 6. Reason borrowed from the structure of making of liuing Creatures, and Plants, with reference to an end. *pag.* 86.

9. The 7. Reasō, that all things do worke most orderly to a certayne end. *pag.* 114.

10. The 8. Reason from the diuersity of mens Countenances and voyces, and frō the Pouerty of Man. *pag.* 145.

11. The 9 Reason, is from Miracles. *pag.* 154.

12. The 10. Realō taken frō Prophesies *p.* 177.

13. The 11. Reason taken frō Spirits. *pag.* 206.

14. The 12. Reason, taken frō the absurdities, rising from the contrary doctrine. *pag.* 216.

15. The 13. Reason drawne from the immortality of the Soule. *pag.* 226.

16. The 14. Reason taken from diuers exāples of diuine reuenge, and benignity. *pag.* 229.

17. The 15. Reason taken from the secret puniffhing of Blasphemy, Periury, and Sacriledge. *pag.* 262.

18. The Argumēts asswered which are broght against the being of a *Prouidence*, and a *Deity*. *pag.* 276.

19. The second Argumēt against the *Diuine Prouidence*, answered. *pag.* 282.

20. The third Argument. *pag.* 186.

21. The fourth Argument. *pag.* 288.

22. The fifth Argument. *pag.* 289.

THE

The second Booke.

WHEREIN is proued the Immortality of the Soule. *Chap.* 1. *pag.*296.

2. The first Reason, prouing the soules Immortality. *pag.* 303.

3. The second Reaso prouing the same. *p.* 303

4. The third Reason. *pag.* 305.

5. The fourth Reason. *pag.* 307.

6. The fifth Reason. *pag.* 308.

7. The fixt Reason. *pag.* 309.

8. The seauenth Reason. *pag* 313.

9. The eight Reason. *pag.* 316.

10. The ninth Reason. *pag.* 317.

11. The tenth Reason. *pag.* 320.

12. The eleuenth Reason. *pag.* 321.

13. The twelth Reason. *pag.* 325.

14. The 13. Reason. *pag.* 326.

15. The 14 Reason. *pag.* 328.

16. The 15. Reason. *pag.* 330.

17 The 16. Reason. *pag.* 339.

18 The 17 Reason. *pag.* 343.

19. The 18. Reason. *pag.* 362.

20. The 19. Reason. *pag.* 368.

21. The 20. Reason. *pag.* 375.

22. The 21. Reason. *pag.* 377.

23. The 22. and last Reason. *pag.* 382.

24. The Arguments obiected against the Immortality of the soule, & their solutions or Answers. *pag.* 388.

25. Of the Punishments of the life to come, out of holy Scripture. *pag.* 413.

26. The Conclusion. *pag.* 441.

THE

THE

PREFACE

of the Authour.

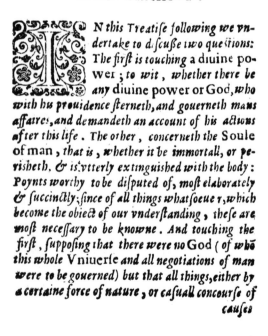

IN this Treatise following we vndertake to discusse two questions: The first is touching a diuine power; to wit, whether there be any diuine power or God, who with his prouidence sterneth, and gouerneth mans affaires, and demandeth an account of his actions after this life. The other, concerneth the Soule of man, that is, whether it be immortall, or perisheth, & is vtterly extinguished with the body: Poynts worthy to be disputed of, most elaborately & succinctly; since of all things whatsoeuer, which become the obiect of our vnderstanding, these are most necessary to be knowne. And touching the first, supposing that there were no God (of whō this whole Vniuerse and all negotiations of man were to be gouerned) but that all things, either by a certaine force of nature, or casuall concourse of

causes

causes had their euents ; then should we be freed of great feare for the things to come, and might securely and without all impunity do what soeuer were best pleasing to our owne dispositions . For then no man were obliged to yield an account (after the death of the body) for things done in his life time ; no man for his sinnes should hereafter be punished ; neither should any reward attend the faithfull and vertuous. Finally , neither of what comportment , carriage , and conuersation a man is , should it be (after the dissolution of the body from the soule) either preiudiciall, or beneficiall vnto him. Since sinne then, should be nothing, but a certaine aëry , imaginary , and a false conceit, of a law violated , & a diuine power offeded.

But now, once acknowledging that there is a God *(through whose prouidence and prescience all things are guided and measured) then it ineuitably followeth , that we ought greatly to feare and reuerence him , and be most cautelous , and wary , that we do not infringe his lawes & sactions ; Since it is most certaine , that he will exact an account after this life , and will inflict due punishments vpon sinners. For it is a point principally iucumbent and belonging to a gouernour , to giue a iust retaliation and retribution to men, recompensing their enormities and vyces with punishments , and their vertues with honours and rewards . All kinds of Gouerments, aswell of the*
worses

The Preface

worser sort, whether they be Tyrannicall, Oligarchicall, *and* Democraticall, *as of the better,* as Monarchicall, Aristocratical, *or* Political, *or any other kind of* Regiment *compounded of these, do vnanimously confirme & warrant this assertion. For it is most euident, that all these haue euer set downe rewards and punishments, grounding themselues vpon these, as vpon certaine foundations, without the which they cannot in any sort subsist or continue. Therefore admitting that there ought to be proposed both rewards and chastisments, thereby to debarre men from vice & incyte them to vertue; It also followeth, that this diuine power is mightily to be feared, of al mē, least they do incurre his indignation, & least they purchase to themselues his iust reuenge. For no man is able to resist him; no man of power to auoyde his power; to be short, no man there is, which liueth not within the boūds of his dominatiō.*

Wherefore euery one is chiefly to be most circumspect, that he doth not deny the existence & being of this power, and that he seeke not to depriue it of prouidence in the disposall of the world, and of all things comprehended therein; except it euidently aforehand can be euicted by conuincing & solid reasons, that no such Diuinity or Power there is; but that the being thereof is suggested & supposed out of a humane conceit, only for Policy sake: for in the intertaining a rash conceit herof,

A man

a man expoſeth himſelſe to the perpetrating of the greateſt offence that can be imagined, ſince gra̅ting the being of ſuch a Deity, the denyers therof ſtand culpable of a moſt heinous blaſphemy, and of ſpirituall treaſon againſt ſo great a Maieſty for as that ſubiect extremly wrongeth his King, who̅ he denyeth to be King, or his kingdome to be ſubiect vnto him; though this his denyall be grounded vpon ſome outward ſhewes of probability: Euen ſo, who auerreth the not being of a ſupreme power (by the which the world and the things therin are ruled) committeth a moſt heinous cryme againſt God, and reſteth guilty of the higheſt diſloyalty againſt ſo powerfull a Deity, though otherwiſe he may ſeeme to ſhadow ſuch his blaſphemy vnder the tecture of ſome weake & feeble reaſo̅s. Which point being ſo, what then remaineth for ſuch a man to expect, then a moſt heauy reuenge to be inflicted vpon him, for his deniall of ſo ſoueraigne, and ſo ſupreme a Power.

Now then, from this it appeareth, how abſolutly neceſſary to man is the indubious and certaine confeſſion and acknowledgement of the being of a God. And indeed the knowledge of the condition and nature of mans ſoule is not much leſſe to be ſearched after: for if it could be proued that the Soule of man were mortall (as the ſoule in beaſts is) the̅ ſhould we not need to ſtand in feare of what hereafter might fall vpon vs; but we

might

The Preface.

might securely lead a careles & pleasurable life, best sorting to our owne desires and sensuality.

Now, if the contrary hereto shalbe demonstrated to be most true (as infallibly it will) the haue we reason to be most anxious, fearfull, and sollicitous, least by our wicked life, and Conuersation our soule after death may incurre most dreadfull and eternall torments. Of both these points I discourse in this treatise; to wit, in the first booke of the Being of a God, & a supreme diuine power. In the second of, the Soules Immortality. The contemplation of voth which is most gratfull, pleasing, and comfortable. For the presence of a Deity & his prouidence wonderfully shineth both in the whole fabrick of the world, and in the creatures contained therein; as also in the most wise disposall and gouernment of the same things. The immortality of the soule is made demonstrable by force of many irrefragable and conuincing arguments. Both these shalbe disputed off, with as much breuity and perspicuity, as possible I can; omitting diuers curious and sublyme points, which might otherwise serue to entagle the Reader, and to diuert his iudgment from the principall scope intended by me; since my desire herein is, that what is here vndertaken, may not be performed out of any idle ostentation, and vanity, but only for the spirituall fruite and benefit of the studious Reader.

SYR

SYR WALTER
RAVVLEIGH
HIS GHOST.

Of the being of a *Diuine power*, or *God*; and of his *Prouidence*.

LIB. I.

N the firſt place here, I will recall to light the names of ſuch of the ancient Authours who haue denyed a *Deity*, or a *Diuine power*, by the which the affaires of men are gouerned; and will produce the chiefeſt argumêts vſed by them heerein. Secondly, I will ſet downe the contrary ſentence impugned by the former Men; and will fortify it with many conuincing & vnanſwerable arguments or demôſtrations. Thirdly, I will anſwere, and ſatisfy the Reaſons vrged by the aduerſaries party.

A

VVho

VVHO THEY VVERE, THAT DENY-
ed a Deity : and what were the reaſons perſwa-
ding them therto .

CHAP. I.

AMONG the Ancients, ſome are found , who denying all *Diuine Power* (by the which the world is gouerned) did take away al Diuinity. Others though granting a heauély & ſupernaturall power, did neuertheles deny the prouidéce of the ſaid power in particuler things (and eſpecially in actions proceeding from mans freewil) moued therto through a ſhew of ſome one or other weake reaſon , which themſelues were not able to anſweare . Thoſe who abſolutly denyed a *Deity* were but few , of whom the chiefe were *Diagoras Mileſius* , & *Protagoras Abderites* (both being ſchollers of *Democritus* , & *Theodorus* comonly called the *Atheiſt* (being a moſt impure & impudent Sophiſter) . To theſe may be adioyned *Bion Boriſthenites* (Scholler of *Theodorus)* of whom we may read in *Suidas* in his Lexicon, and *Laertius l . 2 & 9 . de vitis Philoſophorum* . With theſe former may be alſo marſhalled *Lucian* the ſcorner of all diuine powers, and the bitter enemy of Chriſtians, **who**

who for his impiety was torne afuder with dogs, as *Suidas* witnesseth . *Pliny* also is to be ranged among the foresaid Atheifts; who in his second book c. 7 .doubteth , whether besides the Sun (which he calleth the chiefeft gouernour, & *Numen* of Nature) there were any other power, or any other God;for thefe are his words, *Quifquis est Deus &c. Whofoeuer that God is(if any fuch be)he is in euery part:whole fenfe, whole fight , whole hearing , whole foule, whole mind. & finally whole in himfelfe* : & after refuting the Gods of the Gentils, he further faith: *Deus est &c. He is faid to be a God, who helpeth others, and this is the way to purchafe eternal glory . This path the worthy and noble Romans did tread , and in this* Vefpafianus Augustus, *the most eminent gouernour in all ages, walked with his children, alwaies fupporting the decaying state of men. And that fuch men should be ranged and marshalled in the number of Gods, was the most auncient manner of shewing thankefulnes & gratitude to men wel deferuing.* And then after, the fayd Authour further writeth : *'t is to be laughed at, to fay , That that cheife and fupreme power(whatfoeuer it is) hath any folicitude or care of humane things; for may we not then wel belieue, that then it followeth , that the fayd* Numen, *or Diuine power should be contaminated and defiled with fo wearifome, and fo multiplicious a charge and negotiation?*

A 2   Now

Now *Democritus, Heraclitus, Epicurus,* **and** *Lucretius* acknowledging a *Numen* or diuinity, denyed only all prouidence of the sayd power; since they maintained, that al things did happen either by force of Nature (as *Lactantius* sheweth *l. 2. de ira Dei.c. 9. & 1 0.*) or els by the casuall concourse & meeting of infinit *Atomi,* as is euidently gathered out of *Lucretius:* and according to the iudgment of some, *Aristotle* is auerred to be of the said opinion, who in the 12. booke of his *Metaphysicks cap* 9. writeth, *that it is an absurd thing, that prima Mens, the first mind* (for so he calleth God) *should haue a care of some thinges; & more fitting it were, that he should not see such thinges, as see them.* Yet the contrary hereto he intimateth in the tenth booke of his *Ethicks cap.8* in regard whereof I hould him rather to be freed from that imputation, then otherwise. *Cicero* in his second booke de *diuinatione,* taketh away all prescience and foreknowledg of thinges to come, especially of thinges depending on the freedome of mans wil; & his reason is, in that he thinketh this foreknowledge carryeth with it a necessity of the euent of thinges: vpon which ground he also denyeth all diuination and prouidence. Among men of later tymes many may be foũd denying the Dininity it selfe, but few who deny only the foreknowledge of the said di-
uini"

uinity: for the reafon of Prouidence or foreknowledge is fo infeparably ioyned with
the diuinity, as that they cánot (in the eye of
cleare iudgement) be deuided afunder; for
how impotent and weake fhould that God
be, who were ignorant of thofe thinges,
which euen to vs are become cleare & euident? And how imperfect and narrow an
vnderftanding fhould he haue, that could
not attend to all thinges, which doe fall
out in the world? Therfore it is wifely pronounced by S. *Auftin* (a) in a certaine place
againft *Cicero* : *To confeße that there is a God, and*
withall to deny that he is prefcious, or foreknowing
of things to come, is extreme madnes . Therefore
either prefcience and prouidence is to be admitted, or els all diuinity is to be reiected.

(a) Lib. 5.
de Ciuit.
cap.

Although at this day there be many who
deny in their fecret iudgmentes all diuine
power and *Deity*, yet are they not much
knowne to the world; fince the feare of the
lawes doth impofe filence to thefe kind of
men, and only fecretly among their famili-
ars they do vomit out their *Atheifme*. The errours in Religon (fince all fuch wicked doctrines do finally propend & incline to A-
theifme) haue giuen great occafion hereof:
for once departing from the true religon,
mans vnderftanding findeth nothing, wherin it may firmely and fecurely reft; and then

A 3   the

the vnderſtanding reflecting it ſelfe theron, inſtantly falleth to doubt of the whole my-ſtery of all religion; as if it were a thing for-ged only out of poiicy, that ſo vnder the te-cture & pretext of a *Diuine power*, the people may the more eaſily be contained within the limits and boundes of their duties . And hence it proceedeth that among Heretickes, ſuch as are of ſharper wits doe inwardly doubt of all religion, and either deny , or at leaſt reſt vncertaine, whether there be any diuine and *ſupernatural power at al*; being thus prepared to entertaine any religion , ſo farre forth as it ſorteth to the augmentation & in-creaſe of their temporal eſtates . Theſe men be commonly called *Polititians* , in that they ſubiect all religion to policy, & conſequent-ly by how much the more any religion is conducing to the bettering of their politicall and temporall eſtate ; by ſo much it is by the more eſteemed and practiſed . Among theſe men *Nicholas Machiauel* hath gained the chie-feſt place, as appeareth out of his books writ-ten in the Italian tongue, and particulerly of that entituled *de Principe* , which at this day is read by many.

The chiefe reaſons, whereupon this o-pinion is grounded, are theſe following : If there were any *Diuine power*, by the which **the world were gouerned** , then would it

follow

follow, that improbity, wickednes, & cruelty should not preuaile so much, as now it
doth: neither should it haue so prosperous
successe and euent, nor should it oppresse
and betrample with wrong the vertuous &
innocent, as we fynd that in all ages it hath
done; seeing it belongeth, and is peculiarly
incumbent to the office of a Gouernour, not
to suffer the wicked to rule and sway much,
but to chastice them with diuers punishmēts;
therby not only to cause them to cease from
afflicting the vertuous; but also by amen-
ding their manners, to affect and prosecute a
vertuous life. And for example heereof, let
vs suppose any one Citty, the which the
worst & most wicked mē do daily gouerne,
who without any feare of lawes cōmit ra-
pyne vpon the goodes of their neighbours,
do violate and defile the beds of others, and
without restraint do satisfy their lusts in all
things; who would say that this Citty eioy-
ed a Gouernour that is wise and prouident?
Wherefore since in the whole world there is
such disturbance of order that we can hardly
conceaue a greater perturbation then it is,
to wit, the religious worshippers of God to
be oppressed, to endure extreme want and
other calamities, to liue in a despicable and
contemned state of life, and finally most miserably to dy; and on the contrary syde, the

wicked

wicked to gouerne & fway all, to liue afflu-
ently & abundantly in all riches, to infult o-
uer the vertuous, to wallow in fenfuality, &
laftly to haue a quyet end and death. Now
who would here think(faith the *Atheist*) that
Prouidence (by the which all thinges are
difpenfed, and giuen in an euen meafure)
fhould haue any prefidency, or power in
the vnequall difpofall of thefe worldly affaires ? For from this ἀταξία, and want of
order, and from this confufion of things, the
former men did coniecture, that there was
no fupreme gouernour, which had any care
in the difpenfatiō of temporal bufines. This
argument is the chiefeft for the ftrengthing
of this moft wicked affertion, which preuailed much, not only with fome of former
auncient tymes, but alfo with diuers in our
daies.

Secondly, they obiect, that it is euident
euen by experience it felfe; that mens negotiations & bufines receaue their fucceffe (for
the moft part) anfwerable to the induftry &
endeauours employed in them,& not according to the right & equity of the mater; hēce
(fay they) it procedeth, that many waging
moft iniuft wars haue obtained the victory,
either becaufe they were more numerous &
powerful in fouldiers, or in that they were
more induftrious & painful in their defign-
ments

ments. In like fort fuch men, as maintaine vnlawful fuites, do oftentymes by periuryes and falfe witneffes purchafe the fentence of the Iudge. Finally, we find, that mens owne induftry and laborioufnes doth much more predominate and rule ouer all their mutuall commercements, then the prouidence or influence of any higher caufe. Al which obferuations may feeme to intimate, that there is no fuperiour *Diuyne Power*, gouerning and moderating mens actiõs; but that euery one is left to his owne particuler prouidence, and watchfullnes.

Thirdly, we fee that things confifting of nature, do euer proceed after one & the fame manner, keeping one immoueable courfe & order. Thus the Sunne euer ryfeth & fetteth & rūneth the fame circles, occafioning with his approach, the Spring and Sūmer; with his departure, the Autumñe & Winter: in like fort things natural do grow and after decay or dye, ftill one thing begetting another without ceffatiõ or end, to the perpetuating of the fame *fpecies* or kind, which is a figne that all things are gouerned by the force of Nature, and that there is no other higher power, then *Nature* her felfe, by the which all thefe thinges are effected.

Fourthly, we obferue that man is firft begotten, formed in his mothers wōbe, borne,

increaseth, comes to his full groth or vigour,
growes old and dyes after the same máner, as
other more perfect liuing creatures do, and
that he consisteth of the said members and
organs; therfore there is the like end of más
life, as of other creatures; and as they do vtterly perish away after death, so also doth
man.

Lastly, if there be any supreme spirit, or
diuine nature, it is credible, that it doth not
intermedle with mans affaires, nor busieth
it selfe with things done among vs. First because, this seemeth vnworthy the maiesty of
so great a Deity; for as a mighty Monarch
doth not trouble himselfe with the particuler actions of his Cittizens, workemen, or
bond-slaues, litle regarding what they say,
thinke, or do, as houlding the care of such
small matters to be an indignity to his regall
state: In lyke sort, Men scorne the labour &
busines of Ants or flees, as not regarding their
policy or course they hould. But now in reference & comparison to that *supreme power*,
we men are far lesse inferiour then the Ants.
Furthermore, seing that *Diuinity* is perfectly
blessed, containing all sufficiency within it
selfe, and seeking nothing, that is extrinsecall or externall; why then should it be sollicitous and carefull of our Actions? Finally
the former point seemes true, in regard, that
by

by the meanes of humane things (howfoe-
uer they happen) there is neither any more
neere approach or further diftance from the
fayd Deity. Other Arguments to proue the
fame (then are here alledged) I fynd none;
and thefe former arguments are anfwered &
folued in the fiue laft Chapters of this firft
booke.

THAT THERE IS ONE SVPREME
Power , by whofe Prouidence all things are
gouerned ; is made euident by many rea-
fons.

CHAP. II.

BVT the contrary fentence of this poynt
is to be acknowledged and fet downe,
as an inexpugnable verity; to wit, that there
is *a fupreme Diuyne Power*, by whofe prouidence and wifdome all things (both humane
& others) are gouerned, and this power we
cal God. Now this truth is not to be belieued
only by force of diuine reuelation, but alfo is
made moft euident by many reafons and de-
monftrations, which are moft obuious and
familiar vnto vs , and are to be apprehended
euen by our fenfes. For although a *diuine na-*
ture or *diuinity*, in refpect of it felfe is altogether inuifible, notwithftading there appeare
fo many perfpicuous notes and prints thereof

in-

in ſenſible thinges ſo many footſteps euery
where; finally ſo many ſparcles of this light
or ſplendour are ſhining in euery thing, as
thatwho will diligently inſiſt in the cōtem-
plation of them, cannot poſſibly doubt either of the being of *a God,* or of his *Prouidence.*

Fourteene or fifteene reaſons do occurre
to me, from which this truth receaueth its
proofe,or rather d monſtration, which I wil
briefly here explicate, to wit: firſt, *from the
generall confeſſion of all Countryes, and wiſemen.*
2. *From the motions of the heauens.* 3. *From that,
that thinges corporall and ſubiect to ſight, cannot
receaue their firſt being from themſelues.* 4. *From
the pulchritude and beauty of things, and from the
ſtructure and poſition of parts in reſpect of the whole.*
5. *From the ſtructure of the parts of the world, in
reference to their end.* 6. *From the ſtructure and
poſition of parts in liuing Creatures, and plants, in
reference alſo to their ends.* 7. *From that, that the
actions and operations of all things, moſt directly &
orderly tend to their end.* 8. *From the great diuerſity of faces and countenances of men, and of their
voyces; as alſo from the pouerty, and penury,
wherin the greateſt part of the world are borne.* 9.
From Miracles. 10. *from the predictious and ſupernaturall reuelations of things moſt hidden & ſecret.*
11. *From Spirits.* 12. *From the direction and gouerment of Manners and life.* 13. *From the immortality of the ſoule.* 14. *From diuers examples of ſu-*
                                                    pernaturall

pernaturall reuenge, and benignity, or fauour. 15.
*From the punishments suddainly, and visibly in-
flicted vpon blasphemers, sacrilegious persons, and
periurers.*

THE FIRST REASON IS TAKEN
*from the Confession of all Countries, and of al
wise men.*

CHAP. III.

AS much as we may be inftructed by
History, al Countries (whether barbarous or profeffing learning) haue in all ages
maintayned a diuyne & fupernatural power
to be , which doth know and gouerne al our
actiôs, which vndertaketh the charge of vs,
to whom in dangers, preffures, and afflictions we are to haue recourfe, and from whofe
hand rewards for welldoing, and chaftice-
ments or punifhments for wicked actions are
to be expected . So did the *Iewes* belieue , *the
Egiptians , Ethiopians, Affyrians, Chaldeans, Grecians , Romans , Germans , French , Indians , the
people of China , Iaponians , Tartarians ,* and all
others, not only after , but alfo before Chrifts
comming. Of the truth of which poynt this
is one manifeft figne, to wit, in that all thefe
had their religions, their ceremonies, their
temples, and their Priefts inftituted for the
wor-

worſhipping of a *diuyne Power.* To this *Power.* alſo they made their prayers and vowes , offered vp their ſacrifices and guiſts, and diuers wayes laboured to appeaſe, and pacify the wrath of the ſaid *Deity .* Therfore it followeth, that they all aſcribed to this Power, Prouidence ; aſſuring themſelues , that it tooke notice of their actions that it was able to defend them, to free them from dangers , to imparte to them thinges which they deſired , and to take reuenge for iniuries : ſince otherwiſe they ſhould pray, & offer vp ſacrifices to it in vaine , if it knew not our eſtates nor intermingled it ſelf with our eſtates, nor tooke care for vs . And hence it followeth , that this opinion of a *Deity* is not entertained only by force of Tradition , but is planted in the minds of al, euen by nature her ſelfe. For although all do not agree , whether the ſupernaturall power be one or many; corporal and bodily, or incorporall; finite, or infinite and immenſe; yet all conſpire in this poynt , that there was a certaine *ſupreme intelligence ; or Diuinity ,* which is to be adored and worſhipped, as euen *Cicero* (*a*) witneſſeth, ſaying: *Among men there is no country ſo barbarous, or of ſo iron and hard a diſpoſition , which doth not acknowledge, that there is a God , though they be ignorant, what this God ſhould be :* Which Oratour alſo in another (*b*) place ſpeaking of the ſaid poynt

(a) *Lib* 1 *de Leg.*

(b) *De natura Deorum.*

                                              ſayth

faith, *hoc omnibus est innatum & insculptum* &c.
This thing(to know that there is a *God*) *is con-
naturall to all , and euen engrauen in their soules.*
Now if the acknowledging of this poynt be
incident to all by nature, then it ineuitably
followeth, that it cannot be false : for nature
neuer planteth in the mynd any assent of falshood, but only of truth (since otherwise she
should be wicked , and should peruert the
vnderstanding and reason) for Truth is the
right state , and as it were the health of the
vnderstanding; wheras falshood is a deprauation, and a bad or vicious distemperature
of the same : but the Euill, and Vice of any
thing proceedeth not from the inclination of
nature (but euer against the naturall propension of it ;) therefore an vniuersall assent in
the vnderstanding of what is false, neuer taketh it origin, and first being from nature.

I further add , if it should not be true, that
there is a God; thē should it be not only false,
but also altogether αδύνατον, and impossible,
as implying an irreconciliable contradiction;
for if at this present there be not a *God,* or that
he hath no prouidence of our estates , then is
it altogether impossible, and inuolueth in it
selfe a plaine contradiction , to say, that euer
at any tyme he was , or that euer he had any
Prouidence. For as *Aristotle,* and all Philosophers teach: *In diuinis idem est esse actu, & posse
esse;*

esse ; non esse actu, & esse impossibile. In things that are diuine, it is all one, the same actually to be, and to haue a power to be ; as also actually not to be, or exist, and to be impossible to be. But how is it credible, that, that which is not only false, but also altogether impossible, should be so belieued among all nations, and should be so engrafted in the mynds of euery man, as that all men in all places should (without any externall helpe of instruction therein) entertaine & belieue the same with a vnanimous and general consent and approbation ? And heere is discouered the force of this verity, which is so potent, and hath such a secret agrement and sympathy with mans vnderstanding, as that it is able euen to inuade and possesse (and this without any coaction or constraint) the myndes of all. And of this, heere is an euident signe, in that al countries in suddaine and vnexpected dangers (without any deliberation at all) do recurre & fly to God, imploring his helpe and assistance, saying: *O God succour me, O God helpe me, O God haue mercy on me &c.* Againe, in that all nations belieue, that God knoweth al things, and is able to do any thing, they vpon this acknowledged ground, do pray for fauour for their friendes, and reuenge against their enemies, as *Tertullian* elegantly sheweth in his booke *De Anima testimonio.*

And

And although the truth of this doctrine be not in it selfe so acknowledged and euident to all, as none can contradict the verity, yet it is so agreable to the light of reason, & so probable, as that the mind of má is instantly ready to giue assent therto, & the tongue prepared to confesse the same; and all this through a secret instinct without any precedent deliberation: from whence it appeareth that hitherto neuer any man denyed this verity, but only such, whose naturall iudgement, through some false and weake reason, or through the peruersenesse of his phantasy was mightily corrupted, & as it were darkened with the mist of an erroneous imagination; no otherwise, then sometimes it falls out, that some men haue denyed thinges, as were most euident to their senses: so *Zeno* denyed *motion*, and *Democritus*, *rest*; this later maintaining, that nothing was permanét, but al things were in a continual flux and mutability, and that the world did daily grow, and daily decay. Thus we fynd, that nothing is so absurd, which may not to a depraued iudgment seeme consonant to Reason; and so were the faculties of those few Philosophers mynds infected, who denyed a *Diuinity*, or *Prouidence*, as aboue we said: Notwithstanding it is not to be regarded, what some

B   *on̲y*

one or other do teach herein, but their reasons wherupon they ground so an absurd assertion, are to be weighed, which indeed are found to be most friuolous, weake, and inconsequent, as hereafter we will shew.

To the common iudgment of al Contries and nations herin, we may adioyne the like sentence and iudgment of all most learned Philosophers, who euer flourished in any place or tyme: Since al these most cōfidētly euer maintained a *Deity* and *Prouidence*, as *Augustinus Eugubinus* in his worke *de perenni Philosophia*, largely sheweth. Thus did the Patriarchs teach, the Prophets, and al the wise men among the Iewes;thus the Priests among the Egyptians, the *Magi* among the *Chaldeans*, the *Gymnasophista* amōg the *Indians* the *Druides* among the French, and the chiefe sects of Philosophers among the Grecians; to wit, the *Pithagoreans*, the *Platonickes*, the *Stoicks*, & (as *Eugubinus* proueth) the very *Academians*. I heere omit the most excellent setences of this poynt, which are frequétly found in *Trismegistus*, *Orpheus*, *Museus*, *Homer*, *Hesiod*, *Pindarus*, *Sophocles*, *Plato* and the *Platonicks*, *Seneca*, *Plutarch*, & whō if any be desirous to see, let him peruse the foresaid mentioned Authour.

This opiniō therfore of cōfessing a *Deity*, & *Prouidēce* is fortified with the authorities
of

of al countries, al ages, all religions, all rites & ceremonyes of diuyne worſhip, al Prieſts al Prophets, al diſcipline of *Magi* and Wiſe men, and al the more remarkable Philoſophers of al nations; & finally it is warráted by the force of nature which hath imprinted this truth at his very birth in más ſoule.

Therfore what madnes and blyndnes of mynd it is (for ſome few weake & ſleighty reaſons) to imbrace the contrary opinion? Since this is nothing els, but to preſer and aduance a mans owne priuate iudgment aboue the iudgment of the whole world & of all tymes, and to venditate himſelfe for more wiſe (as enioying a more ſearching and penetrating braine) then any other man liuing. Therfore the Atheiſts do herin diſcouer their wonderfull folly, and inſupportable pryde, which thus hath enchanted them.

THE SECOND REASON DRAVVNE FROM the motion of the heauenly Orbs.

CHAP. IIII.

IN this next place I will alledge certaine Philoſophical reaſons or arguments, & ſuch as are euidét & cleare to the vnderſtáding; pretermitting the moreobſcure, which

may

be taken out of the *Metaphiſicks*. Firſt then
we ſee the heauenly bodies to be carryed a-
bout in their *Orbs* with a moſt rapid and
ſwift motiō. Now this motion cānot haue
it beginning frō any force of nature impreſſed in the heauens, neither from any corporall cauſe; therefore it procedeth from ſome
intelligent and ſpirituall ſubſtance, & this
ſubſtance is God. That it doth not ryſe frō
any naturall inclination of the heauens, is
manifeſt; ſince things which are moued by
a propenſion of nature, direct their motion
vnto ſome one end, the which end once
obtained, they ceaſe from further motion,
and then do reſt, and are cōſerued. Thus al
ſublunary bodyes enioy a power and force
to moue, that if chance they be taken from
their naturall place, they ſtriue by motion
to returne therto; and being returned do
there reſt, and quietly enioy their owne
being. For all things, which ſtand obnoxi-
us & ſubiect to corruption are preſerued in
their owne naturall place; but being out of
it, they periſh, languiſhing (as it were) away
and looſing their ſtate of nature. And there
is no body, which hath an inclination to
motion, ſo, as it ſtill moues without end, &
neuer attaynes to its period, and deſired
place of reſt: for as the Philoſophers teach,
Motus eſt quiddam imperfectum, vtpote via ad
terminum

terminum . *Motion is a thing imperfect in it selfe ,*
as being but only a way or passage to an end, or rest.
But there is nothing , which coueteth to be
euer in its way or iourney(as I may cal it)
but all things desire to haften to their *termi-*
nus , or end , and there to repofe and reft .
Wherfore we may neceffarily conclude frõ
the premifes , that feing the motion of the
heauély Orbs doth not tend, nor is directed
to any *terminus* , or end , where it may find
reft and quyet , that therefore this motion
floweth not from any inclinatiõ of nature ,
as the motion of all inanimate things do ,
which we fee in this world. This poynt is
further confirmed from that, that euery naturall inclinatiõ to motion is directed to the
good of the fubiect or body , which is moued : to wit , that the body may obtaine
therby its perfection and conferuation, and
is not directed to the good or benefit of o-
ther bodyes: for euery particuler thing hath
therefore a force and propenfion to moue ,
that by fuch a mouing, it may obtayne that
place, which is moft agreable to its nature ,
and fo may firmely place it felfe , and reft
there, and not that by a motion it may benefit other bodies . But now the motion of
the heauenly Orbes bringeth no perfection
at all to the Orbes , or to thofe other heauenly bodies (for what doth that continual

B 3   rowling

rowling about of the Orbes profit, or ad-
uantage the Sunne, or the other ſtars?) but
is only beneficiall to the inferiour bodyes,
whiles by this motion it carryeth their vertues and influences throughout the compaſſe of the whole Orbes; and ſo by diſtributing them, cauſeth all things to receaue
vegetation, life, increaſe, perfection, and
conſeruation. Therefore it is moſt euident,
that this motion of the heauens proceedeth
not from any ſecret inclination of nature in
them: for thoſe celeſtiall Orbes cannot apprehend or conceaue their motiō to be profitable to this inferiour world; that out of
ſuch a charitable cogitation and thought
(forſooth) they ſhould thus inceſſantly
moue and turne about: for ſo to apprehend
and reflect vpon the profit of another, is
peculiar to a mynd and intelligence endued with reaſon. From all which it is neceſſarily euicted and inferred, that there is
ſome moſt *powerful ſpirit or intelligence,* which
firſt conceaued this profit in its mynd, and
by reaſon of the ſaid profit firſt ordained &
tempered this motion, of which ſpirit it e-
uer dependeth and is gouerned. Furthermore the great variety of the heauenly motions doth ſufficiently demonſtrate, that
they proceed not from nature, whoſe inclination is euer *ſimple* and *vniforme.* For beſides

fides their motion from the Eaſt to the weſt
vpon the Poles of the world (which is
common to all the Orbes) feuerall Orbes
of euery Planet enioy a proper motion frō
the Weſt to the Eaſt, vpon a different *Axis,*
or Pole, a different way, and with different celerity . The Orbe of *Saturne* per-
fecteth its courfe almoſt in 30. yeares . The
Orbe of *Iupiter* in 12 yeares, of *Mars* about
2. yeares, of the *Sunne* in one yeare , of
Venus in one yeare, of *Mercury* almoſt in like
ſpace, of the *Moone* in 27. daies, and 6.
houres . Behold heere the great diuerſity .
Neither is the poynt here leſſened , if in
place of the motion of the Planets to the
Weſt , we ſuppoſe their motiō to the Eaſt
(though ſomewhat flower) according to
the iudgement of ſome ; becaufe euen
granting this ſuppoſal, yet the ſame variety
is obſerued, the ſame difference of motion ,
and the ſame ſympathy, agreement, & proportion .

Againe, the Planets ſometymes are more
neare to the earth, other tymes more remote
and diſtant ; now they are *ſtationarij* , then
directi , and after *retrograds* : to the demon-
ſtration of which poynts are inuented the
Eccentrick Circles , and the *Epicycles* .

Furthermore many other obſeruations
in the Heauens moſt wonderfull and vnknowne

knowne for so many ages to all antiquity, are lately discouered by the helpe of a Perspectiue glasse inuented by a certaine *Batauia.* As for example, that the body of the moone is spongious, consisting of some matter resembling little locks of woll; that the star of *Venus* doth increase and decrease in light likethe moone, crooking it self into hornes, as the moone doth; and when it *Orbe* is full of light, it is not opposed diametrically to the Sunne, as the Moone is, but is in small distance from the Sunne: from which obseruation it may seeme to be necessarily inferred, that the starre of *Venus* is carryed in a huge *Epicycle* about the Sunne; so as it is sometimes far higher then the Sunne, other tymes much lower. In lyke sort by the former instrument there are obserued, about the starre of *Iupiter* 4. small stars, sometimes going before, sometimes following *Iupiter*: at one tyme they all appeare, at another tyme but some of them, and at a third tyme other some; from whence also we may gather that the said starres do moue in little *Epicycles* about the starre of *Iupiter*. Againe, in the body of the Sunne there appeare certaine spots, which notwithstanding do not euer retaine one and the same place in the Sunne, but daily change their situation; and at one tyme they appeare more in number,

at

at another fewer. From which it is eafily
gathered, that thefe fpots do not inhere in
the body of the Sunne, but are little ftarres,
which interpofe themfelues betweene the
Sunne and our fight, and are moued in
Epicycles about the body of the Sunne. I my
felfe haue often obferued thefe varieties,
with wonderfull admiration of the wifedome and power of God; who hath difpofed the courfe of the ftarres with that ftu-
pendious art and skill, as that they are in no
fort fubiect to the apprehenfion of mans
vnderftáding. I here omit the infinite multitude of Starres, which (being neuer difcouered to the Aftronomers vntill this
tyme) are by the helpe of the forefaid inftrument moft diftinctly feene in the Heauens.

To côclude, in the eight Sphere (wherin the fixed Starres are) there is obferued a
triple motion. The firft from the Eaft to the
Weft, abfoluing its whole courfe in 24.
houres. The fecond from the Weft to the
Eaft, which is thought to go one degree in
a hundred yeares. The third from the South
to the North, and contrariwife; by force
of which motion the beginning of *Aries* &
Libra of the eight Sphere doth defcrybe
certaine fmall circles about the beginning
of *Aries* and *Libra* of the ninth Sphere;

B 5   which

which courſe is perfected in 7000. yeares : Now, who will maintayne, that ſo multiplicious, and ſo various a locall motion ſhould proceed from nature, and not from ſome one moſt Wiſe and Excellent an Vnderſtanding or Power, thus gouerning all the heaués tor the benefit of the ſublunary or earthly bodies, and particulerly of man, to whoſe ne the reſt are ſubiect and ſeruiceable? Neither conduceth it any thing againſt our ſcope, whether it be replyed, that theſe motions are performed by diuers traſient puſhes (euen as the rowling about of a potters wheele is occaſioned by the Potter) or els by certaine ſtable, firme & permament forces, impreſſed in the celeſtiall Orbes (as ſome do affirme) for by whether meanes ſoeuer it is cauſed, it neceſſarily proceedeth from ſome incorporeall cauſe indued with a mynd and vnderſtanding, & not from any peculiar propenſion and inclination of nature. Now this Cauſe (which with ſo powerfull a hand, and ſo many wayes turneth about the heauenly Orbes) we call God, who either worketh this immediatly of himſelfe (which is the more probable opinion) or els by the miniſtery and help of inferiour Spirits, and Intelligences, as many do hould.

THE

THE THIRD REASON, TAKEN FROM that , that Corporall substances, and such as are subiect to the eye and sight , cannot haue their being by Chance , or Fortune .

CHAP. V.

IN the whole course of the nature of things , there must needes be some one cause, of which all therest , in respect of their substance, do depend: and that we call God . That there is such a cause is proued , in that corporeall and bodily things do proceed either from themselues , or casually from *fortune* , or from some incorporeall cause endued with a mynd, vnderstanding and reason . For neuer did any Philosopher set downe any other efficient cause of the world , then some of these three; neither can any other cause differét from these be suggested or imagined , except one will say , that this world is produced of another world , and that other of another , and so still infinitly ; which assertion is in it selfe absurd , seing it implyeth an infinity & interminable progresse and proceeding .

Now , it is manifest , that things haue their beginning neither from themselues , nor from

from *Chance* or *fortune*; therfore it followeth
neceſſarily, that they receaue their production and being from ſome Mynd or Spirit
endued with reaſon.

That they proceed not from Chance, to
wit, from a caſuall concourſe of *Atomies*, or
ſmal bodies, as *Democritus*, *Epicurus*, *Lucretius*
and ſome other did teach, appeareth both
from the ſtructure and forme of all things in
the world; as alſo from the great order and
conſtancy, which is diſcouered in the motion of the heauens, and in the function &
office of other things: for what man, that
is endued with reaſon, will be perſwaded,
that thoſe thinges, whoſe making are accompanied with the fulnes of all reaſon, &
in that reſpect exceedeth the wit of all art
and knowledge, ſhould notwithſtanding
be produced of a meere caſual concourſe of
Atomies without reaſon, and without art?
Since to ſay thus, were as much as to defẽd,
that ſome one moſt faire, ſumptuous, and
ſtately pallace were not made at all by any
artificer with art, but only by a ſuddaine
mingling and meeting together of certaine
peeces of ſtones into this curious and artificiall forme, fallen from ſome huge rocke of
ſtone, ſhaken a ſunder by an Earthquake:
or that the Annales of *Ennius*, or *Commenta-*
ries of *Liuy* were not cõpoſed by any wry-
ter,

ter, but by a ftrange and cafuall concourfe
of letters: for if the parts of the world, and
difpofition of parts, and the bodyes of liuing
Creatures, & plants (in the making wherof
is found all reafon, art & skil in the higheft
degree) can be produced only by a meere
côcourfe of *Atomies* without art & without
reafon; then by the fame reafon, why cannot Pallaces, Temples, Cittyes, veftmêts,
bookes, epiftles and the like (in all which
is difcouered much leffe art, skill, and wit
then in the former) take alfo their making
and being from *Chance*? Therefore, let that
foolifh & abfurd opinion of the concourfe
of *Atomyes* be abolifhed, which feemeth to
be inuented to no other end, then that the
maintainers thereof, fhould not be forced to
acknowledge the world to be gouerned by
diuyne *Prouidence*: againft which *Prouidence* they had a mighty auerfion; it felfe of
neceffity being moft formidable and dread-   *Lucr. l. 1.*
full to a mynd wallowing in all wickednes   *& 3.*
& voluptuoufnes, as is euidently gathered   *Plin. l. 1. c.*
out of *Lucretius* and *Pliny*.   *7. & l. 7. c.*
    That the world and the parts thereof   *55.*
cannot receaue their being from themfelues, is no leffe euident. Firft among fub-
blunary bodyes (as all thofe be, which are
vnder the Moone) thofe which are moft
perfect (as Man & other liuing Creatures)
                    cannot

cannot be of themfelues; for how can thofe
things receaue their being frō themfelues,
which need a preparation and concourfe of
fo many caufes, that they may be borne;
and fo many externall helpes and further-
rances, that they may liue? Or how can that
be of it felfe, which is extinguifhed & perifhed with fo great a facility? Here perhaps
it may be replyed, that thofe bodies, which
be *Indiuidua*, as particuler men, are not of
themfelues, but that the humane nature in
generall (as being eternall, or for euer) is of
it felfe: and that the like may be faid of o-
ther *Species*, or kindes of things. But this is
fpoken ignorantly; feeing the *Species* of any
creature, or body is not a thing feparated
from the *Indiuidua* (as certaine *Platonickes*
dreamed) but doth exift in the *Indiuidua*;
neither hath it any *effe*, or being, in *rerum
natura*, but only by reafon of the *Indiuidua*.
Yea for exáple, *fpecies humana*, or the whole
kynd of men, is nothing els, but the whole
multitude of particuler men, which haue
beene, are, and may be, as they all beare a
liknes of nature among themfelues. Now
then if Indiuiduall and particuler Men do
depend of another caufe, then muft alfo the
whole *Species* or kynd (which is not diftin-
guifhed *à parte rei* (as the Philofophers
fpeake) from the *Indiuidua*) depend alfo of
another

another caufe . This point is further mani-
fefted, in that the whole *Species,* or kynd
may vtterly be extinguifhed or perifhd. But
what dependeth not of another, but hath it
being only of it felfe , cannot be extinguifhed : for what is of it felfe, did neuer begin,
but had euer its *exiftency*; and therefore cannot ceafe or defift to be . That it neuer begun , is proued , in that what once did begin , fometimes was not, and therefore it is
produced (as the phrafe is) *à non efte, ad efte,*
from the not being of a thing , to the being
of the thing it felfe . Now , a thing cannot
produce or caufe it felfe ; and the reafon is ,
becaufe that which doth produce, ought to
precede or go before , that therby it may
draw that , which is to be produced *à non
efte, ad efte .* Therefore whatfoeuer beginn-
neth once to be , is produced of another , &
confequently receaueth not its being of it
felf; for to haue its being of it felfe, is to haue
its efféce without the influxe of any other
efficient caufe . Therefore it is auident that
what is of it felfe , did neuer begin , & therefore fhall neuer end ; and on the contrary
fyde , what did begin hath not its being
from it felfe, but is neceffarily produced of
another .

  Furthermore , euery thing compounded
of matter aud forme , cannot be of it felfe ,
                           but

Cópoun-
ded bo-
dyes .

but neceſſarily is produed of ſome efficient
cauſe, which muſt diſpoſe the matter, and
produce the forme, and ioyne the forme to
the matter; for the matter neither receaueth thoſe diſpoſitions, nor the forme, from
its owne eſſence (ſince they may be ſeparated) therefore this vnion of the matter &
the forme is occaſioned by ſome extrinſecal
cauſe. The ſame may be ſaid of euery thing
conſiſting of parts, for ſeing the parts are
not through any neceſſity vnited among
themſelues, but may be mutually ſeparated one from another, it muſt needes follow, that this vnion proceedeth from ſome
cauſe, which ioyned the parts togeather.

From theſe premiſes afore, it appeareth,
that alſo the Elements, (as the earth, the
water, the ayre, and the fire) are not of thé-
ſelues, but haue ſome efficient begining:
for if thoſe things, which are moſt perfect
for their nature (among theſe ſublunary
bodyes) haue not their being from themſelues, but from ſome other cauſe; then
much more thoſe bodies which are moſt
imperfect (as the Elements are) muſt for
their being depend of another: for to be of
it ſelfe, and not to depend of another, is a
ſigne of greateſt perfection; ſeing, what is
thus in nature, is to it ſelfe the origen and
fountaine of all good, and ſtandeth not in
the

need of any thing externall . Furthermore the Elements are not for themfelues, but for others; I meane as they are parts of the world, and as they afford matter to compounded bodyes , therfore they haue not their being from themfelues; for that Axiome in Philofophy is true , to wit: *Quod habet caufam finalem , ad quam ordinetur, habet etiam efficientem , à qua ordinetur* . What hath a *final caufe , to the which it is directed and ordained , the fame hath alfo an efficient caufe , by the which it is fo ordained;*for nothing is of it felfe, to the end that it may ferue another , but that it may enioy it felfe. Therefore euen in this refpect, that any thing is, *non propter fe , fed propter aliud*, not for it owne felt,but that it may conduce and be ferniceable to fome other thing;it followeth that the fame thing is ordained by fome one, which hath intended the good of another . Befides, in that the Elemēts do enioy this or that magnitude or greatnes, this place or that place, in refpect of the whole fpace and place in the world , they receaue not this from théfelues (feing their effence neceffarily exacteth none of thefe circumftances)therefore they take them from fome extrinfecall caufe, which appointeth to euery one of the Elements their meafure or greatnes , & their place or fituation . To conclude, the

C Elements

Elements are subiect to so many mutations
and changes, and to so great a need of extrinsecall causes, as that in regard hereof
how can it be possibly conceaued, that they
should be of themselues, or be at their owne
fredome and liberty, and in respect of their
being not, to depend of another? These
Materia   former reasons do conuince, that *Materia pri-*
Prima.   *ma* (whereof the Philosophers do teach,
that all things were first made) hath not its
being from it selfe, but from some other
cause. For this *Materia prima* either is not
distinguished from the Elements (as many
auncient Philosophers did hould, who
taught that the Elements are mere simple
bodies, without composition of matter or
forme, and the last subiect of all former) or
els if it be distinguished from thē (as *Aristotle*
with his followers maintained) then is it
far more imperfect then the Elements, as
seruing but for their matter, whereof they
are made. Therefore seing this *Materia prima*
is most imperfect and next to *Nothing*, being
subiect to all mutations, and (as it were) a
seruant to all natural causes, and being of it
owne nature depriued of all forme, wherwith to be inuested, and borrowing all its
perfection from other things, it therefore
cannot haue its being of it selfe, & indepē-
dent of all other causes.

               Now

Now then from all this heretofore obfer-ued, it followeth demonftratiuely, that no Sublunary body hath its being and effence from it felfe, but that all things receaue their being from fome efficient caufe.

Now, that this caufe is incorporeall and intelligent, or enioying Reafon and Vn-derftanding, appeareth feuerall waies: firft becaufe *Materia prima* could not be produ-ced by any corporeall caufe; feing that e-uery action of a corporeall thing euer pre-fuppofeth the fubiect, into the which it is receaued (as *Ariftotle* and all Philofophers do teach,) but before *Materia Prima* was, no fubiect can be imagined, feing it was the firft, and (as I may tearme it) the deepeft, and moft fundamentall fubiect. Againe, if this Caufe were corporeall, the doubtlefly the heaues fhould be this Caufe, fince there remaineth no other corporeal Caufe, to the which it may be afcribed: But the heauens could not produce this *Materia prima*, both by reafon that the Heauens worke not, but by the mediation of light & influence of the ftars, both which qualities require a fubiect into the which they may be recea-ued; as alfo becaufe before this production, the whole fpace, in which now the Ele-ments are, was voyde, as being deftitute of any corporeall body; and then it follo-

C 2   weth

weth, that the heauens fhould produce this *Materia prima in vacuo*, not hauing any precedent fubiect matter to worke vpon, and therefore fhould create it of nothing; but this doth tranfcend the power and force of any corporall nature : Therefore in regard of this abfurdity it followeth, that the caufe of this *Materia prima* muft be incorporall and moft powerfull, as being able to giue it an effence and being, euen from nothing.

From which Collection it further followeth, that this caufe ought to be alfo intelligent, as knowing what it doth or worketh; both becaufe euery incorporall fubftance is intelligent (as the Philofophers teach) as alfo in that it did not produce this *Materia prima*, after a blynd and ignorant manner, but with a certaine finall intention and determination, to wit, that of it all other things fhould be made, and that it fhould be the fubiect of all formes . This poynt is made further euident, in that to a caufe, which is fo perfect, high and potent, the moft perfect manner of working is to be giuen; but the moft perfect manner is by the vnderftanding and the will. Againe the fame is become more cleare , in that there ought to be contained in the caufe all the perfections of the effect, and this *magis eminenter*, more eminently then is in the effect;
I meane

I meane when the caufe is of a different nature from the effect. Wherefore feing Mans nature (which is endued with reafon) and the diuers kynd of liuing Creatures (which enioy fenfe) are the effects of this incorporeall or fpirituall caufe, it moft confequently may be concluded, that all the perfection of thefe (to wit reafon and fenfe) are after an eminent manner contayned in the faid caufe.

That the heauenly bodies haue not their being from themfelues, appeareth firft from their motions; for if their motions do depend of fome other fuperiour Caufe (and that fpirituall) as is afore proued, then can it be but acknowledged, that their fubftance and figure are produced of the fame caufe ; for who is fo voyd of confideratiō, as to thinke, that that Supreme caufe fhould enter into the world (as into an ample and maifterles houfe, wherunto it can pretend no right or title) and fhould challenge to it felfe the gouernment thereof? Can it be thought to be fo impotent, as not to be able to frame to it felfe (as it were) a proper houfe of its owne ? If this houfe of the world belong not to this Caufe, why then doth it affume the regiment thereof? Or why hath it ftored this our inferiour world with fuch opulency & abundance of riches of al kynd,

The heauenly Orbes.

as

as of metals, pretious stones, hearbs, trees, birds, fishes, earthly creatures, and all other variety of things whatsoeuer?

To conclude, if thou considerest the stupendious power, which this cause sheweth in the motions of these celestial Orbs, thou canst not doubt, but that the same Cause is the authour of this whole worke. For although the Sunne be incomparably greater then the vniuesall Globe of the earth and water (as is euicted from the poynt of the shadow of the earth, which reacheth not to the Orbe of *Mars*) yea according to the iudgment of the Astronomers, the Sunne is an hundred sixty six tymes greater then the earth and water; notwithstanding the Sune with its whole orbe is carryed about with such a velocity and swiftnes, that in compasse of one houre it goeth in its motion aboue ten hundred thousand myles; wherupon it is certaine that in the same space of tyme it equalleth the compasse of the earth in its course aboue fifty tymes. Among the fixed starres there are many which are 50. 70. 90. or 100. tymes greater then the whole earth, & (as the Astronomers teach) there is none of them, which is not 18. tymes greater then the earth: and yet they are carryed about with their whole Orbe with such a swiftnes, as that such starres as are

near

neare to the equinoctiall lyne do moue e-
uery houre more then 40. millions of my-
les(euery million being ten hundred thoufand) and fo in one houre moueth more ,
then comes to two thoufand tymes the cõ-
paffe of the earth. Now who is he that will
not here fall into an aftonifhing admiration
of his boundles power , who turneth about
fuch vaft and immenfe bodyes , with fo in-
comprehenfible and impetuous a celerity ?
Or what greater prints, or intimations of
Omnipotency can be, then thefe are? If any
one of the ftarres fhould be carryed about
neare vnto the earth with the like fpeed ,
prefently all things would be diffipated &
fhiuered afunder; the mountaines would
be fhaken and pulled vp, as it were by the
roots , and turned with the earth , and the
fea into very duft . The fwiftnes of a bullet
fhot out of a great peece of ordináce feemes
great; and yet if one confider attentiuely ,
fuppofing the bullet to be carryed the fpace
of a hundred houres with one & the fame
fwiftnes , yet would it not go fo far as once
the compaffe of the earth . For experience
fheweth vs, that in one minute of an houre
it is carryed fcarce three myles, therefore in
one houre 180.myles,in an hûdred houres
18. thoufand myles, which wanteth of the
compaffe of the earth , its circûference (ac-
            C4   cording

cording to the more true iudgmēt of Aſtro-
nomers) being 19. thouſand myles, and 80.
Wherfore from this we gather, that the
Sunne performeth a farre greater courſe
in one houre, thē a bullet would do in fiue
thouſand houres. Now the celerity & ſpeed
of the fixed ſtarres about the Equinoctiall
is forty tymes greater, then the celerity of
the Sunne. Therefore that incorporeal power and vertue, which doth ſo gouerne &
ſterne the celeſtiall Orbes, as that it is able
to driue them about with ſuch a facility,
with ſuch an incomprehenſible velocity,
and ſo long a tyme without any ſlacknes, or
wearines, doth ſufficiently diſcouer it ſelfe
to be the maker and Lord of the ſaid heauens, to whoſe good pleaſure they are ſo
ſeruiceable and obedient; and thus it appeareth that from whence they receaue their
moſt wonderfull motion, from the ſame
cauſe alſo they take their nature and being.
Doubtleſly no man who entreth into a ſe-
rious conſideration hereof, can be otherwiſe perſwaded; ſeing there cannot be a
greater argument and ſigne, that a body is
not of it ſelfe, but dependeth of another,
then to ſhew, that it enioyeth not it ſelfe,
but is made ſeruiceable and obedient to another.

The ſame poynt is alſo proued from the
conſideration

confideration of the diuerfity of the parts,
wherof thefe Orbes do confift. For feing
thefe are altogether diftinct in themfelues,
and haue different qualities, they could neuer meete altogether for the making vp of
one and the fame Orbe, except there were
fome higher power, which did vnyte the
faid parts, diftributing to euery one of thē
their place, their magnitude, their meafure,
proprieties, and influences. And this is further confirmed, in that this different fituation and difpofition of parts, whereby (for
example) this Sarre is in this place of the
Orbe, that ftarre in another place &c. is
not of the effence of them (nether doth it
neceffarily flow from their effence) therefore it proceedeth from fome extrinfecall
caufe fo difpofing them.

THE FOVRTH REASON, FROM THE
beauty of things, and the ftructure and com-
pofition of the parts, in refpect of the
whole.

CHAP. VI.

THE very beauty of things, which
confifteth in a due proportion of
parts, both among themfelues, and
with referēce to the whole, manifeftly fheweth

weth that there is one moſt wiſe *mynd* or *intelligence*. which firſt conceaued, weighed, meaſured and conferred with himſelfe all theſe proportions; and then after externally produced them out. When we ſee any magnificent and ſumptuous pallace, wherein a moſt preciſe proportion and ſymmetry of parts is obſerued, ſo as nothing which belongeth to the exact ſkill of architecture is there wanting; no man doubteth, but that the ſame was builded by ſome one or other moſt artificiall architect. How then cã any one call into queſtion, but that this world firſt had a moſt excellent and wiſe artificer and workeman? ſeeing the parts thereof are ſo perfect, and diſpoſed, and conioyned together with ſuch an exact proportion & ſympathy, and whoſe beauty is ſuch, as that it is therefore called Κοσμ◌, which ſignifyeth adorning, beauty, or comlines.

The heauen being extended aboue, like vnto a vaſt and moſt large vault, couereth and imcompaſſeth all things, leaſt they be ſeuered and diſperſed; It is for greater admiration, beauty, and ornament, diſtinguiſhed with an infinite number of ſtarres, as with ſo many Iewels : certainly a moſt faire and pretious vault or couerture of this worldly pallace. Now what is more pleaſing to the eye of Man, then thoſe blewiſh

and

and purple colours of the Heauens? What more pure, then those shining gems & pretious stones? What more solide, then that adamantine firmnes of the heauēly Orbs; which being neuer worne, nor growing old, haue continued so many ages inuiolable? What is more admirable, then the radiant body of the Sunne, being the fountaine of light and heat? What Nature hath imparted to all these their forme, situation, splendour, and this celestial and vnchangeable beauty & fairnes? They do not receaue them from themselues (since they haue not their being from themselues) but from another. And if from some other thing they take their essence, then from the same they also take their beauty. But this other thing cannot be corporeall; since no corporeall thing can be more powerful and fayre, then those heauenly bodyes are. Therfore that, which doth impart to them all these qualities, must needs be a certaine incorporeall or spirituall substance; whose infinite puissance and incomprehensible fayrnes we are partly able to glasse and see (as it were by reflexion)in so great a worke.

The Earth also, though it be seated in the lowest place, seruing as the flore or pauement of this princely and imperiall pallace, or rather as a channell, wherinto the

excrements

excremẽts of the elements are diſburdened,
yet what pulchritude and beauty hath it?
What delight is diſcouered in the moũtaines, and the vallies thereof, in the ſprings,
floods, gardens, woods, fields of paſture
and graine, orchards, and plaines, couered
with all kind of colours. exceeding al tapi-
ſtry, or other ſuch artificial hangings whatſoeuer, through its variσus and diuers veſt-
ment of hearbs, flowers, and groues? Who
can once dreame, that all things are thus

The va-   diſpoſed of *a Nature voyd of reaſon and vnder-*
riety and   *ſtanding*; ſeeing that the ſoule or mynd of
beauty of   man is not able to excogitate or imagine to
things   it ſelfe any thing more admirable, or beau-
cãnot be   tifull? Neither auayleth it any thing here to
referred   reply, that the Sunne and the ſtarres ſeeme
to the   to be the cauſe of all theſe things. For al-
Sunne.   though without the heat and influence of
the ſtarres (wherby the generatiue and ſeminall power or vertue is ſtirred, and the
vegetatiue humors are prepared) all theſe
things cannot grow, increaſe, and come to
their perfectiõ; notwithſtanding theſe bodyes take not from the Sunne and ſtarres
their originall Cauſe, and reaſon of their
particular ſtructure, forming, and making;
but from ſome intelligent mynd or ſpirit,
which hath impreſſed in the ſeeds a certaine power or vertue, being (as it were)
the

the image of its owne cōceit, by the which
(as by its inſtrument) it diſgeſteth, diſpoſeth, and frameth the body, that it may be
altogether anſwerable and ſorting to the
intended forme. For nether the Sunne nor
the ſtarres can know, of what kynd euery
tree (for example) will be, or what temperature, colour, taſt, ſmell, or medicinable vertue for diſeaſes it will haue, or with
what leaues it is to be couered, with what
flowers to be adorned or beautifyed, and
with what fruites to be enriched; finally
what meaſure it ought to haue, what figure,
extenſions, diffuſions, connexions, and innumerable other ſuch obſeruations ; all
which appeare in euery ſuch particuler
body with admirable artifice and wiſdome:
for there is in euery worke of nature (as
their phraſe it) ſo great cunning, skill, and
ſubtility, as that no art can attaine to the
thouſand part thereof; nor any wit can cō-
prehend the ſame. Who then is ſo voyd of
reaſon, that can be perſwaded, that ſuch
bodies, in whoſe making ſo eminent reaſon
and wiſedome is diſcouered, could yet be
made by any Cauſe that enioyeth not reaſon ?

The Sunne of its owne nature imparteth
its light and heat, and in theſe two ſorts, in
one and the ſame vniforme manner it coo-

perateth

perateth with all ſeedes, to wit in heating
the earth, nouriſhing the ſeedes, ſtirring
vp the ſeminall ſpirit or vertue, and in pre-
paring the humours: therefore this infinite
diuerſity of things, and this proportion &
pulchritude, which is in them, cannot proceed from this Sunne, ſeing his operation
and working is vniforme, and a like vpon
al bodies; but it ought to be reduced to ſome
principle or begining, which may contayne
diſtinctly al theſe things in it ſelfe, through
the force of a moſt working reaſon; which
beginning can be no other, then ſome one
moſt excellent ſpirit, which is the Inuentour and workeman of all theſe things .

Liuing
Nature .

This poynt wilbe made more euident,
if we take into our conſideration the body
of liuing Creatures. Good God, how much
art is in their ſtructure and making, & how
much wit ? Each particular liuing Creature conſiſts almoſt of innumerable parts, &
yet theſe parts haue a moſt exact proportiõ
both among themſelues, as alſo in relation
to the whole, which conſiſteth of them :
which proportion is preciſely found in all
creatures of the ſame kynd ; except ſome
deformity therin happen either out of the
aboundance or defect of the matter, or by
the interuention of ſome external cauſe. As
for example, in mans body there is that proportion

portion, as that the length of it with reference to the breadth is sixfold as much; to
the thicknes (which is taken from the *su-*
perficies of the back in a right line to the *su-*
perficies of the breaſt) ten fould; to the Cubit foure fould; to the ſtretching out of both
the armes, equall; to the foot ſix times; to
the breadth of the hand, 24. tymes; to the
breadth of the thumbe, 72 ; to the breadth
of a finger, 96. times. The like proportion
it beareth to the eyes, the noſe, the forehead, the eares, to the ſeuerall ribs, to the
ſeuerall internall parts, to the bones, the
bowels, the ſinewes, the arteryes, the
veynes and the muſcles. The like certaine
proportions do all theſe parts beare among
themſelues; in ſo much that there are ſeuerall thouſands of proportions in this kynd,
which are to be cõſidered in the fabricke of
mans body. For not only in longitude, but
alſo in thicknes, in conformation, in diſtãce
and vicinity, in ſtrength, and in temperature there ought to be a due proportion in
all parts; in this ſymmetry and proportion
of parts among themſelues, and in reſpect
of the whole, conſiſteth all the comlines &
beauty of the body; in ſo much, that if but
any one due proportion (among ſo mary)
be here abſent, then is there ſomething wã-
ting to the concurrence and making vp of

Mans
body.

that

that pulchritude and fairenes, which is naturally incident to mans body.

We may alfo fynd the like proportion in all other creatures, which confifteth in that ftructure and forme, which is moft agreing to their natures; in fo much, that the very flyes, the gnats, and the little wormes are not deftitute thereof. For the making of euery one of thefe fmall creatures is according to their owne kynd fo perfect, fo admirable, and fo beautifull, as that if the wifedome of all men liuing were contracted in one, and gathered together, it could not find any one part, which might be corrected or amended; and which is more, it were not able in its owne retyred thought and imagination to apprehend the reafon, wifedome, and prouidence, which appeare in the ftructure in any of al thefe or other creatures. Wherupon we may further infer, that fuppofing any one man were fo powerfull and mighty, as that he were able inftantly to make or produce outwardly, what he did conceaue inwardly in his mynd; yet could he not forme any one flye (bycaufe he could not comprehend the reafon of the outward and inward ftructure & compofition of the faid flye) much leffe could he animate it, or giue the vigour of fenfe and motion, or plant in it phantafy,

and

and naturall inclination; since what euery
one of these are, cannot possibly be imagined or conceaued.

But to descend to Plants; what excee-
ding beauty is in all kynd of Plants? How **Plants.**
pleasingly do they apparell and cloath the
earth? How wonderfully doth the earth
thurst them out of her bosome, and yet de-
taynes them by their rootes, least they be
torne a sunder with the violence of the
wynds? How great variety is found amõg
thē, of so many trees, so many youg sprouts,
so many kinds of corne and graine, so many
hearbs growing in orchards, fields, and
mountaines, and to conclude so many fra-
grant flowers in gardens & orchards? And
touching the vse of these plants, the commodity is manifold; some of them seruing
for building and making of diuers instruments, others for the nourishment of man
and beasts, others againe, for the making
of linnen cloath; as also to burne, and for o-
ther necessities of mans life.

Touching flowers, they do also delight
vs with their seueral formes, colours, smels,
as that they deseruedly driue vs into admi- **Flowers.**
ration of their maker. For there is not greater profusion and wast (as I may say) of
prouidence and diuyne art in any body so
base and instantly fading, then is in these.

          D   For

For what diuersity of formes are found in them? They are continued together, diuided, deepe, open or displayed, hollow, rising in forme of hayre, formed like little flocks of wooll, winged, hooked, horned, eared like corne, spherically bearing their leaues, enuironed thicke with leaues like clustered grapes, and many other such like different formes. In like sort they are of one leafe, three leaued, foureleaued, or of more leaues; which leaues bearing themselues in seuerall manners, do occasion infinite other formes of flowers.

Neither is their variety of colours lesse then the variety of formes, as whyte, yeilow, red, bloudy, purple, ceruleous or blewish, and finally all mingled colours whatsoeuer, which in regard of their seuerall mixtures are many in number, and therefore they al become gratefull to the eye. To conclude, euery particular flower is wonderfull fayre, and the seuerall parts of any one flower is disposed in such variety, for the greater beauty of their forme, according to their nature and the different tymes of their growth, as they cannot by any art possible be bettered or amended. Now who considering these things with a serious meditation, will not acknowledge the infinite wisedome of the artificer, and will not ad-

mire

mire, prayſe, and reuerence the ſame?

Touching the odour and ſmel of the flo-wers, there is alſo great variety, and the ſmell in moſt of thē is ſweet; there is ſcarce any one flower which hath not a peculiar ſmell to it ſelfe, different more or leſſe frō all others · In ſome, that are the fayreſt to the eye (a poynt which may ſerue as a do-cumēt to vs mē) the ſmell is leſſe pleaſing; and yet in ſome others there is an equall ſtrife and contention, betwene the excel-lency of their forme or ſhape, & their ſmel.

Now from all theſe obſeruations we cō-clude, that it is a truth more radiant, cleare and perſpicuous, then the Sunne beames are; that all theſe things cannot haue their beginning from a nature, or cauſe voyd of reaſon; but from a moſt wiſe and moſt *puiſ-ſant ſpirit*, or *Intelligence*, which conceaued all theſe things afore in its mynd, & which alſo conferred & weighed together al theſe particulers, to wit the quantity or greatnes of euery pláte, their figures or formes, their proportions, temperatures, vertues, co-lours, and ſmels.

Now then this *Spirit* impreſſeth all theſe in the ſeeds of things, (as the image of his conceite) and then worketh and frameth them according to the ſame. For the ver-tue impreſſed in the ſeeds do not otherwiſe

D 2　　　　worke,

worke, then if it enioyed reaſon; the cauſe
hereof being, in that it is a footſtep of a diuyne conception, and as it were a ſealed
impreſſion thereof. Therefore from this *ſu-*
preme Intelligence, or *Spirit*(as being the firſt
inuenting and informing cauſe)the beauty,
proportion, and perfection of all things
doth take its emanation, flowing, and proceeding.

The be-
auty of
the in-
ward
ſoules or
formes
ofthings.

Neither only this viſible fayrnes, and all
variety (which is ſubiect to the eye) is to
be aſcribed to this cauſe, but alſo all inuiſible beauty(which is inwardly hid in thoſe
viſible things, & can be apprehended only
by reaſon) is to be referred therto. For frō
this inuiſible pulchritude the externall and
viſible doth ryſe: ſince what appeareth externally in theſe corporall things, either in
reſpect of forme, proportion, colour kynd
&c. it cometh altogeather from the internall and inuiſible ſubſtance;which ſubſtāce
is ſo much the more fayre, and to be admi-
red, by how much, it containeth in it ſelfe
more highly and ſimply the reaſon & cauſe
of thoſe externall perfections. In the vegetatiue ſoule, by the vertue whereof trees,
hearbs, flowers and the like (according to
their ſeuerall kynds) do lyue, the reaſon
or cauſe of their ſtructure, & whole forme
or ſhape (which ſo much delighteth the
eye)

eye) is latent and vnſeene . In like ſort in
the ſenſitiue ſoule (which animateth all liuing Creatures) the whole reaſon of the fabricke or forme of the body lyes hidden &
imperceptible by the eye ; the ſame is alſo
latent in the genitall vertue or power , by
the which all theſe things are formed. Therefore how great & bewitching is the pulchritude and ſplendour of theſe ſoules , in
whom all theſe perfections are ſecretly and
ſimply included ? And how ſtupendious &
wonderfull are theſe ſoules in their owne
nature , which after one vniforme manner contayne in themſelues ſo great mul- The ſen-
titude and variety of formes and figures.   ſitiue
    Furthermore , in the ſenſitiue ſoule is ſoule.
not only comprehended the entyre reaſon
of the ſtructure of the body , but alſo of all
the ſenſes , the imagination , the ſenſitiue
appetite , all naturall inſtincts and operations , euery one of which , in reſpect of the
wonders diſcouered therin, tranſcends mãs
apprehenſion. For how great is the power
of the ſenſes ? How far of doth the eye penetrate in a moment , viewing all things &
apprehending the formes of them , and ex-
preſſing them in it ſelfe ? How forcible is
the power of ſmelling in dogs, Vultures,&
many other ſuch like ? And as touching the
imaginatiue faculty , it is neuer idle, ſtill re-
      D 3   uoluing

uoluing with it selfe, and varioufly com-
pounding the formes and fhapes of things,
which it receaueth by the miniftery of the
externall fenfe. The appetite draweth and
inuiteth the foule to thofe things (which
the Imagination afore conceaued) if they
be conuenient; and auerteth it from them,
if they be dangerous and hurtfull. To conclude the motiue power obeyeth the appetite with incredible celerity and fpeed, as
appeareth euen in the motion and flying of
flees.

It were ouer labourfome to profecute al
things in this kynd. Euery power or faculty
hath its obiect, inftrument, operation,
its peculiar máner of working, fo occult, fecret, and wonderfull, as no man is able to
apprehend it; and yet the reafon of all thefe
is contained inwardly in the foules of the
faid liuing creatures; fo as whofoeuer could
perfectly penetrate the nature and the mi-
fteries of the foules, fhould fynd the reafons
of all the reft more clearly. Wherfore I am
fully perfwaded, if one could attayne the
perfect knowledge of one fmall flye, the
pleafure of that knowledge would ouerballance and weigh downe all riches, honours and dignities of Kings. For if *Pythago-*
ras (as is written of him) at his finding out
of a mathematicke demonftration did fo im-
moderatly

moderatly reioyce, as for the tyme he perfectly enioyed not himselfe ; then how much ioy & exultation of mynd will a cleare knowledge of so many and so great misteries bring, which are in themselues discouerable in the making euen of the least flye; they being such as yet the most eminent Philosopher that euer was, could not apprehend them, and such as may serue to entertaine a most sweet and serious speculation of thē, for the space of many yeares ? Verily touching my owne priuate censure, I am of this former opinion (as I said) and I doubt not but all such, as attentiuely consider the workes of God, would conspire and agree with me in iudgment herein.

But now to speake something of the *reasonable soule*; it transcēdeth in beauty, worke and dignity the former by infinite degrees, in the which not only the reason of the structure or making of the body, and of all the senses, but also the faculty of vnderstāding, of recordation or remembring, and of imbracing or reiecting any thing freely (in the which is included true electiō & freedome of will) is contained. By the vnderstanding, the soule cōceaueth the whole world, and frameth to it selfe certaine inuisible images or pictures (as it were) of al things. By the memory, it retaineth al those images

of

of things wrought by the vnderſtanding, and when occaſion is miniſtred, it maketh practiſe and vſe of them. Now, how vaſt & ſpacious are thoſe entrances, which are capable of ſo innumerable formes ? By the will, the ſoule taketh fruition of all things, & diſpoſeth of them according to its beſt liking, yea (and which is more) it maketh to it ſelfe election, or choyce of any courſe of life. Neither is the difference here much to be regarded, whether the ſoule performeth al theſe things immediatly by its ſimple ſubſtance, or by diſtinct faculties & powers, ſeeing the reaſon of all theſe are contained in its ſimple eſſence. Therfore it neceſſarily followeth, that the reaſonable Soule is of wonderfull pulchritude, ſplendour, and perfection; in ſo much, that if it were to be knowne perfectly, as it is in it ſelfe, it would ſeeme to be a kynd of diuinity; in the contemplation whereof, the mind would be (as it were) abſorpt and ſwallowed vp with an incredible pleaſure & delight; ſeeing the eſſence of it ſurpaſſeth by many degrees all corporeall things; as alſo the vegetatiue and ſenſitiue ſoules of Plants and liuing creatures, in worth and dignity.

Therefore out of the premiſes we may gather, that there are foure degrees of beauty

ty

ty of things in this world; The first (which is lowest) is of bodyes, which are *seene by the ye*; the secōd of the *vegetatiue* soule; the third of the *sensitiue soule*; the fourth of the *Rationall*, or *reasonable* soule. Therefore it is euident, that not only the first, but also the rest are formed by some most prudent and skilful *intelligence or mynd*. For if the beauty, which is found in bodyes, be to be ascribed to some such spirit or diuine power, for the wonderful proportions appearing in them: then much more the glorious fayrenesse, which is in the seuerall kynds of soules, which comprehends in it selfe the reason and cause of the bodyes beauty, and which is much more admirable then it, ought to be refered to the same celestiall power.

Furthermore I would here demād, how it can possibly happen, that any cause not capable of reason, wisedome, and vnderstanding, could forme and make in the beginning, so many diuersities of vegetatiue and sensitiue soules; seing euery one of thē is so admirable, and is the Effect or worke of so great a wisedome, as that no humane wit is able to penetrate into the seuerall misteries of it, or beget in his mynd the true and proper conceit or image thereof. To conclude; All the pulchritude and perfection of an Effect, ought to be contained in

D 5   the

the caufe; (for the caufe cannot giue that to the Effect , which it felfe enioyeth not) wherupon it followeth , that all the perfe-ction of liuing creatures, and all the vigour and naturall working of the fenfes , ought to be comprehended within that caufe , by the which they were firft framed: and this not after the fame manner , as they are in the creatures , but after a more excellent & eminent fort, to wit, as the worke is contained in the mynd, or art of the workeman . This poynt is further confirmed , in that there is no caufe (excepting a mynd or intelligence) in the which fo great a diuerfity of things can reft ; but in a mynd or intelligence it may well refide ; euen as the forme of a houfe , and all the meafures and proportions of it are faid to be in the phantafy or vnderftanding of the artificer .

Ad heereto for the greater accefie & increafe of reafon herein , that himfelfe who framed the foule of man, endewing it with reafon , vnderftanding, and frewill, cannot poffibly want reafon , vnderftanding and frewill; but muft haue them in more perfect and excellent manner . For how can he want reafon , vnderftanding , and will , who firft made and gaue reafon , vnderftáding and will ? The Prophet therfore truly faid , *Qui plantauit aurem &c. He which*
planted

plantd the eare, shall he not heare? Or he that *Pfalm.93.*
formed the eye, shall he not fee? efpecially feing
thefe are fuch perfections, as the hauing
of them is not any impediment to the fruition and enioying of greater perfections;
fince it is far better to be indued with vnderftanding and frewill, then to want the,
or to haue any thing which may be repugnant to them: from all thefe confiderations
then it is moft euident, that there is a certaine *fupreme Intelligence*, *or Spirit*, which is
the inuentour, authour, and architect of all
thefe vifible, and inuifible beautyes, in
which fpirit, as in its caufe al pulchritude &
fplendour doth eminently exift, & this fpirit we call *God*, who be eternally bleffed,
prayfed and adored.

THE FIFTH REASON DRAVVNE FROM
the ftructure and difpofition of the parts of
the world, with reference to their ends.

CHAP. VII.

EVEN as, not any of thefe things,
which are fubiect to our fight, taketh its being from it felfe, but from
fome efficient caufe; fo nothing is made for
it felfe, but with refpect to fome extrinfecal
end, to the which end the whole ftructure
of

of the thing, as alſo al its parts, and faculties
of its parts, are (after a wonderfull manner)
diſpoſed and framed. Theretore of neceſſity
there muſt be ſome one moſt *wiſe mynd* or
ſpirit, which aforehand conceaued in it ſelfe
all thoſe ends, and ordayned proportionable and fitting meanes to the ſaid ends. For
Nature, which is not capable of reaſon, nor
endued therwith, as it cannot conceaue or
comprehend the ends of things; ſo neither
cã it diſpoſe or ſet downe ſutable meanes to
the ſaid ends; ſince this is a chiefe worke of
art and wiſedome; we will make this manifeſt firſt in heauenly bodyes. The Sunne,
excelling in fayreneſſe all viſible things, is
not for it ſelfe (for it can not apprehend, or
refleϭ vpon its owne beauty) but for the
good & benefit of other things, to wit, that
it may enlighten the world, and cheriſh al
things with its heat; not much vnlike, as
the hart is in man, and other liuing creatures, which is not for it ſelfe, but for the good
of the whole body; for as the heart is in the
body endued with life, ſo the Sunne is in
the whole body of the world, which wanteth life. This then being thus, the Sunne
ought to haue a certaine proportionable
meaſure of light, and quantity, as alſo a determinate place in the world, leaſt that the
light being ouer radiant, ſhyning and great,

                                                                    or

The Sun
not crea-
ted for it
ſelfe.

or it self in place ouer neere, it should burne
the earth ; or on the contrary side the light
being too remisse & smal, or too far of from
the earth , should not sufficiently lighten
it, or heat it . Now , this disposition of a fitting quantity , light , and place, cannot be
assigned by any , but only by such a mynd
or spirit , as is able to consider the end and
the meanes , and of iudgment to set downe
a sorting and conuenient proportion betweene them .

But if the Sunne be made not for it selfe,
but for some external end, then much more
the same may be verifyed of the rest of the
starres , of the heauenly Orbes , and of all
other corporeal natural bodyes. This poynt
may be further fortifyed by this ensuing
reason : *That , which is for its owne selfe , ought
to be of that excellency and perfection , as nothing
can be more excellent , for the good whereof this
other may be ordained ;* This is euident euen
in reason , since otherwise it should not be
for it self, but for that, for the benefit wherof it is disposed . Furthermore it ought *to be
of such a nature, as that it may conceaue & enioy
its owne goodnes;* for if it hath no sense & feeling hereof , it is nothing aduantaged by
such its excellency. For what can the domination and gouerment of the whole earth
profit a mã , if he neither can take any pleasure

The sta-
res , the
Orbs and
all other
bodyes
created
for the
vse of a
reasona-
ble soule

sure therby, nor knoweth that he hath such a principality, or rule belonging vnto him? Therefore it is an euident signe, that, what că not perceaue its owne good, is not made for it selfe, but for some other thing, to the which it becomes profitable. But to apply this now; no corporeall nature is so excellent, but it may be ordained to some other thing more excellent & more worthy; for the degree of a reasonable nature transcéds and exceeds much in worth the degree of a corporeall Nature, and this to the former for many vses becomes seruiceable. Againe a corporeal nature cannot haue any feeling of its owne good, but resteth only in being profitable and expedient for some other thing: Therefore it followeth, that not corporeall or bodily nature is made for it selfe, but euen of its essence & being, is ordained to some other thing, to wit, to a reasonable nature, for whose behoofe and good it exilteth. From which it may be gathered, that if there were no reasonable nature, then all the corporeall nature should exist, as in vayne & bootles, as not being able to bring any benefit to it selfe, or to any other thing; euen as the fruition of great riches should be altogeather vnprofitable, if the man possessing them, should haue neither knowledge, vse, nor feeling of them.

The

The fame poynt is further made euident
frō the motion of the celeftiall Orbs, which
motion bringeth no benefit to the heauens
themfelues, but is wholy applyed to the
good and vtility of man, & of thofe things,
which are commodious to the vfe of man.
For firft the motion of them is fo tempered,
that all Countries of the earth (excepting
fome few, which are beyond 66. degrees
neere to the Poles) enioy within the fpace
of 24. houres both day and night; this being fo directed to the moft gratefull alteration and change of day and night. Furthermore the Sunne by his proper motion
vnder the *Eclyptick* euely cutting the equinoctiall lyne, and declining fometimes to
the fouth, or at other tymes to the north,
more then 23. degrees, caufeth the foure
feuerall tēperatures of the yeares, (I meane
Winter, Spring-tyme, Summer, and *Autumne*)
all thefe being moft accommodate and fitting for the good of fuch things, as the
Earth bringeth forth. For the *winter* fo worketh by its cold, that the fpirit and heat
(which is within the feeds and buds) being inwardly receaued, all things may be
more ftrengthned with in, that fo they may
better gather humour and nourifhment;
that they may faften their rootes in the
earth and finally that all fuch things may
inwardly

The mo-
tion of
the Hea-
uens or-
dayned
for a rea-
fonable
foule.

The 4.
feafons
of the
yeare.

inwardly ſwell, therby to burſt out in due
tyme . The *ſpring* through its pleaſing and
tépered heat calleth all things forth, drawing out buds, leaues, graſſe, flowers, and
the like. The *Summer* with its greater heat
conſumeth the ſuperabundát humour, diſgeſteth crude and raw things, extenuateth
and refineth things groſſe, openeth paſſages
in the bodyes, diffuſeth or powreth in the
ſpirit, & bringeth fruites to their maturity
and rypenes.

To conclude the *Autumne* with its, humour and moderate heat, tempereth a new
all things, correcteth the drynes and heat
of things, which the ſummer aforehád beſtowed; it alſo diſpoſeth the earth to new
ſeedes and new grothes; laſtly it repaireth
the decayed ſtates of liuing bodyes, through
want of naturall heat; Now out of all theſe
obſeruations, who ſeeth not, that all this
motion of the Sunne, and the heauenly bodyes was firſt ordained, & euer after is perpetuated and continuated to the benefit of
man, & to the grouth, increaſe and fuller
aboundance of all liuing creatures, & other
bodies, which may in any ſort be ſeruiceable to the vſe of man? For no other benefit
of it can be aſſigned thé this, nor any other
cauſe can be alledged, why the motion of
the Sunne, and the other celeſtiall Orbes
ſhould

should be in any such, and such sort.

Now if any enter into consideration of
Wynds, raine, snow, and frosts, he shall easily
discouer, that these are ordayned for the
good, emolument, and benefit of liuing
creatures, but chiefly of *Man*,

And first of *Wynds*; the vse of them is various and great, for they ventilate and fan
the ayre, and so make it more wholsome
to be breathed in; which if it should continue vnmoued and vnshaken, would putry-
fy, and being by this meanes affected with
some pestilent quality would kil both men
and beasts: For such close places (we may
obserue) wherin the wynds blow not, are
become most pestiferous and noysome. Secondly, the wynds serue to carry the clouds
about through the ayre, and so to disperse
and distribute them to seueral countryes &
regions: for without the help of the wynds
the *mediterranean* places, and such as are
farre distant from the sea, would be euer
destitute of cloudes and showers; and so
would become ouer hoate, barren, and in-
habitable. For seing from coasts and places
far remote from the sea, there cannot be
drawne vp sufficiēt store of vapours, which
may serue for clouds and raine, except they
being eleuated frō other places, be thither
carryed by force of the wynds, the said *me-*

E   *diterranean*

diterranean countryes would be continually
scorched with the sunne ; and be deprived
of all rigation and watering. For it is the
sea , which chiefly miniſtreth matter for
clouds, out of whoſe vaſt boſome (being
directly and continually oppoſed to the
Sunne) great abundance of vapours are attracted vpwards , by the heat of the Sunne;
which being after by force of the cold gathered into Clouds, are laſtly reſolued into
ſhowers of raine ; wherfore , except the
wynds did carry theſe clouds vnto another
place, all raine would fall into the ſea, from
whence the matter of it doth ryſe ; and the
whole earth through want of watering
would remaine barren and vnprofitable .

Neither this aboue would happen , but
alſo all *fountaines* & riuers would in a ſhort
tyme be drawne dry : for theſe take their
begining and continuance from the *ſnow*, &
ſhowers, which fall vpon the mediterranea
and mountaſious places . For the Snow ,
which during the winter falleth vpon the
hils , melting by little and little through
the Suns heat , and diſtilling into the hol-
lowes and concauityes of the hils , doth in
the end cauſe ſprings or fountaines. In lyke
ſort the waters of *ſhowers* , being receaued
and drunk vp into the higher places of the
hils , and after many wyndings to and fro
vnder

The be-
ginning
of riuers
and wel-
ſprings.

vnder the earth meeting together, do in the
end, fynding an iſſue or paſſage, breake out
into fountaines or ſprings. Now, of *ſprings*
being mixed with other waters (whether
proceeding of ſnow or of ſhowers) & running into one common channel, are begotten *Riuers*. And hence it followeth, that
during the ſummer (when it but ſeldome
raineth) riuers are greatly decreaſed, and
except they be ted with ſnow water, they
are ſometymes dryed vp. So as if for the
ſpace of two or three yeares it ſhould neither raine nor ſnow, it would follow, that
all riuers and almoſt all fountaines would
ceaſe their runing through want of matter.
But theſe things are ſo diſpoſed and gouerned, that for certaine ſeaſons ſo great ſtore
of raine and ſnow may fall, as that therby
the ſprings and riuers may be continually
maintayned and ted.

Furthermore the wynds are neceſſary to
dry vp the vnprofitable humour of the earth
to recreate and refreſh the bodyes of liuing
creatures, to rypen fruites, to the turning
of mils, and ſuch machines or workes, and
finally to the vſe of Nauigation; for admitting there were no wynds, all Nauigation
would almoſt ceaſe. But what great profit
doth ryſe by Nauigation to Man? For by
this, what merchandize is in forraine coun-

tryes, which conduce th either to the commodities of mans lyfe, or to the vse of phisick, or to the delicacy of nature, the same is most easily transported throughout the whole world; and what is peculiar to few, is by this meanes communicated & imparted to all mankynd.

Neither is the profit of the *showers* & *raine* inferiour to that of the wynds: for it cooleth the ayre, refresheth the bodyes of liuing creatures, perpetuateth and continueth springs & riuers, ministers drinke to beasts, watereth the earth, and maketh it fruitful; for without showers of raine the earth would become dry, barren, depriued of all beauty & ornaments of trees, grasse, hearbs and flowers, and finally not fit and commodious for the habitatiō of man & beasts. Showers receaue their fecundity, and fruitfulnes from a double cause: first by the mixture of a viscous and fat matter, which is exhaled and drawne vp with the vapours from the earth and the sea; for the sea being fertil, hath a certaine fatnes, with the which fishes are nourished. Therefore while the Sunne eleuateth vp the more thin parts of it (which are vapours) it withal attracteth a certaine oyle and fat matter, which being mingled with the vapours, & after throgh cold condensd and thickned into rayne,

doth

The profit of showers.

doth water the earth. The same thing also hapneth, when vapours and exhalations are drawne vp through the Suns heat from a fenny earth, frō gardēs, fields, & woods. Secondly, showers take their fruitfulnes from the spirit and heat included and impressed in the cloud or shower by the beames of the Sunne: for this spirit or heat causeth all things to grow and increase. And to the end, that the fall of showers should not ouerwhelme with an ouer great and impetuous force & weight, the tender buds and flowers, therefore the *diuyne prouidence* hath ordayned, that they do not fall ouer abundantly and precipitantly, but that frō a great height they should distil by little & little through a large tract of the ayre, wherby they being deuided into infinite most small drops, do besprinkle the earth with a pleasing moisture and humidity. And to the end, that what is thus falen vpon the earth, should not by the heat of the Sunne be instantly dryed vp & consumed, before it could penetrate and descend to the roots of plants; therefore for the most part, certaine dry remnants of clouds do intercept the beames of the Sunne, vntill the earth do drinke and suck vp the raine, and transmit it to the rootes, for the better nourishing of the fruite which it bringeth

E 3   forth.

forth .

Also *Snow* (which is as it were the froth
of clouds) is accompanied with no small
benefit ; for besides , that it affords matter
The pro- for the continuance of springs and riuers ,
fit of descending from the highest mountaines ,
Snow it doth couer the earth (as it were) with a
fleece of wool , and by this meanes keeping
the heat of the earth within , it hindreth ,
that frosts , penetrating ouer deeply the
earth , do not extinguish the seminall vertue resyding in rootes ; and thus , Snow is
one cause of the earths great fertility of
plants . Snow also hath in it selfe a fecundity and fruitfulnes , in regard of the ayre included in it , which shining with infinite
bubles, giueth that extraordinary whitenes
to the Snow .

Frost in like manner is most profitable to
all things , for by a repercussion & beating
The pro- backe , it keepeth within , the spirit & heat
fit of of the earth , and of liuing creatures , not
frost . suffering it to euaporate and vanish away .
And from this it cometh,that in colder cou-
tryes , and such as are subiect to frosts , men
are of a more robustious & greater stature ,
and longer lyued , then in hoater regions .

Now these , to wit, *Wynds, showers,*
snow , frosts, and the like come not promis-
tuously in any tyme of the yeare, but are so
distributed

diſtributed by certaine ſeaſons thereof , as
they moſt aptly agree and ſort to the begetting , growing, increaſing , and perfecting
of plants and liuing creatures , and to the
perpetuating of their *ſpecies* and kynds, and
further do ſerue moſt cōmodiouſly to Mens
vſes . From all which it is euen demonſtratiuely concluded , that all theſe are ordained and inſtituted by a moſt *wiſe*, and moſt
powerfull mynd or ſpirit , for the good and ſeruice of liuing creatures, and chiefly of *Man*,
to whom all the reſt are ſubiect .

And that the *Elements* are for the ſame
cauſe made, and do to that end enioy ſuch
their peculiar ſituations , and their proper
formes and figures , which now they haue,
doth abundantly appeare from the conſideration of the earth and water . For if we
conſider preciſely things , as they ſhould be
in their owne nature, the earth ought to be
exactly round , and the water ought on euery ſyde to couer & encompaſſe the earth;
Seing all things, that are ponderous and
heauy , ought to deſcend equally towards
the Center of the earth; and by how much
one body is more heauy then another; by
ſo much it ought to be more neere to the
center , and lower in place then the other .
Therefore the *earth* ought to be vnder the
waters , and the waters ſpecially to be po-

The wonderfull diſpoſition of the Elements

wred

wred about it. But we fee that thefe two
Elements are far otherwife fituated : for a
huge portion of the earth, to wit, all that
which is not couered with the fea, and all
the immenfe weight and heape of mountaines, is far higher, and more remote from
the Center, then the water is. For there rũ-
neth a mighty vaſt channell through the
middeſt of the earth of an infinite profundity, deuided into feuerall paſſages, which
running diuers wayes and in fome places of
greater breadth, in others of leſſer, do make
Ilands. Into this channell all the Element
of water is receaued (that only excepted,
which being extenuated and made thin,
turneth into vapours) that fo the earth as
free from being couered with water, might
be made feruiceable for the habitation of
men and other creatures, and for the groth
and increafe of things.

Furthermore, the *Earth* is fo fafhioned
and brought into that forme, that from the
sea towards the mediterranean places, it by
insensible degrees lifteth it felfe vp, & rifeth
higher, vntill it end into mountaines and
rockes : in which poynt confiſteth a moſt
admirable art of the *diuyne Prouidence*. For
firſt by this ſtructure of the Earth, it is made
free from all perillous inundations, which
by little and little, and in long proceſſe of
tyme

The con-
formatió
of the
Earth.

tyme by the influence of the starres, or force of the wynds might endanger al the Earth. For we see by experience, that such bordering parts of the earth, as are neere to the sea, and do not much exceed the Sea in height, are often vtterly ouerflowed with the deaths of the Inhabitants, and losse of all goods. Furthermore if this easy ascent & rysing of the Earth were not, there could not be any riuers: for if the *superficies* of the earth were equally distant from the *Center*, (as in a globe perfectly round) then would there be no fall of riuers; for the water cannot flow, except it fyndplaces morelow and neere to the Center: And if the Earth should suddenly be lifted vp into steepe heights, then would the fall of riuers be more impetuous and violent, then were requisite; neither could riuers being so precipitious and downfall be commodious to mans vse; neither could they runne continually through defect of matter. I here omit the danger of inundations, which often do chance (to the great losse and detriment of the inhabitants) when abundance of raine aud melted snow being gathered together, do suddenly and precipitantly fall from some great height. Therfore the Earth ought to ryse in height by little and little, and by insensible increasings from the

E 5

mouthes

mouthes of the riuers (where they runne
and difgorge themſelues into the ſea) euen
to their ſprings and to other mediterranean
places. Now if we inſiſt in the ſpeculation
of *mountaines*, we ſhall fynd; that in nature
there is no neceſſity of them , but only for
the behoofe and benefit of man . For they
firſt ſerue to breake the force of wynds ,
which might be very domageable to all
creatures, if all coaſts were plaine & euen,
and no hinderance were interpoſed to ſlac-
ken their ſtrength . Hence it proceedeth ,
that wynds are more impetuous and boy-
ſterous in the open Sea , where all is plaine
and eauen without any obſtacle , then in
the middle places of the Earth .

Mountai-
nes .

Secondly, Mountaynes & high hils ſerue
for bounds of regions and kingdomes , for
they are (as it were) the limits or cloſures
of great kingdomes , by the which the ambition of men and deſire of further enlar-
ging their Regality is bridled and reſtrained, leaſt it ſhould inceſſantly exerciſe it
ſelfe in vexing and ſubduing their bordering neighbours . Therefore the ſafety of
kingdomes is much preſerued , and the infinite miſeries and preſſures ſtill attending
vpõ wares by the difficult & inacceſſible ,
paſſages of the mountaines , are much hin-
dered. Great hils do furthermore ſuppedi-
tate

tate and minister matter for building , as
stones , lyme , wood , tyle or slate , with
many other things either necessary , or at
least very commodious to mans life. For
almost all metals and diuers kynds of pretious stones are digged out of the bowels and
veynes of mountaines . There also do grow
vpon mountaines diuers rootes of great
vertue, and infinite kynds of hearbs, as also
most excellent wynes and oliues . Lastly
they containe the origins , and beginnings
of springs and riuers , and they perpetuate
& stil continue them by feeding the with
matter and store of water .

Now let vs next descend to the *quality of
the Earth and Sea*; For this is not found to be
such, as the nature of these Elements(being
considered in it selfe) doth require, but such
as may best sort to the preseruation of liuing
Creatures and commodity of man . For if
we precisely consider the nature of these
bodyes, the Elements ought to be simple or
without mixture of other bodies, vniforme
and in euery place of the same vertue , operation & affectiō . For the *earth* in its owne
nature is vehemently dry , and moderately
cold; the *water* extremly cold and moyst ;
the *ayre* moyst and moderately hot ; and all
these are naturally depriued and voyd of al
sapour or tast, colour, and odour or smell .

The qua-
lityes of
the earth
and the
sea.

But

But this poynt is far otherwise ; for there
are many diuersities & differences of soyles
of the earth ; for they are hoat, cold, tempe-
rate , such as may be crûled away or brokē
into small peeces , light, ponderous , fatty,
vnctious , dry ; In colours blackish, reddish,
yellow , whyte, as also of seuerall tasts, and
odours or smels , and fit and commodious
for the bringing forth of seuerall things: according to those verses.

Hic segetes, illic veniunt fælicius vuæ ;
Arbores fœtus alibi, atq; iniussa virescunt
Gramina ; Nonne vides croceos vt Tmolus odores,
India mittit ebur , molles sua thura Sabæi ?

Therefore seuerall soyles & earth haue
their peculiar fecundity & quality impressed in them , by him who firtt created this
Element. Neither can we ascribe all this
diuersity to the Sunne and the starres; seing
that vnder one and the same Climate there
are some places more desert & barren, other
most fertill ; and such of these places as are
fertill, do not bring forth the same kynds
of plants & other liuing Creatures, though
they receaue one and the same aspect & influence from the Sunne and the starres . In
like sort, the earth doth not produce all
kinds of metals and minerals in one and the
same place, but diuers in diuers places. For
in one place it bringeth forth stones , in a-
nother,

nother, chalke, red lead, in a third, brasse, tyn and lead, in others gold, siluer, & pretious stones. Therefore the earth in diuers places receaueth diuers vertues, forces and operations, that therby it may minister to Man all kynd of riches, which not only côduce to an absolute necessity of mans life ; but also to a greater conueniency, delicacy and splendour thereof; which poynt doth turne to the greater honour, glory, & laud of so munificent a Creatour.

In lyke sort, the *Sea* hath its fruitfulnes altogether most admirable ; & this diuers ; according to the difference of places. For not in each part of the Sea all kynds of fishes are found ; for some kynds do breed in the North, others in the South seas ; Some also only in the East, & others in the West seas.

Furthermore all the sea (meere contrary to the nature of that Element) is of a strãge saltnes. Now from whence doth this come? Or what power & vertue gaue this saltnes to it ; and to what end? The reason is ridiculous and absurd, which some Philosophers haue inuented hereof, to wit, that this saltnes cometh by reason of the Sunne beames, by the which the bottome of the sea is scorched and burned ; and that adustion and burning causeth saltnes (say they) is

The saltnes of the sea.

proued

proued from the experience in burnt aſhes :
That this reaſon is moſt inſufficient, is euident: for how câ the bottome or the groûd
vnder the ſea (being couered with ſuch an
infinite ſtore of waters ; that in ſome places
it is 500. or a thouſand cubits deepe) be ſo
burnt by the Sunne, as that from them all
the whole ſea ſhould contract ſuch a bryny
ſaltnes ? For the Sunne burneth not but
only by reaſô of its light, which light doth
not penetrate in the water further then 15.
cubits (as diuers Swimmers vnder water
aſſirme) and the light is ſo faynt, that the
heat thereof can hardly be felt, but a little
vnder the water. Now, that ſaltnes ſhould
proceed of aduſtion, it is required, that the
aduſtion be ſo great, as that it diſſolueth
the matter, & reduceth it to its beginning,
as experience ſhoweth. Neither doth aduſtion and burning properly cauſe ſalt in o-
ther things, but rather openeth and diſcouereth it ; And therefore we ſee, that of ſeuerall bodyes the ſalt is ſeuerall, and taketh
its ſeuerall vertues & operations from the
bodyes ſo ſtrayned & refyned, as the Chy-
mickes do experimentally proue. In like
manner the ſpirit of euery thing (or the oyle
which is extracted out of it by fyre) doth
aforehand lye hidden in the thing it ſelfe.
Furthermore it ſalſity or brynenes proceed
from

from this aduftion , then ought the Sea to
be dofy , more and more falt ; wherupon it
wouldfollow, that the fifhes as not éduring
that temperature, would in the end dye, as
it hapneth in the Lake *Afphaltites* (which is
called *Mare mortuū*) fince the nature of fifhes requires a certaine temperature of the
waters . To conclude the increafe of this
faltnes in the Sea would be noted at leaft in
feuerall ages , but no fuch augmentation
hath hitherto bene obferued . Of the lyke
improbability is that fentence , of the firft
origin *of mountaynes* , which teacheth , that
the firft proceeded of Earthquakes , by reafon that the ayre , and other fuch fpirituall
fubftance, which being included in the bowels of the earth , did aduance and lift vp
the higher part therof . This opinion might
with *fome probability* be maintayned , if it
were deliuered only of fome certayne little
hils. But it cannot with any fhow or colour
of lykelyhood , be verifyed of that great
multitude of moft huge mountaines , poffeffing many *mediterranean* places , and extending in length 800. or 1000. myles. But
omitting many other ftrong reafons, by the
which this fiction is refuted, I couclude that
the faltnes of the Sea was firft giuen to it by
the *authour and maker of it* , who as he implanted (contrary to the courfe of nature) a
                                    fecundity

tecundity in the earth for the bringing out
and nouriſhing of plants, and liuing Creatures, ſo the like he beſtowed vpon the ſea
for the production, ingendring and feeding
of fiſhes.

From all which ſpeculatiõs it is moſt neceſſarily gathered and inferred, that al theſe
things (aboue mentioned) were ſo diſpoſed and ordained for the vſe and benefit of
Man, by ſome moſt *wiſe and moſt powerfull
Intelligence*; ſince all things (euen beſides
their naturall condition) do ſerue, and become obedient to the vſe of mans life, and al
do finally propend and are directed to this
end; Neither can there be rendred any
other reaſon, why they ſhould be ordered
in ſuch ſort, as they are, but only for the
emolument, commodity, and ſeruice of
Man.

Neither it is in any ſort preiudicial to the
being of a *diuyne Prouidence*, that by reaſon
and meanes of impetuous wynds, hayle,
thunder, earthquakes, infection of the ayre,
inundation of waters, drouthes, & the like,
men do often ſuffer great calamities & miſeries; ſince theſe things do more euidently
demonſtrate the being of the ſaid prouidence. For as it is the property of a Prouident and wiſe Prince, ſo to diſpoſe his lawes, tribunals or Iuſtice ſeats, towers, prouiſion

The Ca-
lamityes.

uifion of warres &c. that they may be directed to the good and fecurity of his fubiects, as long as they liue in due allegiance and duty towards him; and the fame things alfo to turne to their chaftifings and punifhments, if after they fhould once endeauour to fhake of the yoke of fubiection: Euen fo although that *fupreme Power* or *fpirit* hath finally created the heauens & the Elements for the feruice of man; yet hath he fo tempered thefe things, that withall they may ferue, as fcourges for the caftigation of finners; which chafticement may neuertheles be beneficiall to fuch, who know to make true vfe thereof, as hereafter we will fhew.

Some here may obiect (contrary to our former doctrine) that fuch things, wherof we haue intreated before; haue not their euét from any particuler end, to the which they are by any intelligent caufe directed, but only by reafon (as the Philofophers phrafe & dialect here is) *neceffitatis materiæ*, through the nature of the matter forcing or caufing fuch effects : as for example it is naturall, that through the heat of the Sunne vapours and exhalations be attracted from the Earth & the Sea; the which being eleuated aboue, are repelled backe by the cold of the midle Region, & fo do caufe wynds, or els being gathered into clouds, do mini-

F　　　　　　　　　　 fter

ſter matter for rayne, ſnow and haile, from which ſprings and flouds do after take their ſource and beginning.

I anſwere hereto and confeſſe, that ſome of theſe things may ſeeme to take ſuch their euents from their matter, whereof they are made: But this diſcouereth a greater and worthyer diſpoſall of the *diuyne Prouidence*, by the which the vniuerſall cauſe of things (to wit the motion of the Sunne & ſtarrs) is ſo ordayned and gouerned, as that without the cōcourſe of any other efficiēt cauſe, it can occaſiō the foreſaid things, as wynds, raine and the like, at ſuch tymes and in ſuch ſeaſons, as are moſt conuenient for the producing and nouriſhing of plants and liuing creatures, and for the benefit of man. And therefore theſe effects do thus fall out, not only throgh the inforcemēt of the matter, but withall through the various aſpect and applicatiō of the vniuerſal cauſe. Add herto for the greater fulnes of our anſwere herein that the diſpoſition and placing of the Sea and the earth, the firſt beginning & large extenſion of mountaines, the channels of riuers &c. cannot be referred to any neceſſity of matter or force of nature, but are neceſſarily produced by art and Prouidence as is aboue ſhewed. And thus it falleth out that (for example (*Egipt*) being deſtitute of

of raine) is in the summer tyme so watered
with the inundation of *Nilus*, & therby so
couered ouer with a tat & vnctious slyme,
as it becometh most fertill. In like sort one
of the Iles of the *Canaryes* (called *Ferri*)
wanting altogether sweet water, is supply-
ed heerein by *diuyne Prouidence* from a tree
there growing; whose nature is such, as that
it daily distilleth (like vnto a spring or foū-
taine) a certaiue sweet humour, which
serueth for drinke both to man, and beasts.

Now besides the heauenly and Elemen-
tary bodyes (of which we haue spoken a-
fore) there are found three perfect kynds of
mixed bodies, to wit liuing Creatures,
Plants, and all such things as are to be digged out of the bowels of the earth; al which
no doubt were first created and made for
the vse of Man; considering, that we see
they are subiect to Man; he ruling ouer thē,
and applying them at his pleasure to his
owne vse and benefit.

From all which, this one true resultacy
or conclusion may infallibly be gathered ; The
that all this aspectable world, with all the world
things, which it containeth, was first made why
for the cause of Man ; and that it serues for created.
the tyme, as a most ample and fayre house,
furnished with all things seruing either for
necessity, or pleasure and delicacy; in the
F 2   which

which man is placed, to the end, that he acknowledging *a diuyne and ſupernaturall power* to be the authour of this world, may loue, reuerence, and adore the ſaid power; and that he may vſe theſe things according to the true vſe and preſcript of Reaſon; whether they conduce to the maintenance and ſuſtentation of his body, or ſolace and comfort of his mynd, or to the health and increaſe of knowledge.

For ſeing the ranke of things intelligible and endued with Reaſon, is the higheſt and moſt worthy among al things created, it followeth, that man (as being an intelligent and reaſonable creature) is of a more eminent nature, degree, and order, then any other thing in the whole world. Therfore man ought to be the end of all things in the world, and they to exiſt, and be for his vſe. For man only conſidereth al things in the world, apprehendeth all things, and vſeth and enioyeth all things. Man only alſo feeleth and diſcerneth the ſweetnes & beauty of al things, who being (as it were) a certaine ſecondary *Numen,* or diuyne power, doth produce and create by the help of his vnderſtanding al this corporal world in himſelfe, after an incorporeall manner: for without man to apprehend them, in vaine were all this ſo great beauty and artifice

(marginal note) Man the end of all viſible things & of the whole world.

artifice of all things, in vayne so wonderfull a disposall of them; in vaine so stupendious a structure and composition of all: finally in vayne were such variety of formes
colours, smels, sapours, and temperaméts.
For if man were not, then there were nothing left, which could discerne or apprehend these things, admire them, praise the,
vse them, or take any pleasure of them. For
al other liuing creatures are seruile & mancipated to the senses of tast and feeling, and
do not apprehéd any thing vnder the shew
and forme of good, but what is agreable &
sorting to their belly, or venereous pleasure, & this also after a brutish máner. Therefore as that house, wherin no man doth
inhabit, and of which none is to make any
vse or benefit, (though it be otherwise
stored with all abundance of furniture and
domesticall necessaries) is not to be prized,
but to be reputed, as a needles Edifice or
building; Euen so this world (though thus
beautifyed (as it is) with such variety of celestiall and terrestriall bodyes, and al other
things accompanyng the same) should but
exist in vayne and fruitlesly, if there were
no rationall and intelligent nature, to reside
and dwell therein, who were able to apprehend, obserue, and discerne the admirable workes therein, and to take fruit and

pleasure

pleasure of it, both in regard of temporall commodity, as also of speculation & knowledge.

Now then from al these Considerations it is most cleare, that this world was made for man; and consequently that there is a *Prouidence*, which did create the world to this particuler end. For it could not exist by it selfe to this end, neither could it re-ceaue from it selfe al this disposition, by the which it is so wonderfully accommodated to the vse of Man (as is aboue shewed:) Therefore the world hath its being, its forme, its disposition, its motion, and its forces & vertues from an *intelligent nature*, which we call *God*.

THE SIXT REASON, BORROVVED FROM the Structure or making of liuing Creatures, and Plants, with reference to an end.

CHAP. VIII.

THAT the Prouidence of this *diuyne* and *supreme Power*, is not only in generall and confusedly; to wit, as it ordaineth the foresaid generall causes to the production of sublunary things; but also, that it is in particuler and most perfectly, as distinctly belonging to the least things,

is

is euidently conuinced from the structure
and making of liuing creatures and plants.
For the seuerall parts and members of them
are framed with such exquisite artifice and
skill, and with such a proportion, and so
apt and fit to performe their functions and
ends; as that no art or wisedome can add
any thing therto, or correct or better the
lest thing therein : which poynt is a most
absolute demonstration, that al these things
were first excogitated, inuented, & made
by a most *wise spirit, or mynd* ; and who first
distinctly and separatly considered all particulers aforehand, and then after most curiously produced and brought them forth,
through his admirable and stupendious art.

This we will make euident by some examples, & first we will a little insist in the
speculation of *Mans body*. Well then : Man
could not consist of only one bone, because
then he could not bend himselfe, nor vse
his members to seuerall motions and functions; Therefore he is framed of many bones;
some being greater, some lesse, and others
most small, of all which every one in particuler hath that magnitude, shape, firmnes,
and connexion, which the strength of the
body, the facility of mouing, and the vse
of the members requireth. The bones of the
head are in number eight, of the higher iaw

*The Cō-
sideratiō
of Mans
body.*

Bones.

F 4 twelue,

twelue, of the lower, one. The teeth are
thirty two, the ridge or fpine of the backe
confifteth of 32. *Vertebres*, or ioynts. The
bone of the breaft is compofed of three bones.
The ribs are 24. of which fourteene comming from the backe bone, do arriue to, &
touch the bone of the breaft, and are implanted in the fame bone for the more firme
keeping of the Heart and the longs. The
other ten do not proceed fo far, to the end,
that laxity and loofenes may be left to the
ftomack and belly. Euery feuerall fingar
confifteth of 3. fmall bones, and the thumbe
of two. The hands with the fmall bones of
the wreft, by the which they are tyed to
the bones of the cubit or arme, do confift
of twenty fmall bones. In the feet there are
no fewer bones, and thefe are connected
together after a wonderfull manner. For
fome of them are infixed & driuen in (like
nailes (as the teeth of the iawbone are:)
Others are inferted, and as it were fowed
in, as we fee in the bones of the fcull. Some
againe are faftned in manner of a box, and
are tyed with ftrong ligaments, as the bone
of the thigh in the hollownes of the hip.
Others do mutually enter & penetrate one
anotherin forme of the hinge of a doore
(which connection is called in Greeke
γιγγλυμωδις ευναφι:) to conclude others are
                                        knit

knit togeather atter other forts, as is beſt
fitting to the firmnes and motion of the mē-
ber. Furthermore with what moſt ſtrange
skill are thoſe little bones (which are tearmed *Seſamina*) interpoſed in certaine places
for the more eaſy mouing of the ioynts ?
Briefly euery bone is made fit and apt to its
end and function, that it cannot be conceaued, how it could be made more commodious. For there is nothing in vaine, nothing redundant or ſuperfluous, nothing
deficiēt or wanting;finally nothing which
is not moſt neceſſary and expedient to its
end, wherunto it is made.

In like ſort, theſe bones could not be couered with one continued and vndeuided
maſſe of fleſh; for ſo they would be vnfit
to the vſe and mouing of the members;and
therefore they are fitted with ſeuerall parcels of fleſh (which we cal *Muſcles*) & with
theſe parcels the bones are couered, and of   *Muſcles*
them the body is framed after a wonderfull
manner. There an are in mans body more
then *ſix hundred muſcles*, as long muſcles,
ſhort, broad, narrow, thicke, thin, ſtraight,
crooked, ſharpe,obtuſe, ſtreit and round,
plaine or eauen corned:they are alſo either
of a ſimple figure and forme, or els of a multiplicious & diuerſe ſhape. Againe they are
placed either one vpon another, or neere

to another; As also either directly, oblique-
ly, or transuersly, & this most wōderfully;
for by the meanes hereof euery member exerciseth its mouing. *Galen* wryteth, that in
mans body there are more then two hundred bones, and that euery bone hath more
then forty *scopi* (as they are called) which
may wel and deseruedly be obserued in the
framing, disposing, and connecting or knit-
ting together of the bones ; therefore to the
end, that the only bones of Mans body may
be aptly framed and formed, there are more
then eight thousaud *Scopi* to be considered .

Furthermore there being more then six
hūdred nuscles, whereof euery one hath tē
scopi, & therefore only in the muscles there
are six thousand , for thus writeth *Galen* ;
*Eadem ars &c . The same art is to be seene a-
bout all the bowels, & indeed about euery part; so
as if one consider the scopi, which the structure of
mans body hath, the multitude of them would rise
vnto some myriades.* And hereupon *Galene*
concludeth , that mans body is framed by
some most wise and most puissant workeman.

It was not sufficient , that mans body
should consist of bones and muscles ; but
withall it was needfull , that it should haue
naturall heat , by the which it might liue; &
bloud,

bloud by which it might be nourished ; & *spirits*, by the which it might moue and exercise its senses ; for without this spirit the soule could neither vse any sense , nor the body moue it selfe ; for seing the spirit is of a most attenuated and thin substance (as a thing betwene the most subtile soule and the grosse body) it is therefore the immediate and next instrument or *Organum* of the soule, by meanes whereof the soule causeth in the body motion and sense, and without the which there can be no distribution of nourishment made through out the whole body .

Therefore the *diuyne Prouidence* hath fabricated and made three principall parts in mans body , by the which these operations may be performed , to wit, the *Hart*, the *Liuer* and the *braine*. The Hart is ordained for the *vital heat*,and spirits of the whole body; the Liuer for the sanguineous , bloody and *naturall spirits* ; and the braine for the *animal spirits* . To these three other externall instruments & parts of the body are seruiceable. To the Liuer belong the teeth , the *Esophagus* , and the stomacke to affoard the matter of blood , or a certaine concocted iuyce , which is called *Chylus*. The *Intestines* or entrals do serue partly to trasmit & send this *Chylus* through the *Mesaraical* veynes to the

The principall parts of the body

the Liuer , and partly to deonerate & diſburden the body of the excrementall part of meat and food . Furthermore to the Liuer belongs that veſſel, called *folliculus fellis*, the receptacle of *gall* , that therby , after the *Chylus* is once turned into blood , it may draw to it ſelfe, & containe the more ſharpe matter or ſubſtance of nouriſhment , which matter would be otherwiſe hurtfull to the body; The *Liene*, or *Splene* conduceth, that it may attract to it the more groſſe and ſeculent parts of blood . The *Reynes* , that they may ſucke vp the raw , and redundant wheiſh matter, being mixt with blood, and after they do ſend it through the veſſels of vryne to the bladder to be auoided in conuenient tyme . The *Longs* are ſeruiceable to the Hart , wherby the Hart is refrigerated and cooled , and the vitall ſpirits recreated and refreſhed through the often attraction and expiration of new and freſh ayre .

Now, the *ſpirits* are engendred after this ſort . The meate being once concocted, the beſt iuyce of it is transferred to the Liuer; This tranſmiſſion or ſending it thither is made partly by the vitall compreſſion or cloſing of the ſtomacke , and partly by the vertue of the veynes of the Inteſtine called *Ieiunum* , and other innumerable veynes , which being placed in the *meſenterium*, or in the

The engendring of the ſpirits.

the midle of the bowels, haue a power of
fucking to them. The Liuer then receiuing
the *Chylus* through a fistula or hollow pipe,
turneth it (throgh its owne natural difpofition) into blood; and after that, the more
thin parts therof it chāgeth into a vapour,
which commonly is called *fpiritus naturalis*:
this vapour diftendeth, enlargeth, and openeth the veynes and pores of the body. One
part of this blood the liuer by meanes of
vena caua (which proceedeth or ryfeth from
it felfe) fenderh to the heart; Then through
the heate of the hart, this blood is wonderfully extenuated and refyned ; firft in the
right ventricle of the Heart , and after in *the*
left ventricle, & fo a great part therof is conuerted into a moft fubtill and thin vapour;
of which vapor one part is fent frō the Heart to the brayne by a great Arterie;& there
being elaborated againe, clarifyed & tempered in that fould of fmall arteries (which
is commonly called *rete mirabile*) it becomes *fpiritus animalis*: the Animall fpirits do
ferue only to *fenfe* and *motion* , which are
peculiar functions of a liuing Creature .
The reft of thefe fpirits (being mingled
with moft thin and pure blood) the Hart
diftributeth through out the whole body
through the Arteries, conferuing and maintaining herby the natural heat of the body :
and

and this spirit is vsually tearmed *spiritus vitalis.* And here now we are briefly to shew, how both kynds of these spirits and bloud is dispersed throughout the whole body; that therby we may the better apprehend by *how admirable, and wonderfull a Wisedome* all these things are thus disposed.

Our body consisteth of *heat* and *moisture*; The heat dayly consumeth and spendeth the moisture, vapouring it away into ayre; as the like appeareth by water exposed to the Sunne, or to fyer, which by little and little vanisheth away. And thus all the members and entrals of mans body would soone decay and dry away, if there were no instauration and repairing thereof made by nourishment. The immediate & next nourishment of the body is blood; and therefore it is requisite, that blood be distributed through the body, that all parts of it be nourished therewith. The Liuer is the shop (as it were) of bloud. Therefore from the Liuer there are drawne two great veynes, the one going vpwards, the other downwards the body; both which do after brách and diuyde themselues into seuerall lesser veynes; these againe into lesser and lesser, till they end in most small veynes, and to the eye scarce visible. These veynes go towards the bowels & to the muscles, & in them

How the spirirs are distributed through out the body.

The distributió of the bloud.

them they are terminated and implanted.
Seing then that there are aboue six hundred
muscles , and that for the most part many
small veynes do run into euery muscle, it
cōmeth to passe, that besides those inuisi-
sible veynes (which for their smalnes are
called *vene capillares*, as resembling in quā-
tity the haires of a mans head) there are
some thousands of veynes, or rather branches of veines, which do rise and take their
beginning from the two former great veynes .

Now by this meanes it is effected , that
there is not the least part of the body , but
there is nourishment brought to it . The
making and vertue of the veynes is wonderfull : for they consist of *fibræ*, or small
strings, and these are direct, oblique , or
transuerse By the direct *fibra*, they attract
and suck blood; by the oblique they retaine
and keep it ; and by the transuerse they
transmit it further to the muscles and other
extreme parts. The same art and prouidēce
is obserued in the concauityes & hollownes of the *intestina*, or bowels : they haue
the power of keeping bloud , which once
bursting out of them, doth instantly putri-
fye, and ingendreth diseases as we may obserue in Plurisyes, Contusions, and inflā-
mations. The wheish humour is mingled
                                    with

with bloud, for the more eafy diftribution
of it, which humour after is either diffipated into ayre through heat, or els is purged
away through fweat. The blood is alfo
mingled with a little gall for the more at-
tenuating and making it thin, left otherwife it fhould coagulate and thicken. Finally the bloud is in like fort mingled with
that fpirit, which is called *fpiritus naturalis,*
that it may open the pores, and let in the
nourifhmét, for there is no part of the body
which is deftitute of *Pores*.

In bones, mufcles, bowels, finewes,
veynes, arteryes, membranes, and grifles,
there is *vis affimulatrix*, an affimulating power; by the which all thefe parts do con-
The di-   uert the nourifhmét fent to them into their
ftribu-   owne fubftance, nature, and kynd.
tion of
the vitall   As the Liuer doth fuppeditate and mi-
fpirits   nifter blood to all parts of the body, with
the which it is nourifhed, as alfo naturall
fpirits; fo the *hart* doth giue heat and vitall
fpirits, by the which the natiue heat is cherifhed, ventilated, and cooled: to which
end there proceed from the hart two *Arte-*
ries, the one going vpward, the other downeward; both which deuyde themfelues
into many branches, and thefe againe into
other leffer, vntill they end in moft fmall
fibræ, iuft after the manner of the veynes a-
boue

aboue specifyed . The smallest branches of
the Arteryes are implanted in all the Muscles , and all the bowels, therby to bring to
them heat and spirit .

Furthermore , as in those bodyes, which
haue hoat bloud, the hart doth continually
beat it selfe with those two motiõs , which
are called *systole* and *diastole* : By *diastole* or
dilatation of it selfe, it drawes in new ayre
to temper the heat , and refresh the spirits ;
by *systole* or compression of it selfe , it expels
all fulignious vapours; so are all the Arteryes throughout the whole body at the
same instant moued with an incessant and
continuall vicissitude , in dilating and con-
tracting themselues , euen for the foresaid
ends . And this ventilation is of such moment , as if it be interrupted (as sometimes
it is by an afflux of humours) then presently is a feuer inflamed , and set on fyer.

The *brayne* affordeth *animall spirits* which
is diffused throgh all parts by meanes of the
nerues or *sinewes* ; as bloud and naturall spirits are by the veynes , and heat ,and vitall
spirits by the Arteryes . But because such
store of sinewes, which were to be deriued
to the bowels and all the Muscles , could
not proceed from the brayne, which is contained in the head ; therefore the *diuyne
Prouidence* (being the maker of Man) doth

*Systole
and
diastole .*

*The di-
stributiõ
of the
Animall
Spirits .*

G　　　　　　　　　extend

extend and draw out the substance of the
braine(enclosed in its owne membranes &

**The pro-
duction
of the
brayne
and its
skins .**

skins)from the head by the *vertebre* or ioynt
of the necke , throughout the whole spine
or ridgebone of the backe , so as the *medulla
spinalis*, or the inward substance of the back-
bone is nothing els , then a certayne continuation and production of the braine. Now
to the end , that these *animall spirits* should
not be dryed vp or vanish away , & so man
should suddenly dye; therfore the brayne is
inuolued and couered with a double skin ;
the one being more thin, which is the more
inward, and next to the brayne ; the other
more hard , which is the outward , & next
to the bone of the *Cranium* or skull . In like
sort & with the same skins the *Medulla spinalis* is inclosed .

The sinewes proceed from the braine &
from the *spinalis medulla,* & from the double

**Six payre
of sine-
wes from
the
brayne .**

membrane of them . From the braine there
are six paire of nerues or sinewes , wherof
fyue are directed to the organs or instruments of the fiue senses, therby to deriue to
them the animal spirit chiefly for sense, and
secondarily for the mouing of the muscles
of the head. The sixt paire or sinewes is extended out of the head, to certaine Muscles
of the necke , of the *larinx* of the breast ,
and the orifice or m outh of the stomacke ,
which

which beareth a great sympathy with the
hart. From the *spinalis Medulla* and its membranes, there do rise thirty payre of syne-
wes ; whereof euery payre being after de- **Thirty**
uided into many branches, are in the end **payre of**
inserted in the muscles, as the like afore we **sinewes**
said of the veynes and arteryes. When they **from the**
come vnto the muscles, they run into a sin- **spina**
newy matter, which they call *Tendo*, and **dorsi.**
with maketh the head of the Muscle. Thus
are the animall spirits transmitted and sent
from the braine and *spinalis medulla*, through
the concauities of the sinewes to the instruments of sense, and to the Muscles : by the
helpe of which spirits the soule moueth the
muscles ; and the muscles (being thus moued) do moue euery member, as also by
the meanes of the said spirits (as by its instrument) the Soule performeth the operations of both the externall and internall
senses.

The Composition of the sinewes is most
admirable ; for as the braine consisteth of **The**
three things ; to wit the *medulla* or marrow **Compo-**
therein & the two skins, within the which **sition of**
it is inuolued ; so in like sort doth euery **the Sine-**
sinew, proceeding from the braine : for the **wes.**
inward *medulla* or marrow of the braine, is
like to the substance of the braine ; & this
medulla is couered ouer with two tunicles

or skins; ſo as the Sinewes ſeeme to be nothing els , then the production or continuation of that *medulla* , and of theſe membranes or skins, whereof the braine conſiſteth. And by this meanes it is effected , that the braine is (after a manner) throughout the whole body, & in euery part therof, which hath ſenſe and motion . For firſt it is placed in the head, wherin are all the organs and inſtruments of ſenſe. From the head, it (being accompanied with the two foreſaid skins) is extended through the ſpine of the backe ; from the *ſpina dorſi* , or ridgbone of the backe, it goeth into the ſinews , which being diſperſed throughout the whole body , are implanted and inſerted into all the muſcles .

In like manner, the Hart by meanes of the Arteries , which imitate the nature of the hart; & the Liuer , through the veynes which retaine the vertue and power of the Liuer , may be ſaid to be diffuſed throughout the whole body, & to exiſt in the leaſt part of it. Therfore with what wonderful artifice and Prouidence are thoſe three principall members, to wit the *brayne, hart*, and *Liuer* , (by the which ſenſe, motion, the dilatation & compreſſion of the hart or Arteryes , and Nutrition , are performed) extended throughout the whole body ,&

How the three principall mēbers are throughout the whole body .

do

do exit (after a certaine maner) in al parts thereof? I omit innumerable other poynts, which might be deliuered and set downe touching the structure, and vse of the parts of the body .

But I haue somewhat largly insisted in discoursing of the vse & end of these three principall members, in that the serious côsideration of them hath seuerall tymes moued me to an admiration of the *diuyne Power*, who so strangly hath compacted and framed them. For let the wisedome of all men and al Angels meet together , & they are not able to excogitate or inuent any thing so wel disposed & directed to its end, and so sorting and agreable to the nature of the thing it selfe, as these things are .

Neither only in Man , but in the *species* or kynds of other liuing Creatures the artifice and skill of these three members are found: for seing all liuing Creatures enioy sense and motion ; it is therefore needfull that they haue *animall spirits*, and consequétly a *brayne* sorting to its nature , which is the shop of those spirits ; as also that they haue sinews deryued from the braine, by the which the spirits are deferred and carryed to the Muscles . In like sort becaufe al liuing Creatures are nourished, it is requisite , that they haue a *Liuer* , which prepa-

The thre p incip Member are foud in other liuinge Creatures .

G 3   reth

reth and concocteth the nourifhment , and *veynes*, by the help of which , the nourifhment is transferred to each part , as alfo
naturall fpirits , feeing by the benefit of
thefe the aliment penetrateth all parts of
the body .

Finally , becaufe the forefaid Creatures
are to be cherifhed with a certaine natiue
heate of their owne ; wherby they may
liue , it is expedient , that they haue a *hart*,
from the which the natiue heat and vitall
fpirits are difperfed ; and arteryes , by the
which they are fo difperfed. Now thefe
three principall mébers are moft appofit-
ly and aptly framed and difpofed in liuing
Creatures , not after one and the fame maner , but after different forts according to
the different nature of the faid Creatures ,
and therefore they are found in *flies, gnats,
fleas*, and the leaft wormes . For thefe fmall
creatures haue their braine, their Liuer,
their finews , arteryes , and veynes fabricated and made with wonderfull fubtility:
their inward parts are not confounded in
themfelues , nor of one forme , but they
haue feuerall perfect organs & vnmixte;
they being of different temperature, different faculty , different vfe, different forme,
different connexion, and of different place
or fituation ; yet made with fuch an invifi-
ble

ble tenuity and smalnes, as is incomprehensible to mans wit. And this poynt is fully manifested by the sharpnes of their senses, their swiftnes of motion, & their strange and great industry and sagacity.

Now, if we consider the externall and outward parts of liuing Creatures; how wonderfully is euery part appropriated to its peculiar vse & end? How easy, expedite, and quicke functions and motions haue they? And how great variety is there of them according to the variety of their kinds? *Birds* are made with small heads, & sharpe becks the more easily therby to cliue and pierce the ayre; with crooked pounces, wherewith to hold fast the boughes of the trees, wherupon they sit; with fethers growing backward, that their flying be not hindred; which feathers ly close to the body, whyle they fly, that the ayre may the lesse enter among them; their wings are most light, and so framed, as they may easily open and close for flying; being fitted with a soft hollownes to receaue ayre in while they flye, and to couer their body straitly and comely. Such of them as feed vpon flesh, haue most strong & hooked beckes to teare the flesh asunder, and sharpe and crooked tallants to apprehend and hould it. Such as feed vpon the water,

The externall parts of liuing Creatures.

The shape of Birdes.

G 4   ter,

ter, haue log necks; that they may dyue in
to the water the deeper with their head,
To conclude, how many colours are there
in seueraii kynds of byrds? How pleasant
is the beauty of their wings? How great is
the difference of their sound and voyces?
How sweet is the singng of some of them?
And euen in some of those, which haue
but a very small body, how shrill and pi-
ercing is the sound they make?

The making of *forefooted beasts*, becaufe
they go vpon the ground, is farre differét
from the former. Such as feed vpon flesh
and liue vpon preying, haue the members of their bodies fit and accommodated
for prey: In their mouth they haue two
teeth aboue, and two below, long and
strong to hold, and teare a sunder; their
clawes sharpe and faulked, or hooked to
hold fast; which clawes, when they goe,
they so beare, that they are not worne; &
in catching their prey, they stretch them
out, like fingars.

The making of fourefooted Beasts.

Those other beasts, as feed vpon hearbs,
leaues, or fruits, haue their teeth and hoofs
otherwise formed. For the order of their
teeth are eauen and equall, one not being
lóger then an other, of which the further-
most are sharpe to cut the grasse, or the
new buds of trees & flowers; the inward-
most

moſt are broad & blunt to grynd and make
ſmall the meat . Their hoofs are firme and
plaine , that they may ſtand firmely , & that
their feet be not ouerpreſſed with the
weight of their body . Their neck of that
length , as ſtāding vprightly they may graſe
vpon the graſſe: and ſo accordingly Camels
by reaſon of the hugenes of their body, haue
a very long necke ; But in an Elephant it is
otherwiſe, to whom a long necke would
become deformed , and would haue made
that huge weight of his body to be vnapt to
the defence of himſelfe . Therefore an Elephant hath a moſt ſhort necke , yet in liew
therof a long ſnout with the which(as with
a hand)it taketh any thing , and reacheth it
to his mouth . Now, who ſeeth not , that all
theſe things are thus purpoſely diſpoſed and
framed with wonderfull wiſedome & conſideration ?

And to come *to Fiſhes:* How fitly and pro-
portionatly are then bodies framed to lyue
in the Element of water ? The head of moſt
of them is narrow , the better therby to cut
the water ; the tayle broad and ſpread out ,
which ſerueth (as a ſterne) to guyde the fiſhes motion with an extraordinary celerity
and ſwiftnes . They haue alſo cloſe to their
belly certaine fins (wherof ſome haue two,
others foure or more :) theſe ſtand inſteed of

The ma-
king of
fiſhes .

oares (as it were) by the helpe whereof they
either moue in the water , or ſtay their mo-
uing:vpon their backe they haue a certaine
finne like vnto a skin , which they ſtretch
out , that they may ſwin with their bodies
downeward , and that they may not eaſily
be caſt vpon their backs . Their gils which
they haue vpon the ſide of their chawes, do
ſerue for the caſting out of water; both of
that which they dayly draw in to the refri-
geration of their hart , as alſo of that, which
entreth into them, whyle they are in taking
of their food and nouriſhment . And therefore ſuch fiſhes as want theſe gils , haue inſteed of them certaine holes , by the which
they diſburden themſelues of this water .
And without this help of auoydance, it is
certaine, that they would be preſently ſuf-
focated and choaked , as wanting all reſpiration . Their Scales grow backward , to
the end they may be no hinderance to their
ſwiming which, when the fiſhes are in motion , cloſe neare together . Such fiſhes , as
breath not much , want lungs or lights, and
haue their hart thinly couered ouer , neere
vnto their mouth , that it may be eaſily refrigerated and cooled by the attraction of
water . Thoſe of a ſtrong reſpiration haue
lungs (with which the hart is couered) and
other inſtruments fitting to the ſame end

To

To conclude the kynds of fishes and variety
of their formes is almost innumerable; euery
one of them hauing their outward and inward parts and members most aptly framed
to their vses and ends; so nothing is there
to be found, which is not disposed with all
reason, wisedome, & prouidence. Neither
is this variety of formes & elegancy of structure to be found only in the bodies of fishes
but also in shels, with the which the small
fishes (though imperfect in nature) are couered. Of these *Shels*, their beauty, and variety is wonderfull, although they serue to
no other vse, then to couer and arme the
small bodies of their fishes. For there is no
where greater shew of diuyne arte and skil,
then in these, especially where there is produced such variety without any seed, and
only out of a formed Element, as appeareth
from the testimony of (a) *Pliny* himselfe. *Tot
ibi colorum differentiæ &c.* So many *differences
of colours in Shels, so many figures and formes,*   (a) l. 9. c.
as plaine, hollow, long, horned, as the moone, ga-   33.
thered together in a round forme, smooth, rough,
&c. with many other formes by him recyted, & then after he further writeth: *Nitor
& puritas &c. The shining & purity is incredible
in diuers of them, exceeding all mettals of gold and
siluer, and not to be corrupted, but in a most long
space & tyme.*

This

This further is worthy of consideration
in liuing Creatures. To wit, To man, in
that he is endued with reason, there is giuē
at his birth, neither any thing to cloath his
body, nor any weapon for his owne defēce,
but in place of these; Hands are giuen him,
with the which he may make to himselfe
all kynd of vestmēts or weapons, to weare
or lay by at his pleasure. But to beasts, because they cannot make and procure these
things to themselues, they therefore receiue
thē euen frō a most *benigne and diuyne Prouidēce*, and they increase with the increasing of
the beasts, neither do they all at any time
need any repayring. For weapons, are giuen
to some Hornes; to others Teeth; to others
Clawes; to others strength in their feet; to
others a sharpe dart in their tayles; to others
a venemous poyson in their teeth or their
hoofes, and this endangereth their Enemies
either by touching or breathing. Of others;
their safety doth lye in their speedines of flying away; or in their naturall craft and de-
ceipt, or in the hardnes of their shels, wherwith they are couered, or in the pricks of
their skins, which some of them can cast
from them against their enemies. Insteed of
Cloth (wherwith they are couered) some
haue haire, others wool, fethers, scales, a
sharpe & hard pil or rynd, shels, & a smooth
skin,

The na-
turall
weapons
and co-
uerings
of beasts.

skin, yet of sufficient hardnes. Furthermore their is in euery liuing Creature a vertue or power, by the which all these veapons and vestments (as it were) are framed in conuenient places, formes, and colours; and this out of the earthly & grosser part of the nourishment or meat, otherwise improfitable, and but to be purged away. Therefore we may worthily admire *Gods Prouidence* herein, which turneth the matter (otherwise hurtfull for the nourishing of the body) into such necessary vses.

I heere pretermit the most diuers formes and shapes of those liuing creatures, which are commonly called *Insecta*; as flies, gnats, and the like; as also all little wormes, with the which the ayre, the earth, the fields, the riuers and standing waters do abound in the Summer time. Al parts or members in them are wonderfully faire, all most exactly framed, and all most perfectly agreing and fitting to the functions, for which they were made. Among so many kinds of which small liuing bodies, there is not one so base and vyle, which is not able to procure an astonishing admiration in whom behold them attentiuely. Yea by how much the creature ie more base and abiect, by so much the more the art of *diuyne Prouidence* shineth in the fabricke and making of it.

The

The like Prouidence is shewed in the making of *Plants*, which comming out of the earth do remaine fixed to the earth; wherof there are many kinds, & most diuers formes of the said kynds. Nothing is in thē, which is without the height and fulnes of reason: All their parts most aptly sort to their ends. The rootes (whether it be a tree, a young bud, or an hearb) do serue to fasten the whole plant to the earth, and to sucke from thence humour for the nourishing of al its parts. The vertue of the rootes, is strange, seing the greatest trees that are, though neuer so much diffused, and spred out into brā-ches, are by their rootes so affixed to the earth, that no force of wynds can leuell thē with the earth. The Barke or outward rynd (seruing as a cloathing to them) defends them from cold and heat, and from the en-counter of any other domageable thing. The Bowes and branches are directed for the greater increase of fruites. The leaues serue partly for ornament, and parly for the safty of the fruits, least they perish through heat and showers. The fruit serues for the continuance of the seed, and in most of them for food of men and other liuing creatures; and therefore they are more full of suck, and there is greater store of them, then the con-tinuance of the seed requireth; as appeareth

in

The fa-bricke or making of Plāts.

in apples, peares, mellons, and many other
kynds of fruits. Plants do want Muscles, because they want motion, and do cleaue im-
moueably to the earth. All parts euen from
the lowest peece of the roote to the highest
of the leaues are ful of pores: they haue a power of sucking in, and what they sucke in,
they do assimilate & make it the same with
the substance of the tree. The leaues and
fruyte do hang by a little stalke, which consisteth of many *fibræ* or smal strings; through
the staike all the iuyce passeth, which after
is dispersed through the pores of the *fibræ*,
into all parts of the leaues and fruites in a
most strange manner. The stalkes do not ad-
here or cleaue to the boughes by any *fibræ*,
which are continued to the boughes, but by
such as are inserted in them, and glewed or
ioyned together through the force of a certaine humour; The which humour being
once dryed, the fruyt and the leaues either
freely of themselues, or with very small
pulling do fall downe. In the *Medulla* or
marrow of the Plant there is a genitall power or vertue, and therfore it is called μήτρα
or in Latin *Matrix*; the which marrow being taken away, though the tree do beare
fruite, yet is this fruite destitute of seed.
Euen as the roote, the stocke of the tree, and
the boughes or branches do consist of the
barke,

barke , the wood , and the marrow ; fo the fruite confifteth of the barke of that part which is commonly called *Pulpa*, and of the feed. The fucke and humours of the earth being attracted by the roote , and difperfed by the *fibra* into the body and the boughes, and perfectly concocted , the watery parts being improfitable to the tree , or to that woodden fubftance (whatfoeuer the plant be) and going to the furtheft parts of the boughes , are turned into leaues; the very parts into flowers:that which is more groffe and better tempered is partly changed into the fubftance of the plant , and partly into fruite ; and thus no fuperfluity remayneth which is to be purged away; though the cõtrary fall out in liuing Creatures . Some of thofe plants (which afcending high are through their height weake) do either fold themfelues about fome other thing(as hops, Iuy , and many other fuch like plants) or els they haue certaine wynding twigs or ftringes , wherwith (as with hands) they take hold of ftaues or fuch things,fet purpofely to fupport them , that they fall not ; as Vynes, Pompions, and fome others. But to be fhort , it were a labour infinite & endles to repeat and fet downe all the miracles (as I may truly tearme them) which appeare in the ftructure and making of Plants .

Now

Now from all these foresaid speculations I conclude, that seing the parts of liuing creaures and of Plants haue a double end; the one as they are *parts*, of which the forme & structure of the *whole* dependeth; the other as they are organs and instruments ordained for certaine functions necessary to the safety of the whole; and to both these ends they are made so apt and proportionable, as that it cannot be conceaued, how more exactly and wonderfully they could be framed; it is therefore euident, that all those parts were made by some one *supreme* and most *wise spirit or intelligence*, who first conceaued in himselfe all these ends, and considered aforehad the meanes best sorting to the said ends. For it is altogether impossible and with true reason incompatible, that there should be so wonderfull and admirable a proportion & conueniecy of so many innumerable *Media*, or meanes, to so innumerable ends, except the meanes and the ends had bene aforehad most exactly weighed and compared together.

This reason most perspicuously conuinceth, that there is a *most wyse, and diuyne Prouidence*, & that this Prouidence hath a care in the least things: seing that euen in Gnats, Myse, little wormes, and the least hearbes it hath framed innumerable parts, and innu-

H

merable

merable inſtruments to the complete & perfect forme of that little creature or ſmal plãt; as alſo it hath diſpoſed all the functions and ends moſt agreing to its ſafety & health. For *Prouidence* is diſcouered in nothing more, then in an apt diſpoſition and contriuing of meanes to their Ends; and this ſorting of meanes cannot be performed without an abſolute and perfect working of Reaſon. Wherfore ſeing this diſpoſall is moſt perfect and admirable in the leaſt Creatures, it followeth, that it is more cleare then the ſunne beames, that a moſt diſtinct *and remarkeable Prouidence* had it ſole hand buſyed in the making and creating of the ſaid ſmall bodyes.

THE SEAVENTH REASON: THAT ALL *things do worke moſt orderly to a certaine End.*

CHAP. IX.

VVE haue proued in the precedent Chapters, that there is a *diuyne Power*, frõ the nature and diſpoſition of the parts of the world, & from the ſtructure & making of liuing Creatures and plants; Now, in this place we will demonſtrate the ſame from this conſideration, that all things do worke for ſome one end or other. For there is nothing idle
in

in the world, all things tend & direct their operations and working to some end, and that to the benefit of the worker, or of some other. And they incline and bend to their ends so ordinatly, and with such conuenient wayes and passages, as that it cannot be bettered by any art whatsoeuer. Wherfore seing the things themselues can neither perceiue the ends, wherunto they are directed, neither the meanes, nor the proportion of the meanes, by the which they are directed; it is therefore most certaine, that all things are directed by some *superiour Power*, who seeth and considereth both the meanes and the ends. For it is impossible, that a thing should particulerly & ordinatly in its owne operation ayme at one certaine end, except it either knoweth the end, and the meanes conducing to the said end, that so by this knowledge it may guyde its operation, or at least be directed by some other, which knoweth all these things. Thus (for example) a Clocke, whose end is the distinguishing the houres of the day, because it neither knoweth this end, nor is of power to dispose it selfe to this end, is therfore necessarily to be directed by some vnderstanding mynd, which knoweth these things, and can make distinction of houres.

That all things tend to some one end or

other

other, firſt it is euident in the *motion* of the
Heauens, and in the illumination & influx
of the ſtars, and in the fecundity and fruitfulnes of the ſea and earth (as is ſhewed afore.)
Secondly in the *parts and members* of all liuing Creatures and Plants ; ech part wherof we haue already made euident, to haue its
peculiar vſe and ſunction, neceſſarily for the
good of the whole. Thirdly, the ſame poynt
is to be manifeſted in *all ſeedes*. Fourthly in
the induſtry, *and labour of liuing Creatures.*

And firſt , this informing Vertue or Power, which is in ſeedes , doth moſt clearly
worke for ſome end , to wit to frame and
forme the body of a liuing creature, or a
Plant. Now, this it effecteth by ſo multiplicious and ſtrange an art, and by ſo long and
well diſpoſed a worke, as it is impoſſible it
ſhould be wrought by any more wiſe a mā-
ner . And certainly if this ſeminall vertue
were any Intelligence indued with reaſon
and diſcourſe, it could not proceed with
greater order, artifice , and wit. Vpõ which
ground *Hypocrates* in his booke entituled
περί αρχῶν, *num* 1. writeh, that this ſeminall
vertue or naturall heat , by the which all
things generable, are framed and made , is
eternal, and indued with an vnderſtanding,
for thus he ſaith : *Videtur ſanè &c. That which
we call (calidum) ſemeth to me to be immortall,*
and

The ſe-
minall
vertue or
power.

and to vnderstand, *see, heare, and know all things both present & to come.* Of this opinion he was, because he thought, that those things could not be made without great art and vnderstanding, which were wrought by the force and vertue of the naturall heat.

First then, the more grosse part of the seed by force of this heat and spirit, is extended into *fibræ*, or little strings, into the which *fibræ* this spirit entring doth partly hollow them into fistules or pypes; and partly causeth them to be spongeous, in some places more thin, in others more solid and firme; and thus doth it forme the extreme parts, making them fit, and bynding them, as the necessity of the bones and members may seeme to require. From the other portion of seed and from bloud, it frameth the three principall members, to wit the *Brayne*, the *Harte*, and the *Liuer* ; drawing out of the *fibræ* matter for the making of veynes, arteries & sinewes. The spirit entring into thē doth hollow, dilate, extend, and deuyde them into seuerall branches; then it deduceth and draweth them through the whole body, that they may carry nourishment, as also vitall and animall spirits to all parts. In the meane tyme euery small portion or part of the body doth attract bloud, and conuert it into its owne substance; the spirit still for-

The manner, how the seminall vertue worketh.

H 3   ming

ming euery thing by little and little, and giuing each part its due figure, meaſure, proportion and connexion with other parts: ſo
as from the ſeauenth day after the conceptiō
the forme of the whole body and diſtinctiō
of all parts euen of the fingers, doth appeare.
Now how manifold and various is this labour in framing of ſo many bones, veynes,
arteryes, ſinewes, and Muſcles, in the apt
diſtribution, deduction, or drawing out,
& termination or ending of euery part, each
of them keeping its due forme, temper, meaſure, place, ioyning together and inciſion?
What mynd or vnderſtanding can be intent
to ſo many things at once? What Art may in
the leaſt part ſeeme to equall this? Who therfore conſidering all theſe things, can doubt,
but that there is ſome one moſt *wiſe* & moſt
poten: *Mynd or Soule*, by whome all this operation and working is directed, and to whō
all this admirable artifice is to be aſcribed?
If an indigeſted & informed heape of ſtones,
tyles, lyme and wood ſhould begin to make
to it ſelfe a houſe, directing it ſelfe in the doing thereof, and framing all parts thereof,
as the Art of Architecture requyreth, who
would not affirme that a certaine Vnderſtã-
ding, skilful of building, were inuiſibly and
latently in the ſaid things, that they could
ſo artificially diſpoſe themſelues? Or if a
                                        penſill

pensill being imbued with diuerse colours,
should moue it selfe, and first should but rudely
draw the lineaments of a mans face, &
after should perfect euery part therof by framing
the eyes, drawing the cheeks, figuring
the nose, mouth, eares, and the other
parts (seruing in them all a due proportion,
and fitting colours, as the exact science of
painting requireth;) no man would doubt,
but that this pensill were directed herein by
an intelligent spirit. But now, in the framing
of euery liuing Creature far greater
art and wit is desired, then in any humane
worke whatsoeuer; since the skill whereof
transcendeth by many degrees all mans skill
and artifice; for it arriueth to that height of
perfection, as that the worke cannot in that
kynd be possibly bettered; neither can the
parts of it (whether internall or externall)
haue a more pleasing proportion and connexion.
Therefore who is so voyd of Reason,
that can enter into any dubious and vncertaine
consideration with himselfe, whether
all this molition and laboursome endeauour
in framing a liuing Creature be directed by
a power indued with reason & wisedome,
or no?

Furthermore, there are three things here
to be considered, among which there ought
to be a great proportion; to wit the *Soule* of

H 4　　　　　the

The proportion betweene the internall forme & the body, and betweene the body & the seminall vertue.

the liuing Creature, the *body*, and the *Seminall vertue*. And first, the Soule ought to be most proportionable to the body. For such ought the small body of any little Creature to be, as the *Anima* or soule of the same doth require to performe its proper functions; wherfore how great the difference is of Soules, so great also the discrepancy is of bodyes, if we insist in the figure, the temperature, and the conformation of the Organs; therefore in the nature of euery soule the whole formall reason is contained, so as that if a man did perfectly know the nature of the soule, from it he might easily collect, what the habit, figure, and temperature of the body ought to bee. But who is ignorāt of the nature thereof, must consequently be ignorant of the other; for in some one particular or other he shall euer be wanting, and neuer attaine to the due proportion in knowledge thereof. As for example, if the question be touching the small body of a flye, how many feet it ought to haue, how many flexures or bendings in their legs, or thighes, what difference betwene euery flexure, what temperature, proportion & connexion; how many sinews in euery thigh, how many veines, what proportion to its little nayles; of which things many are for their smalnes not to bee discerned by the eye.

eye: for in the small body of the flye, there
may be found seuerall thousands of proportions, as necessary, that its soule may rightly
sort to the body; to all which no man can
attaine, except he first doth penetrate and
consider in his mynd the nature of the soule,
in the which the reason of all these (as in
the root) doth ly hidden and secret. Againe
the *Seminal power* ought to haue most perfect
proportion with the **body**, that it may produce such a body in al respects, as that soule
doth require. Therefore, who first caused
and made this seminall power, ought aforehand to haue the whole structure of the
body exactly knowne vnto him, that so he
might sute and proportion this seminall seed
to the body. For as in the soule (as in the
finall cause) the whole reason of the fabrick
of the body lyeth, and therefore the body
ought in a perfect proportion to be accommodated, and made fit to the soule; In like
sort the reason of the making of the same is
latent and hidden in the seminall vertue, or
power, as in the efficient cause. Wherupon
it followeth, that there ought to be as an
exact proportion betwene the structure of
the body and the seminall vertue, as is betwene the efficient cause & the adequate effect of the said Cause.

Now, from all these premisses it is most

clearly

clearly demonstrated, that these three, to wit the *Soule* of euery liuing Creature, the structure of the *body*, and the *seminall vertue*, haue their source from one and the same beginning; which beginning cannot be any nature depriued of reason & vnderstanding: seing a beginning voyd of reason could not among different things set downe congruous proportions; much lesse so exact and so infinite proportions, as are betweene the body and the soule, and the seminall vertue and the making or fabricke of the body. For to performe this, requireth a most perfect and distinct knowledge. Therefore it is concluded, that there is an *intelligence* or *spirit* both most *wise* and most *powerfull*, which through its wisedome is able to excogitate and inuent, & through its power is of might to performe all these things.

The reason, why this seminall vertue might seeme to be indued with a mynd or vnderstanding, is, because this vertue is a certaine impression, and (as it were) a foot step of the diuyne art and skil; and therefore it worketh, as if it had a particuler art and knowledge in working. Euen as if a painter could impresse in his pensill a permanent power and vertue of his art, and that therupon the pensill should moue it selfe, and draw the images, as if there were an art and vnderstanding

The seminall vertue is the impression of a Diuyne Art.

vnderstanding in the Penfill. Furthermore
it may be here prefumed, that this *diuyne fpi-*
rit or *Intelligence* doth conferue this impreffiõ
with his continuall influxe, and doth cooperate with it thus working with his generall concourfe.

Euen as in liuing creatures thefe three, to
wit the Soule, the body, and the feminall
vertue do meet and confpire together in a
wonderfull proportion; fo do they a like in
euery kind of Plant : for in the *Anima* and
foule of euery plant the whole reafõ of the
ftructure of the body of the Plant, as alfo
of the leaues, flowers, and fruite is contained.

The like may be faid of the feminall power. For the forme or foule of the Plant is
a thing fimple and vncompounded, & fuch
alfo is the feminall vertue. For the whole
difference, & the whole multitude of figures, colours, fmels, iynes and proportions,
which is difcerned, either externally in the
body of the Plant, or in the leaues, flowers,
fruits, rootes, barke, or iuyce and marrow,
proceeds from the feminall vertue & from
the forme or foule of the Plant : and therefore all thefe things are internally after a
fimple and inuifible mãner moft ftrangely
contained in them both. If therefore flowers
do appeare externally faire to the eye, and
                              admirable

admirable for their great variety of figures
colours, and proportions; then how much
more fayre and pleasing is the *internall forme*
(to wit the soule) and the *seminall vertue*,
from which all that visible beauty floweth,
and in the which after a wonderfull particuler and ineffable sort it is wholy contained?

Neither do only the seeds of things
(which worketh after a naturall manner, &
without any reflexe, or knowledge of its
owne working) tend to a certaine end in
their working; but also liuing Creatures do
the lyke, when they worke by their imagination. For all liuing Creatures are moued
and inclined to their sense of gust & feeding,
and to the act of generation; and these they
performe, not thinking at all or conceauing
the end, wherunto those functions do tend
and are directed. For neither are they stirred vp to the act of generation through the
desire of hauing young ones, neither do they
eate with intention of producing their liues
and conseruing themselues; but they apprehend the working of these two senses after
a confused maner, vnder the forme of a de-
ctable thing, and in this apprehension they
are stirred therto. And yet doubtlessly these
actions haue a further intention and end.
For neither eating, nor the act of generatiõ

The
working
of liuing
Creatn-
res are
directed
to an end

are

are ordained for pleasure; since this is to perpetuate and continew the kynds of liuing creatures, and that to defend and maintaine the particuler life of euery one. Therefore it is needfull, that there be some one *superiour Mynd* or *vnderstanding*, which knowing and intending these ends, doth direct bruit beasts to the said ends, and which giueth to euery liuing creature (according to its nature) fitting organs and instruments, by the which it may come to those ends.

To conclude, there appeareth in many irrationable creatures a certaine particuler industry, by the which they either take their meat, build their nests, bring vp and defend their ofspring, and this in so industrious and witty a manner, as that (if they were indued with reason) they could not performe the same actions better, & the end (for which they thus do, and to which all this is finally intended) they apprehend not, but rest absolutely ignorant of it.

The Industry of irrationable Creatures.

The *Spider* (for example) weaueth her web with wonderfull art, & (lyke a hūter) layeth her nets for the catching of flies; the threeds of her web are most synely and curiously wrought, and the further they are distant from the midle or center of the web, they alwaies by degrees do make greater Circles; and the connexions or insertions of

The spyder.

one

one threed with an other (still obseruing a
precife diftance) are moft ftrange. She conceaueth the aptnes of her web to hold faft
with the fynenes of the threed? And when
her web is wrought, fhe prouydeth her felfe
of a little hole to lye in (lyke vnto the cuftome of fowlers) left fhe fhould be efpyed.
When the flye falleth into the web, the
fpider inftantly runneth therto, taking hold
of her, and hindering the motion of her
wings, left fhe fhould fly away, then prefently fhe killeth the flye, taketh it away, &
layeth it vp againft tyme of hunger. Now
fuppofing the fpider were indued with reafon, could it do all thefe things with better
art and order, and more fitly tending to her
defigned end?

The *Bees* worke their fyne hony-Combs,
distinguifhed on each fyde with little cells
or roomes of fix corners, which they frame
with their fix little feete. And then they
flying abroad, and lighting vpon flowers
and hearbs, they gather from thence the
fweet dew of heauen, and lay it vp in thefe
fmall roomes, to ferue for their prouifion in
the winter tyme. How they deuyde the labour herein among themfelues is moft admirable, for fome of them bring part of flowers with their feete; others water with
their mouthes; others againe ferue to build,
worke,

The in-
duftry of
Bees.

worke, and frame their cels within, and do
disburden such bees, as come loaden to the
Hyue. When their Cels are full of matter,
then do they couer them with a small membrane or skin, least otherwise the liquour
therin should flow away, when any part of
their Combs is ready to fail, they support it
with a partition wall (as it were) made of
earth in forme of an Arch. All the Bees do
rest together, they labour together, & conspire together to performe one generall
worke; helping one another according to
their facultyes & powers. I here omit what
authours haue written of the strange policy
and gouerment of Bees, obserued curiously
by diuers.

If we come next to *Emmets* or *Ants,* what
sedulity and industry is found in them? And
how much care is taken for the tyme to
come, and yet they want all knowledge of
the tyme to come? They make their habitation and dwelling places in little concauityes of the earth, themselues thus labouring
the earth, which habitations for greater security & quietnes are ful of many wyndings
and turnings. Here they bring forth their
Eggs, and hither they bring in the sommer
their winters prouision; they indifferently
communicate in their labours, as bees do, &
haue a kynd of politicall gouernment and
care:

The in-
dustry of
Emmets.

care : they do firſt knaw and byte the corne, leſt it ſhould take roote againe (ſee herein the wonderfull prouidence of God in theſe ſo vyle Creatures.) The corne being moyſtened with rayne, they lay out to the Sūne, by which it is dryed, and after they hord it vp againe. They carry their burdens with the pinſers (as it were) of their mouths ; It is alſo ſtrange to obſerue, how in ſo great a concurſe of them of many hundreds or thouſands, they meeting one another in a moſt ſtraite way, are no hinderāce or let to their paſſages, and they only of all liuing Creature (excepting man) do bury one another.

The *Silkwormes* do worke out of their owne bowels , their graues or ſepulchres , **The Induſtry of the ſilkworme.** the wolly fertility of their bellies miniſtring them matter therto; In this graue they being ſhut vp (as it were dead) at length appeare and come forth in another ſhape ; imitating herein a ſecond birth or generation through a ſtupendious *metamorphoſis* and change : their forme is lyke to the gardenworme commōly called a *Canker* ; they eate and feed almoſt continually, only they reſt from feeding, & attend the concoction of their meat two ſeuerall tymes , till they grow greater. Comming to a iuſt quantity or bignes , and their body being diſtented and ſtretched out with meat, they reſt againe for better concoction.

cochion . Then they begin to weaue with a
continuall paine and indefatigable labour ,
vntill they haue shut vp themselues within
their worke . The fynenes and yet the firmnes of the threed thereof is strange . They
draw out the threed with the small nayles
of their feet; they wynd it into a partly round
clue , but of an ouall figure , wherein they
close themselues vp . Now how great industry and Prouidence is found in this worke?
And from this their working commeth that
so great aboundance of silke , wherein the
world now offendeth so much in wast and
luxury .

The *Hedghog* goeth vnder the Vyne tree ,
and by shaking the vyne casteth downe such
grapes , as are ripe ; when great store of the
are falne downe , he contracteth his body
into a round compasse, & so tumbling him
among the grapes , and they sticking vpon
his pricks , he carryeth great store of them
into his den to feed himself and his whelpes
withall. The lyke he doth for the gathering
of Apples. Neither is the industry small in
Cats; for with what silence of pace ,do they
rush vpon birds , & with what obseruat eye
do they light vpon my ce? And it is said,that
their excrements they hyde and couer ouer
with earth,lest otherwise they be discouerd
and betrayed by the smell thereof.

I　　　　　　　In

The industry of fishes.

In *fishes* also there is a great shew and outward appearance of reason and prouidence, yea euen in such as are thought to be most dull of nature, as appeareth in the fish called *Polypus* (as hauing many parts resembling feete, or armes) being accustomed to feed vpon shel-fishes. These fishes, after they perceaue, that his feete are within their shels, do presently shut and close them, and thus by this violent compression of the shels they cut of the feete of the said fish. Now this danger to preuent, the *Polypus* is vsed to cast within the shels a little stone; that so the shels not closing together, he may without any danger feed of the fishes within them.

Oppianus l. 5. de piscatu a Aelianus l. 8. c. 6. Plutarch de prudentia animal.

The *Whale* (as diuers ancient authors do wryte) being of an imperfect eye-sight hath a little fishe, as his guyde, which goeth before him, least he should fall vpon any narrow rocke. Many fishes, which are more slow of their owne nature to seeke their prey and food, haue diuers little things hãging about their chawes, in shape like to small wormes, that so the lesser fishes being allured thither vnder the shew of meat may be the more easily taken of other fishes. The fish *Sepia*, when she perceiueth her selfe to be touched, doth darken the water with a kind of humour and moysture; as blacke as Inke, that so hyding her selfe in the darknes thereof

thereof she may better escape. The shelfish
called *Pinna* is euer ingendred in mudy waters, neuer goeth without his companion,
which they call *Pinnoter*; This *Pinnoter* is a
small shrimpe. The *Pinna* desirous of prey,
and being altogether blynd, offereth (as it
were) his body to little fishes to feed vpon.
The fishes assaulting him in that number as
is sufficient for his nourishment, and the *Pinnoter*, or his companion giuing him notice
thereof by a little touch, the *Pinna* doth kill
all the fishes with a hard and violent compression of them; so feeding himselfe after
vpon them, and giuing part of them to his
fellow. The fish *Torpedo* being immersed in
mud and durt, hydeth himselfe, that the fishes should not flye from him, the which
then swimming ouer him, and being be-
numd through an inward quality proceeding from him, he after catcheth them.
Other like relations of fishes are reported by
Pliny, *Plutarch Oppianus*, and others.

And next to come to *Birds*, in whom there
appeareth no lesse prouidence, then in the
former creatures. And first, with how
much care, skil, and forecast (as it were) The In-
do they build their nests, that they may be duſtry of
fitting for their rest in the night tyme, & for Birds.
the nourishing and bringing vp of their
young ones? They worke them for the most

part in trees, or thickets of brambles and quſhes, therby to be far from the danger of men and beaſts. The outward ſide of their neſts are cōmonly but playne, as of bryars, twigs, or boughes. This matter they diſpoſe in forme of a hat turned vp ſide downe, and faſten one part therof with an other, with clay, ſo as it can hardly be diſſolued; next they lyne the inward part therof with ſome ſoft matter, as moſſe, hay, or the lyke, ſtraitning by degrees the hollownes of it towards the entrance; Laſtly for the more ſoftning of it, and for the greater heat, they ſtrow it within with downe of feathers, ſmall hayre and the lyke, ſo as the birds may lye therin with eaſe and heat. And although all birds do retaine this forme in generall for the diſpoſall of the matter of their neſts, yet euery kynd of them hath his owne peculiar frame, and different manner of architecture (as I may call it;) as among vs we find ſeuerall kynds of building, to wit the *Corinthian*, *Dorick*, *Tuſcane*, *Gothick*, and ſeuerall other ſorts thereof.

There is beſides in birds and many other liuing creatures, an extraordinary care of bringing vp and feeding their young ones; I meane of ſuch Creatures, as being but newly borne, cannot prouide for themſelues: for they ſeeke out of euery place food fitting
for

for their brood , and bring it to their nests ;
yea diuers of them not finding sufficiét store
of meate for themselues , and their brood ,
are content to suffer hunger , therby to giue
the greater quantity to the other . Next obserue with what earnestnes of mynd they
defend their ofspring from their enemies ;
for they presently raise théselues, interpose
their body, swell, rouse vp their fethers in
terrour to their Enemy, & do oppose to him
all their weapons , as their beackes , teeth,
nayles , hornes, clawes, and what other instrument they are able to fight withall. And
some of them , where they see their force
cannot preuaile , do vse strange sleights for
diuerting their enemy from their nests,som-
times with shew in suffering themselues
to be taken, that so with short flights they
may the better draw their aduersary from
their nests, and if their nests be found , how
much then lamentation doth appeare in
many ? With what dolefull cryes do they fill
the ayre? And what incõsolable griefe doth
afflict them for the tyme ?

To conclude, there is in all liuing creatures a strange industry for their owne preseruation . Many haue their safety in their
flight, others in their weapons , and some in
deceipts. The *Hare* being in danger, and
willing to stay securely in some one place ,
will

will make his laſt bounces and leapes wonderfull great, that therby the dogs by ſuch
his iumping may loſe their ſent of him. And
for the ſame cauſe they ſotimes wil ſwimme
ouer Riuers, becauſe their ſmell ſtayeth not
in the water. The like and greater cunning
doth the *Fox* vſe for ſauing his iyfe.

In *Ægipt* there is great ſtore of *Serpents*:for
the better remedy of this inconuenience,
there is by Prouidence of the higheſt a little
creature called *Ichneumon*, lyke vnto a *dor-
mouſe*;this (being the others natural enemy,
and ready to fight with it) doth firſt roule
& tumble himſelfe in myre and durt, which
after is dryed and hardned with the ſuns
heat. The *Ichneumon* thus armed with the
dryed myre (as with a breaſt plate) cometh
to his denn, and prouoketh him to fight.
The ſame little beaſt alſo entring into the
chawes of the *Crocodyle*, (when he is a
ſleepe) and penetrating his body doth kill
him by gnawing and eating away his bowels.

In lyke ſort irrationable creatures do
know ſuch kynd of meates, as are hurtfull
and dangerous to them, as alſo the remedy
and cure of their diſeaſes and wounds. *Dogs*
when they haue ſurfetted with eating, do
procure a vomit by eating of graſſe, & ſo do
purge their infectious humour.

Beaſts
know
what is
hurtfull
to them,
and what
medici-
nable.

The

The *Ringdoue*, the *Chugh*, the *Vzell*, & the *Partridge* do purge their yearly corrupt humours by eating of the leafe of a bay tree ; *Swallowes* haue taught vs that the hearbe *Celandine* is medicinable for the eye sight ; for they do cure the sore eyes of their young ones by causing them to eate thereof. The *Hart* being wounded with an arrow yet sticking in him, doth cast it out by feeding vpon the hearbe *Dictamnum* ; and being stroken by a Serpent, cures himselfe by eating of crabfishes. The *Barbarians* do hunt the *Panther* with a piece of flesh coloured with the iuyce of a venemous hearbe, but she perceauing her iawes to bee shut vp with the force of the poyson, seeketh to feed vpon the bowels of a dead man, which is to her the onely cure for this disease. I omit innumerable other things touching the customes of liuing creatures, which are made knowne to vs, partly by the diligent inquisition & search of man, & partly by the ofte experience had of them: all which is relaed vnto vs by good and approued authours.

Now from all these obseruations it is euident that the operations and working of liuing Creatures (yea when they perfourme the same by the interuention and help of their imagination) do most ordinately and regularly tend to a certaine end. But if they

I 4   ayme

ayme to ſome ſuch deſtinated end, then it
neceſſarily followeth, that they are directed
thither by ſome cauſe. But the beaſt it ſelfe
cannot be this cauſe; in that irrationable
Creatures do not know the ends of their
owne operations, neither can they apprehēd
or diſcourſe with themſelues; that this thing
is profitable and conducing to that end; or
that this is to be done for that reſpect, or the
like. As for example, the *Spyder* knoweth
not to what end his web ſo wouen is profitable, or with what order he is to proceed
in making of it. Neither do the *Bees* know
why their honycombs are made in ſuch a
forme, or what benefit and good they ſhall
reape therby. Neither doth any other ſuch
liuing creature know, why he eateth or
drinketh, or begetteth little ones, or feedeth
and nouriſheth them, or flyeth away from
his enemy, or defendeth himſelfe from him:
finally he knoweth not the end or reaſon
of any thing he doth; and yet he performeth
his operations, in ſuch an order, and with
ſo great an induſtry and reaſon, as if he were
indued with the true vſe of Reaſon. In ſo
much that ſome of the ancient Authours
maintained, that all liuing Creatures had
reaſon, though they were depriued of all
ſpeach or láguage, which might be knowne
to vs. And of this very point and ſubiect did
Plutarch

Platarch wryte a booke . But this opinion is most false, and ridiculous.

Therefore it is necessarily to be granted, that there is a certaine *Spirit* or *Intelligence* presiding and ruling ouer bruite beasts, and gouerning their actions; which well knoweth what is conuenient to the safety and defence of their liues , and to the propagation of each one of their kynds , and by what meanes they are to attaine vnto the same . By which *Intelligence* all the actions of irrationable creatures are directed to their proper , seuerall , and distinct ends . For here is first needfull an exact and distinct knowledge of all these ends , which agree to euery one of them according to their *species* and kynds , as also of the meanes conducing to the same ends. Secondly it is requisit to know what proportion ought to be of euery meane to its end . Lastly what instinct is necessary to seuerall functions ; and to the many *series* or degrees of their functions . Now all this knowledge being presupposed & granted as necessary, it was easy for that *supreme Architect* , & *Maker of all things* to imprint in ech liuing Creature peculiar and accommodated instincts , to all these meanes and Ends.

Now, that beasts and al other irrationable Creatures by force of these instincts do so

I 5   proceed

proceed in their actions , as if they were indued with an vnderstanding ; the reason is,
because these instincts are certaine impressi-
ons of the wisedome and reason of the *diuyne
prouidence* , and hereupon those creatures do
no otherwise direct their operations , then
the diuyne Prouidence it selfe , if it were
planted in them , or would vse them , as its
instruments would direct them . For two
wayes may a thing be directed by reason &
art in its working, & in tending its working
to some end . One way immediatly , as the
instrument is moued by the artificer : thus is
the pensill moued by the paynter . A second
way , by the mediation of some power or
vertue impressed , which impression is a
certaine printe or imitation of reason ; And
in this later manner are irrationable creatures moued by the *diuyne Prouidence* . Therefore these Creatures are guyded by reason
in all their operations , yet not by reason inhering or really being in them; but by reasō
inuisibly assisting and gouerning them ; and
not as bare and naked instruments immediatly moued by the workeman , but by the
meanes of a certaine impressed vertue ,
which vertue retaineth the forme of art in
working. And in this sense the Philosophers
were accustomed to say : *Opus nature est opus
intelligentie*,because an intelligent spirit directeth

*why na-
turall
instincts
guyde
boasts
like
Reason .*

recteth nature in all things through a certaine impressed vertue .

The like we fynd, that humane art begetteth and causeth in beasts;for we see that *Dogs* & *apes* are taught by mans labour to dance with distinct paces to the pleasure of the beholders, and gaine of their maisters . This dancing is gouerned by Art, not that this art is inherent in the Dog or Ape, but that in a sort it doth gouerne them, & hath impressed in their phátaíies a certaine print of it selfe through often practice; and many other things are dogs taught especially touching hunting. In like sort *Birds* and diuers other Creatures pleasingly performe many things, and yet they know not why they performe them, or why they do thus, rather then otherwise, or to what end they so doe, though all these he who thus taught them, well knew. Now if man can transfer a certaine imitation and shew of his art vpõ irrationable creatures to effect certaine functions, and for certaine ends & proiects; thẽ how much more easily may that *most wise & most powerfull spirit and vnderstanding* (which we call *God*) plant in all creatures a print of his Art and Prouidence, which extendeth it selfe to al things necessary to the conseruation of their lyues, and future propagation of their kynds?

Man,

Man, in that he enioyeth reaſon and a certaine generall Prouidéce (by the which he gouerneth himſelfe, ſetteth downe his owne end, and diſpoſeth of fitting meanes for the ſame end) hath no need of theſe naturall inſtincts, which other creatures haue. And although diuers men in regard of their peculiar temperature of body, haue peculiar inſtincts both for the ſtirring vp of ſeuerall motions and paſſions of the mynd, as alſo for inclyning them to certaine artes; yet they are not to gouerne themſelues by theſe inſtincts, but by the guyde and force of reaſon, which is granted vnto them. But other Creatures(becauſe they are depriued of reaſon) cannot gouerne themſelues, nor direct their particuler operations to ſutable & cóuenient ends; therefore they ſtand in need of a certaine prudentiall inſtinct , by the which they are to be directed both in the perform ance of their working, as alſo in the directing and diſpoſing of it to an end. Therfore Man hath an vniuerſal prudence or wiſedome, by the which he leuelleth all his actions to his end; But other Creatures haue (as it were)a certaine ſparke of prudence, or rather a peculiar inſtinct lyke vnto prudéce, in certaine peculiar workes of their owne. This inſtinct , ſo far forth as it artificially performeth its worke , (as the web in the Spider,

Spider, and the hony combe in the Bee) is a certaine participation of diuine art, & this not vniuersally but particularly ; to wit as it is confidered in this or that worke . In like fort as it fittingly directeth its working to an end , it beareth the shew of diuyne Prouidence .

Now this inftinct in beafts cōfifteth chiefly in the difpofition of the phantafy, by the which it is brought to pafle , that it apprehendeth after a certaine manner a thing , as conuenient or hurtfull, according to tyme & place , and as occafion ferueth . Secondly it confifteth in the inclinatiō of the Appetite , and in a certaine dexterity , or habil(ty of working .

From all thefe confiderations thē I hould it fufficiently demonftrated , that there is one *Supreme Intelligence*, Mynd, *or Spirit* , whofe wifedom is equally paralelled with his power , by whom not only the principall parts of the world were framed, and difpofed to their particuler ends ; but alfo all the membeis , and leaft parts of all liuing Creatures and plants , as alfo the feed of all things, by whofe fweet prouidence the operations of al liuing Creatures are moft cōgruently and orderly directed to their defigned ends . Out of which poynt this refultacy or collection alfo rifeth , to wit, that his

prouidençe

prouidence extendeth it selfe to the leaft things; and that nothing is made without the fame, feing nothing can haue its being or effence without its vertue or inftinct cōmunicated and imparted by the forefaid *Intelligence*, or *Mynd*.

But here it may feeme to be replyed, that granting, that Gods prouidence hath collated vertue & power to all things to worke, yet followeth not, that his prouidence therfore ftretcheth it felfe forth to all the operations and workings. Euen as he, who teacheth a Dog to dance, or a Parret to fpeake Greeke, doth not (becaufe he fo taught thē) know all things, which after they may do by reafon of their teaching. To this I anfwere, and fay that here is a great difparity and difference; for *Man* may be far remoued and diftant from his worke, and then he knoweth not, what his worke performeth; But God cannot depart from his worke, but alwaies remaineth within the fame; both becaufe God is euery where, filling all places whatfoeuer; as alfo in that he is to preferue, fupport, & fuftaine his owne worke; fince otherwife it would inftantly decay, vanifhing away like a fhadow. For though a Wright (for example) building a houfe, and after departing from it, the houfe remaineth by it felfe to be feene; yet neither the

world

world nor any thing of the world can haue
its subsistéce & being, after God hath with-
drawne himselfe from it . And the reason of
the difference here, is diuers; first because the
Wright maketh his worke in a matter or substance , which he neither made , nor ought
to conserue , but which God made & conserueth ; the Wright doing nothing therin ,
but either by way of adding to, or taking God is
from , or placing all things in a certaine or- euer pre-
der . But now God worketh in that matter, sent to
which himselfe only made, and he only can his
destroy or preserue it . Secondly , because workes ,
God made all things of nothing , eleuating
& aduancing euery thing to its essence and
being ; and therfore all things may againe
reuert & turne to nothing; euen as a heauy
body being by force lifted vp from the earth
doth of it owne nature declyne towards the
earth againe . Wherfore as this body is continually to be supported , that it doth not
precipitate and fall headlong downewards;
euen so all things being first created by diuyne power, need to be sustentated by the
said power, that they be not reduced againe
to nothing . And here I do not vnderstand
by the word *Nothing* , any positiue inclination (such as the heauens or the earth is) but
a defect of power or hability to retaine its
owne being ; because it hath no power preseruing

ſeruing it ſelfe but only from God. Thirdly, becauſe all things haue their dependance of God after a perfect manner, as the light of the ayre depends vpon the Sunne, and the intentionall *ſpecies* or formes of Colours vpõ their obiect, or as the ſhadow vpon the body expoſed to the Sunne (as the ancient Philoſophers do teach and eſpecially the Platonicks:) for we are not to thinke, that there is leſſer (but rather far greater) dependency of things created, vpon God, being the moſt vniuerſall cauſe, then is of theſe effects vpõ their particuler cauſes. Therefore all things do need a continual preſeruation and a continual influxe; in ſo much that if God ſhould but for a moment withdraw or diuert this ſubſtance-making beame (for ſo doth *Dionyſius* call it, terming it ὑσοποιὸν ἀκτῖνα) then would all things inſtantly vaniſh away, & returne to nothing. I omit diuers other reaſons, which here might be alledged; Only it ſufficeth here to ſhew, that God can in no ſort be abſent from his worke; from which poynt it neceſſarily may be concluded, that nothing can be concealed and hid from his Prouidence, ſeing that himſelfe is moſt intrinſecally & inwardly preſent to al things.

THE

THE EIGHT REASON FROM THE
diuerſity of Mens countenances and voices,
and from the pouerty of Man.

CHAP. X.

THESE two things (I meane thé
great diuerſity of faces and voyces
of Men, and the penury that Man is
ordinarily borne vnto (may be no ſmal in-
ducements (if they be rightly conſidered)
to proue the care of the *diuine Prouidence* .
And touching the fiſt ; The *diuerſity of faces*
is ſo multiplicious and almoſt ſo infinit in
Man, as it affordeth no ſmal argumét therof;
for without this variety neither could iuſtice be obſerued, neither could any forme of
a common wealth conſiſt. For ſuppoſe Men
to be in countenance alyke, as ſheepe, crowes, ſparrowes, and many other liuing
Creatures of the ſame nature are, then
moſt ineuitable perturbation and tumults a-
mong Men would enſue ; for neither could
maryed Men diſcerne their owne wyues frō
other women, neither the Parents their
children, neither the creditours their deb-
tours, the friends their enemies, nor the
magiſtrate the delinquents, nor the ſubiects
their Princes ; and therfore each Common

The di-
uerſity of
faces.

K   wealth

wealth would be extremely infelted with adulteries, incefts, frauds, proditions, murthers, and all other wickednes whatfoeuer; fince fuch lewd mifcariages might then be perpetrated with all impunity & freedome from punifhment; for euery one might through a refemblance of face giue himfelf for whom he would, neither could the miftaking be eafily difcouered. This poynt is moft euident to any that ferioufly weigheth the fame, and diuers examples of thofe men do witnes no leffe, who côfyding & refting vpon likenes of face and fauour, haue attempted to inuade other mens beds, patrimonies, kingdomes; fometime with good euent, at other tymes in vayne, but euer with great trouble and tumults. Therefore it is euident, that the difference of faces is moft neceffary, that the lawes of iuftice and of the Commonwealth may not be tranf-greffed, and peace and tranquility obferued.

If it be here replyed that this difference of faces commeth only by chance & cafually, and not from any Prouidence fo difpofing the fame: I anfwere, that it is abfurd to affirme that to haue its euent by chance and fortune, which preuayleth fo much in preuenting of iniures, & in côferuing of iuftice among Men; fince, otherwife it would follow,

low , that all iuttice and true policy which
is found among Men , fhould be grounded
only vpon chance; and that foitune fhould
be the foundation of all Commonwealthes.
Furthermore what proceedeth from chance
is not perpetuall, but rarely hapneth ; and
is not found in all , but in tew only, (as
Ariftotle and other Philofophers do teach.)
As for example , that a man is borne with
fiue fingers, cánot be faid to come by cháce,
but it may be fo faid of him, who is borne
with fix fingers . And anfwerably hereto ,
we fynd, that difference of countenances &
faces is not a thing ftrange and rare, but very
ordinary and common ; which almoft alwaies, and in all places is incident to Men .
Therefore it is n ᴐt a thing to be afcribed to
chance , but to Prouidence, which hath ordained the fame , the better to preferue iuftice and ciuill life betweene Men , which
without this variety of faces could moft
hardly be obferued. But on the other part ,
if the nature of Man and the propagation of
him were fo difpofed , that Men fhould bee
commonly borne lyke in faces , and that no
diffimilitude fhould be betweene them , thē
might this diuerfity of faces well be attribu-
ted to chance , but the contrary we fee, falleth out ; for diffimilitude and vnliknes is
ordinary , and likenes and refemblance of

faces but rare; Therefore, that Men are like,
is to be imputed to chance; that they are vnlike, to Prouidence. And here I vnderſtãd
by the word, *Chance*, a rare and extraordinary concourſe of cauſes, which notwithſtanding is gouerned by the mighty hãd of
Gods prouidence: for in reſpect of his prouidence (which incompaſſeth all things
within the largenes of it owne Orbes) nothing can be ſaid to be caſuall; but only in
regard of ſecondary cauſes, whoſe knowledge and power of working is limited.

In irrationable Creatures there is for the
moſt part ſo great a parity and likenes of the
indiuidua and particulers of one kynd, as that
with difficulty any difference can be obſerued: For ſeing it importeth not much, whether they be like or vnlike, nature followeth that which is more eaſy; and therefore
maketh them like, ſo as to the eye there appeareth no markable & notorious differéce
or vnlikenes: for it is more facile and better
ſorting to the courſe of nature, that bodyes
which internally are of one and the ſame
nature and ſubſtance, ſhould alſo be indued
with the ſame externall qualities, thé with
diuers and different; And when occaſion
requires, that among theſe creatures, one
ſhould be knowne from another (as in
ſheepe, goates, horſes &c. it is an eaſy matter

ter to set on them a marke for their better distinguishing.

Neither among Men is there only this variety of faces (for their better discerning of
one from another) but also of *voyces*; so as
there is no lesse difference among them in
sound of *voyce*, then in Countenance. For
seing a precise and distinct knowledge necessarily conduceth to the preseruing of iustice; therefore the *diuyne Prouidence* hath so
disposed, that there should be a disparity &
vnlikenes not only in *faces*, but also in *voyces*;
that so by a double sense (to wit by sight &
hearing) as by a double witnes, one man
should be made knowne from another. For
if but one of these disparities were, then perhaps some mistaking might be ; but where
both of them do ioyntly concurre and meet,
it is almost impossible, that men heerein
should be in both deceaued. Only difference
of Countenances were not sufficient, because matters are often menaged in darknes; as
also some mens eye sights are so weake and
imperfect, as that they cannot exactly discerne the lineaments and portrature of the
face ; besides among some men (though but
seldome) there is a great resemblance of vi-
sages; so as in distinguishing of them the eye
may be deceaued. And therefore this want
is heere fully supplied with the like dispari-

ty of mens voyces; to the end that such mē, which could not be knowne one frō another by their faces, might neuertheles be eafily distinguished by the sound of their tongues.

But to proceed further in this generall subiect, it is euident, that the consideratiō of *Pouerty* (wherwith the world laboureth) affordeth a strong argument of a *diuyne Prouidence*; Since *Pouerty* is that, which preferueth all entercourse among Men, as furnishing man withal ornaments and delicacyes of this life; as on the contrary side affluence and abundance of riches leadeth man to all dissolution and turpitude of life. For suppose, that all things, which are in any sort necessary to mans life, were fully and promiscuously giuen to al men without any labour and induſtry on their parts; then it is cleare, that two mayne inconueniences would instantly follow : to wit, an ouerthrow and decay of all artes, and all other splendour now appearing in Mans life; and an vtter deprauation and corruption of manners & integrity of conuerfation. For granting the former position, no man would learne any mechanicall arts, or learning would practice them.

No man would vndertake any laborious and painfull taske, nor be seruiceable to
any

any other; since no man would performe thele things, were he not forced therunto through want & penury. And so we should want all rich attyre, all fayre and stately edifices, all costly furniture for houses, all magnificent temples and Churches, all Cittyes, Towers, Castels, and other such fortifications. In like sort, then would ceale all agriculture and tilling, all nauigation, fishing, fowling, & all trafficke for merchãdize; againe there would be no noble and potent men, as being deftitute of all seruãts and followers. Moreouer, all differences of degrees and orders (which are necessary in euery common wealth) would be taken away, and consequently all reuerence and obedience. Therefore whatsoeuer in the whole course of mans life, is faire, gorgeous, magnificent, and to be desired, all the same would be wanting, if men were not poore: and nothing would remayne but rudenes, barbarisme, and sauageneffe.

To this former inconuenience may be adioyned another of greater importance, to wit, an extreme corruption of manners and an opening the sluce to all disorder & dissolution of life. For it is obserued, that such lasciuious courses do commonly accompany idlenes and abundance of wealth; an example of this we may borrow from the men liuing

K 4   uing

liuing before the deluge , (whom lasinesse,
opulency and fulnes of temporalities did o-
uerthrow) as also from the inhabitantes of
Brasile, who (by reason that the country af-
forded them abundantly without labour ,
through the natural temperature of the Climate , all things necessary)are altogeter become mancipated and slaues to Epicurisme ,
lust, and all vicious sensuality .

Two things then there are , which chiefly hurt , & depraue all conuersation of life;
to wit idlenes , and affluence of riches. This
later ministreth matter to all vices ; the first
giueth opportunity and tyme for the practi-
zing of the . But both these are taken away
by pouerty;the one(to wit abundance)imme-
diatly , seing want is nothing els then the
want and not hauing of riches ; the other (I
meane idlenes) in that whiles penury afflicteth and presseth men , they are (for the
further preuenting thereof) willing to vndergo any labour and paines . Therfore penury serueth to man , as a spur , wherby a
flothfull nature is pricked and stirred vp to
industry and toyle ; which while it is who-
lely imployed, bent, and intent vpon its designed worke and taske , is freed from dangerous and vicious cogitations , and consequently hath not leasure and tyme,to spend
the tyme in sensuality . From this then it is
                              euident ,

euident, how healthfull and medicinable
Pouerty is to mankynd; since it extinguisheth
and cutteth away the nourisher of all vices,
possesseth and forestalleth the mynd with
hurtles thoughts, and filleth the world with
all ornaments and commodityes. For what
in humane things is to be accounted as fayre
excellent, and to bee admyred, is the handy
worke of pouerty, and is chiefly to be afcribed to it. Therefore it was truly said of
one authour, Η᾿ πενία σοφίαν ἔλαχε, that is, *Penury and want begetteth wisedome*. This argument is handled copiously by *Ariſtopahnes* in
Pluto; and we do euidently discouer in it
Gods prouidence, by the which he so sweetly
and moderatly gouerneth mankynd.

THE NYNTH REASON, IS FROM *Miracles*.

CHAP. XI.

TO the former argument we may adioyne this next, which is drawne from
miracles, which do irrefragably demonſtrate
a *diuine power*: for if euents haue, and do happen, which cannot be ascribed to any corporall cause; then is it euident, that there is
some one inuisible & greater *vertue* or *power*,
from whom all such ſtupendious actions do

K 5   proceed;

proceed; and this *power* we call *God.* Now, that there are, and haue bene many such, which transcend the limits and bounds of nature, is most cleare from reason it selfe, from the frequent testimonyes of most approued histories, and from the ioynt confessions and acknowledgment of al countryes. Among which great number I will heere insist in the most remarkable and notorious of those, which haue bene effected either before or since our *Saniours* Incarnatiõ. First then may be the *creating of the world* of nothing; for seing this cannot be made of it self (as is proued aboue in the third & fourth reason) then must it necessarily be made by some other agent; but it is an incomprehēsible miracle, to wit, the producing of so huge a worke out of nothing, and such as could be accomplished only by that *power* & *wisedome,* which is most infinite and illimitable.

The second may be the *framing and making of so many liuing Creatures and Plants,* and the first institution of so many seuerali seedes, by the which they are propagated & increased; as also that great fecundity of the earth and the sea, by the cooperation whereof, one Creature or seede is multiplyed in a short tyme into seuerall thousands.

The third. The *most swift motion of the heauens,*

uens, and the gouernement and difpofall of this inferiour world by meanes of this rotation and fpeedy turning about of the faid celeftiall bodies . For by this is occafioned the moft pleafing and gratefull alteration and change of day and night , with the fecret and ftealing increafe and decreafe of them in length . By this alfo are effected the feuerall tymes of the yeare ; fo as all creatures & plants are by this meanes brought forth & after become mature , rype , and perfect in their due tymes. In like manner by this motion of the heauenly Orbes , the fieldes are beautifyed and enriched with flowers , the paftures with graffe , the woods with trees and leaues , and the trees with fruit : finally by the mediation of the forefaid. motion is wrought the flux and reflux of the fea , the blowing of wynds , the darckneffe of the clouds , the conueniency of fhowers , the benefit of fnow , the firft rifing of fprings , the current of riuers, the wholfomnes & ferenity of the ayre , and the benefit proceeding from thunder , & diuers other *Meteors*.

To thefe may be addreffed the *deluge* and inundation of the whole world , the fafety of men and beafts by the Arke , the cloud or burning Sulphur with the which the Citty *Pentapolis* was confumed , the plagues of Ægipt , the diuifion of the fea , the fubmer-

fion

ſion & drowning of the Egiptians, the *pillar of the cloud and fyre*, the heauenly meate or *Manna* giuen to the people of Iſrael for forty yeares ſpace, the wels ſpringing out of rockes through the ſtriking of the with a Rod; the infinite multitude of quailes ſet into the Camps; ſo many apparitions of God euident to all men; ſo great caſtigations and puniſhment of rebellious, incredulous, and miſbeleeuing people, deſtroyed ſotymes through the opening of the earth, other tymes through fyre, or touch of ſerpents; ſo many admirable and vnexpected victories. To theſe in lyke ſort, are to be adioyned, the ſtaying of the Sūne in the midle of its courſe for the ſpace of ten howres; the retrograde or going back of it diuers degrees; the force and burning of the fyre ſuſpended and reſtrayned, and the preſeruation of the ſeruāts of God put into a burning fornace; the fury of Lyons ſuppreſſed that they hurt not the true worſhippers of God, the dead recald & raiſed to life, and the wicked and impious by the peculiar hand of God, wonderfully chaſtiſed.

From all which it is a moſt cleare and illuſtrious truth, that there is a certaine *ſupernaturall* and *diuyne power*, which ſeeth all things, gouerneth all things, and weigheth all things in an euen ballance of iuſtice and Reaſon;

Reason;& which seuerly punisheth the perpetrators and workers of iniquity, & vndertaketh a particuler charge and defence of the vertuous, often effecting for their good and safety many things, aboue the ordinary and setled course of nature.

Neither in these miracles can there be cōceaued the least suspition of any imposture or deceit; *first*, because the authour, which wrot all these(some few excepted) was indued with extraordinary wisedome, and grauity, and was accounted the greatest Prophet that euer liued in any age among those, who either florished for sanctity of life, or praise of wisedome. *Secondly*, because there were many predictions set downe by him in his works, as in *Genesis* 12. & 49. the *Numbers* 24. *Deutron.* 32. and 33. all which seing we fynd by the euent to be most true, we may rest assured, that he was most faithfull in his relation of other things *Thirdly*, in that euery one of the things recyted aboue, are so particularized with all their circūstances of tymes, places, persons, names occasions, effects, with such an order and so sorting to the nature of things, with such a consequence of matters, and so agreeably to piety and probity of Manners, as that euen an eye witnes of the same passages & occurrents could not deliuer them with greater
exactnes,

exactnes. Now who forgeth things, auoydeth (for the most part) many circumstáces;
or if he addeth them, then is the fiction easily discoured by them: for what he wryteth, is either not agreable to the tyme,
place, nature of things themselues, or other
more certaine and approued historyes, or els
some contradiction is found in the matter it
selfe, as falleth out in the fabulous historyes
of *Homer*, *Nonnus*, *Virgil*, *Ouid*, *Amadis*, &
many other such like. *Fourthly* in most of the
things aboue related, the authour (to wit
Moyses) was not only present at the performance of them; but was the chiefe man in
the action pertorming the same, as the instrument of the holy Ghost, and therefore
had best reason to know them most precisely. *Fiftly*, if he had written differently from
the truth (especially to ching the plagues
of *Ægipt*, the deuyding of the Sea, and the
actions performed in the wildernes) he
might easily haue bene conuinced of tal-
shood by many hundred thousands of witnesses, who were also then present with
him. For all these things were red openly
before the whole multitude, & were also
to be read ouer againe euery seuenth yeare
in the presence of the people, as appeareth
out of the 31. chapter of *Deuteronomy*. *Sixtly*,
all the former things, as then being best
ne

knowne throughout all the East , were recorded in Hebrew verse by *Dauid*, who was
a King and a Prophet, and who was later
in tyme then *Moyses* , more then 450. yeares ; which verses euen from that tyme to
this very day , are continually sung in the
publicke prayers , almost throughout the
whole world by the Iewes , where they
enioy the vse of their religion, and by Christians for the space of 1600. yeares . Yea after the dayes of *Moyses* there did almost in e-
uery age rise vp among the people of Israell
certaine Prophets and venerable Men who
being guyded by the assistance of the holy
Ghost , did gouerne , teach, and reduce the
erring people to the law of *Moyses*; which
men, did euer worship Moyses , as a diuyne Prophet and worshipper of the highest
God .

　All which , as beinge worthy and pious
Men , and in what credit & estimation they
were had , may appeare from the consideration both of their actions and writings . For
their actions were such , as exceeded al humane forces , and necessarily required the
ayde of the Almighty : such were those acts
performed by *Iosua, Debora , Gedeon, Sapson ,
Samuel, Dauid , Nathan , Salomon , Abias* Si-
lonites , *Elias , Elizæus , Esay , Ieremy, Daniel ,
Ionas , Iudith , Esther , the Machabees* , and by
　　　　　　　　　　　　　　　diuers

diuers others. And their writings were re-
plenished with diuers predictions and Prophesyes of things to come, which through
long succession of many ages, had their answerable accomplishments and fulfillings: a
poynt so worthy of obseruation, as that the
lyke cannot be found in any history or Writings of other nations. *Seauenthly* euen during the law of the Iewes from the tymes of
Moyses, there was euery yeare an acknowledgment of the effecting of these former
wonders celebrated by diuers ceremonyes,
festiuall dayes, sacrifices, and other rytes,
least the memory of them should in tract of
tyme perish and be abolished: for the feast of
the *Passouer*, and the Sacrifice or the *Pascall
Lambe* was performed in thankesgiuing for
the peoples deliuery out of *Ægipt,* and for the
preseruation of those Iewes who during
their stay in Ægipt, were saued from the
slaughter, which was made vpon the first
borne of the Iewes. And for the same cause
was offered vnto God all the first borne of
things. The feast of *Pentecost* was in memory of the law giuen vpon the fiftith day after their deliuery. The feast of the *Tabernacles* was celebrated, in recordation that the
people liued forty yeares in the desart in
Tabernacles. Furthermore the *Arke of the
Couenant* was kept and preserued, the which
                                        Moyses

Moyses by the commandement and direction of God made, and in the which the *Rod
of Aaron* which bloffomed, and the *veffell of
the Manna* ; and the Law written in two ta-
bles of ftone by the hand of God, and deliuered by *Moyfes*, were fafely laid vp; all
which benefits of God and his wonderfull
workes were celebrated with the finging of
diuers Canticles and fongs. To conclude
the very bookes themfelues of the teftamēt
were with great diligence and publick authority in a holy, publick, and moft fecure
place (as diuyne Oracles) preferued, leaft
otherwife they might by any deceit be corrupted and depraued.

Eightly, for the greater acceffion of Reafons to the former, it may be added, that
thofe wrytings of the old teftament are full
of wifedome, piety, and grauity ; in which
are found no vanity or improfitable curiofi-
ty ; For all things there are fet downe moft
ferioufly and moft aptly for the informing
and rectifying the mynd with vertue and
piety, for deterring it from all wickednes,
and for it voluntary imbracing of godlines,
iuftice, benignity, manfuetude, patience &
temperance ; and all this with wonderfull
documents and examples of moft excellent
men alledged to this end: a courfe far contrary to that, which is taken in the wrytings

of

of Philoſophers, in the which many vayne curious and improfitable paſſages are found, as alſo ſometymes many wicked, prophane and impure inſtructions are to be read. For they in their bookes, by reaſon of the then commō vſe, do permit the wo rſhip of idols, though they were perſwaded that there was but one *ſupreme diuyne Power*. In like manner they permit fullination, repyning and ſecret hate againſt ones Enemy; as alſo fornications, filthy luſts, a vayne deſire of glory, and other internall vicious affections of the mynd. And though ſometymes in their wrytings they commend vertue & reprehend vyce, yet do they not bring any mouing and forcing reaſon, therby to deter men from vyce, and perſwade and moue them to the practice of a vertuous lyfe. For the ſplendour and inward beauty of vertue, as alſo the turpitude and vglines of vice (which two ſole points are vſually aledged by Philoſophers) are but weake incytemēts to the mynd; therefore that Man may haue an abſolute dominion ouer himſelfe and his paſſions there is need of more vehemēt perſwaſions. And hence it is obſerued, that very few men haue bettered their mynds (ſo far forth I meane as concernes piety) by reading of their labours, though many by that meanes haue arriued to a great **pryde and e-**
                                    lation

lation of spirit ; but it is certaine, that from
the wrytings and doctrine of *Moyses* & from
the other sacred bookes of Scripture innumerable men haue come to wonderfull holines, and haue enioyed great familiarity
with God himselfe ; so as they were most illustrious and celebrious for the admirable
workes performed by them.

To conclude this poynt, if any one will
seriously contemplate and confer together
the mysteries of the Iudaicall and Christian
religio, he shall clearly see, that such things
as were done by the Iewes, did serue but
to adumbrate and shadow the mysteries of
our Christian fayth, according to the words
of the Apostle 1, *Cor.* 10 *Hæc omnia in figura*
&c. *All these things chanced to them in figure: but*
they are written to our correction, vpon whom the
ends of the world are come. Wherfore we are
able euen from those poynts, which Christians do daily professe and practise, to proue
that the Iewish discipline and doctrine was
agreable to the truth. From all which pre-
mises it is most cleare, that credit and fideli-
ty is to be giuen to the bookes of *Moyses* (&
not in that degree only, as is exhibited to
the Commentaryes of *Cesar*, the History of
Liuy, or any other prophane authours) but as
to certaine most vndoubted Oracles, writtē
by the speciall concurrency and assistance of

L 2   the

the holy Ghoſt. The like may be auerred of other holy bookes of Scripture (whether they be hiſtoricall or propheticall) ſeing the ſame reaſons and arguments, which are alledged for the writings of *Moyſes*, are alſo preuailing for them.

Now let vs deſcend next to the miracles of the new teſtament: good God, how many and notorious did our Lord here liuing in fleſh, performe? He clenſed the lepreus, he raiſed vp the paralitick, he caſt our deuils in the poſſeſſed, he cured all languors and diſeaſes, he reſtored ſight to the blynd, hearing to the deaſe, ſpeach to the dumbe, going to the lame, and life to the dead. He alſo commanded the wynds, reſtrayned tempeſts, walked vpon the waters, and finally fed diuers thouſands of men by a ſudden multiplication of a ſmall quantity of bread. He wrought all theſe not in priuate, but openly in the ſight of the whole world; ſo as all *Iudæa* tooke notice thereof: neither could ſuch as were emulous and maligning of his glory contradict the ſame.

He alſo did them, not with much endeauour, or with any long preparation aforehand; but only either by his word, or by the gentle touch of his hand. To proceed further, we know, that in his death the Sūne was obſcured, the earth trembled, rocks & **ſtones**

ftones broke afunder, the veyle of the teple
did cleaue in two, and the dead did rife out
of their graues; many thoufands of me were
witnefles hereof, which might (& would
no doubt) charge the Euangelifts writing
thefe things in feuerall tymes and places,
with facriledge, if they had diuulged fictios
and forgeries: fince to lye in poynt of Religion is facriledge in the higheft degree.

But to omit all other things, how ftupe-
dious a miracle was it, that our *Sauiour* co-
uerted the world by the meanes of twelue
men, and thefe ignoble, poore, defpicable,
and ignorant fifhers, (notwithftanding the
gainfaying of the power, wifedome, and
eloquence of the whole world, as alfo the
great reluctation to flefh and blood, mans
corrupt nature, and an inueterate and wicked cuftome ?) For his doctrine was not
to perfwade men to an eafy religion, and
fuch as was indulgent to fenfe, but to a pro-
feffio moft hard, feuere and repugnant both
to mans vnderftanding and his manners: for
it taught, that he, who was nayled vpon
the Croffe was *God*; that riches, honours,
pleafures, and what els is to be prized in
this world, ought to be contemned; that
we ought to tame our flefh, bridle our defires, beare our Croffes, loue our enemies,
render good for euill fpend our blood and

life

life for Chrifts fake, and finally pray for all
fuch, as do in any fort, perfecute or wrong
vs.

How difficult a labour was it, to perfwade the world (blynded afore with Idolatry, and placing all its felicity in riches, honours, and pleafures) to the imbracing of
thefe matters; and this againft the cuftome
and authority of their forefathers, againft the
vfe of all Countries, againft the common
iudgment of all mankind, againft the fenté-
ces of the Philofophers, againft the edicts,
comminations, and threatnings of Princes,
with a refolute neglect of all commodities
or difcommodities of this life, of honour or
contumely, of wordly allurements or torments, how great foeuer? And yet Chrift
performed all thefe great affayres by his A-
poftles, being but poore and ignoble men,
reducing by their meanes the whole power
& wifedome of the world vnder his yoake
and gouerment. Now the Apoftles were a-
fore moft rude, feartull, pufillanimous, ignorant of heauenly mifteryes, ignorant of
the tongues, and indeed altogeather vnapt,
for fo high an enterprife. But behold, after
the Holy ghoft once defcended downe, they
inftantly became moft wife, fearles, mag-
nanimous, skilfull in all the tongues, hauing
the courage to vndertake fo great an ex-
ployt,

ploye, and after performing the same most
gloriouſly and happily. Theſe things are of
ſuch an infallible truth, as that no man had
the forehead to deny them. all ancient Hiſtoryes recording thē ; for the whole world
proclaimes and witneſſeth, that it was firſt
conuerted to Chriſtianitƴ by certaine fiſhers
& that no torments (how exquiſite ſoeuer)
of Tyrants (by the which themſelues and
infinite othes were conſumed) could hinder
the beginning, progreſſe, & increaſe of ſo
worthy and heroicall a buſines. Neuer did
the like happen in another country. Which
miracle being deeply weighed, is not only
of force to the iuſtifying of the being of *Gods
prouidence*, but alſo of the *diuinity of Christ*, &
of the truth of Chriſtian religion. Furthermore the Apoſtles had the guilt of working
miracles, which in ſome ſort was moſt
neceſſary ; ſince the world could hardly
haue bene induced to entertaine ſo ſtrange
and diſpleaſing a doctrine, except in were
waranted therunto by ſome moſt wonderful ſignes & prodigyes. Therfore they gaue
ſight to the blynd, ſtrengthned the Paraly-
tickes, rayſed the lame, cured all kynds of
diſeaſes, reſtored the dead to life, & effected
many other ſuch ſupernaturall things, as appeareth from the *acts* of the *Apoſtles*. From the
Apoſtles tymes euer after, there paſſed not

ouer any one age, which was destitute of
miracles, if we do belieue Ecclesiastical historyes.

Now nothing can be answearable hereto
to take away the authority of these miracles,
but that they were not true, but only forged; or if true, performed by the helpe of
the deuill. But with what colour or shew
of truth, can it be said, that they were meere
forgeryes, seing this answere is not warranted with any reason? For from whence
is it knowne, that they are forged? belyke
because they are miracles, and being miracles they seeme impossible to be wrought.
But here the Atheist is to proue, that they
are impossible, (which he cánot) since the
performance of them implyeth no true and
reall contradiction. That they are not accomplished by the force and power of nature, we all grant, and from thence do proue,
that there is a *diuyne and inuisible power*, more
potent then nature, by the hand wherof all
these are wrought. Furthermore to say, that
they are feigned, is implicitly to take away
all credit of histories, all memory of antiquity, and all knowledge of former ages:
since by this answere all ancyent historyes
whatsoeuer shall be said to be forged, and to
be reiected as mere fables; seing no historyes
are written more accurately, diligently, &
with

That the
former
Miracles
cannot
be said
to be
forged.

with greater inuestigation & search of truth
then are the miracles aboue recyted, especially since the Church hath bene euer most
sollicitous and carefull, that false miracles
should not be ventilated, and giuen out for
true; for here we speake only of those miracles, which the Church acknowledgeth for
certaine & euident. *Thirdly* who condemne
all these miracles for fictions, do charge all
Christian Prĳnces, magistrates, and all the
Christian world of madnes, and extreme
simplicity, in suffering innumerable fictiõs
& lyes to be obtruded vpon thē for so many
truthes; they not hauing so much perspicacity and clearnes of iudgment, as to be able
to discouer the deceit. They also no lesse
do charge all Ecclesiasticall Prelates, generall Councels, all Deuynes, & all wise men
of sacrilegious imposture, in that they do
commēd such commentitious & lying narrations for true miracles, they by this meanes most egregiously deluding the whole
world.

Fourthly, diuers of these miracles are recorded, by so graue authours indued with
learning and sanctity, and with so many
particuler circumstances, as that all possibi-
lity of fraud is taken away. In things, that
are forged, the forgers are accustomed pur-
posely to declyne and auoyde the circum-

L 5   stances

stances of names, and especially of tymes and places, for the better concealing of their lying. *Fiftly*, there was presented no iust and vrgent cause, why these should be falsly inuented. For why should the authours willingly stand obnoxious to so great a sacriledge? Or with what hope or reward should they vndergo the aspersion of so foule a blemish? No man doth any thing, but there is some reason which induceth him so to do. What then was the motiue, that incyted so many Authors, (*to wit, Eusebius, Socrates, Sozomene, Ruffinus, Gregory Nissene, Basil, Ierome, Austin, Sulpitius, Gregorius Turonensis, Optatus, Theodoret, Damasus, Gregory the great,* & many others, who haue written of miracles) to perpetrate so heinous a wickednes? Certainly no true cause hereof can be assigned: for what graue and religious man had noe rather suffer death, then deliberately to wryte one lye, especially in these things, which belong to religion? since thus doing he doth not onlypurchase an eternal infamy among men, but also is most wicked, hateful and abhominable in the sight of God.

Sixtly, if the foresaid miracles were but inuented, then might the authours of them be easily conuinced of forgery by the men then liuing in that age, since the lyues and actiōs of Saints were for the most part diuulged

ged throughout the whole world, at that
tyme , when they were wrought ; for the
radiant splendour and light of such extraordinary vertues cannot be obscured , much
lesse wholy eclipsed ; But there can be alledged not any one Man , who either in the
dayes of those Saintes , or in the tymes immediatly ensuing , durst charge the wryters
of the said miracles with any fiction therein.
Sequently , Mans nature is of it selfe incredulous and full of suspicion , when it questioneth of any new miracles ; and hereupon it
examineth all things concerning the same
most precisely and particularly , least there
be some imposture latent & hidden therein.
Besides there are neuer wanting mē which
are emuious of the glory and honour of o-
thers , who prying into each particuler , do
euer labour (as much as in them lyes) either
wholy to call in question such miracles , or
at least to depresse and lessen the worth thereof.

Now to come to the second branch of the
former answere . If it be said , that they are
performed by the worke of the deuils , then
in thus answering , it followeth , that there
are spirits, or incorporeall substances, which
are more excellēt, then these visible things,
and consequently it is to be granted , that
there is one *supreme Spirit* , excelling all the
                                             rest

reſt in power and wiſedome, & this we call God, as hereafter ſhall be proued. But to proceed further againſt this ſecond part of this Anſweare, I ſay; that theſe ſtupendious workes cannot with any ſhew or pretext of reaſon, be referred to the power of the deuils; for to reſtore ſight to the blynd, going to the lame, to cure the paralitcks only with their word, and to raiſe the dead to life, do far tranſcend and exceed the power of the deuils, who cure diſeaſes only by the mediation of naturall cauſes; to wit, by applying the vertue of hearbs and other medicinable things, as philoſophers & deuynes do teach. Furthermore thoſe holy men, by the miniſtery of whō theſe miracles are performed, were euer in moſt deadly hatred with deuils, and they ware ſo far from vſing them as a meanes, as that they proclaimed open war againſt the Deuils; for they ordinarily diſpoſſeſſed mens bodyes of them, ouerthrew their worſhip, diſcouered their deceites, confuted their doctrines, ſcorned & contemned all their preſtigious artes, and finally deſtroyed their kingdome and gouerment. Such were in the beginning all the Apoſtles, and their ſucceſſours, and infinit others. For againſt theſe and ſuch others no power of Deuils, no Arts magicke, no machinations, and endeauours of wicked ſpirits,

As S. Auguſtine l. 3. de Trinit. c. 8. teacheth.

rits, nor any prestigyes, or sleights could preuayle. Besides how can we with any probability thinke, that so many learned Doctours, so many Prelates, so many Princes, finally so many wife and prudent men were become so stupid and blockish, as not to be able to discerne true miracles from adulterate and forged wonders, and the illusions of the deuill from the hand and worke of God? Belyke only the Pharisyes, the heathen persecutours, & prophane Atheists haue this guift of distinguishing miracles from the prestigyes and deceites of the deuill; and all other men are blynd, toolish, and in this poynt depryued of all sound and perfect iudgment.

This indeed was long since the calumny of the Pharisies againit our Lord, & of the Heathens againft Martyrs; who when they were clearely conuinced with supernatural signes and miracles (as plainly seeing them daily wrought) and being then conscious of their owne inward wickednes, did buift forth into horrible blasphemyes; attributing those things to the deuill and art magick, which were effected only by the mighty Luke 11. hand of God. Now the Reason, why God vouchsafeth to worke miracles in diuers places is manifold. First, he doth this, that hereby he may manifest his presence & prouidence.

uidence to al men . For if during the space of
many ages whatsoeuer was wrought , was
encompassed within the limits of Nature,
then might men (perhaps) be induced to
thinke, that there were no diuine Power,
who had a care of humane affaires , & vpon
whome the charge of them were properly
incumbent ; but that all things had their e-
uent by a secret impulse and force of nature.
For although this is euidently disproued by
many reasons , as from the motion of the
starres , from the fabricke and making of
bodyes , from the innate direction of euery
particuler thing to its certain end (as is shewed aboue) yet many do not sufficiently &
seriously penetrate these matters , but are(as
it were) blynded herein through the daily
and continuall seeing of them ; for how admirable a thing is it , that from some few
graines of corne so great an increase should
rise ? From a formeles seed , so fayre and so
seuerall kynds of bodyes both of liuing Creatures and of Plants should be framed? From
a small roote so huge trees should grow ?
And yet few there are , who do admyre
these things; and few who do acknowledge
Gods wonderfull power and prouidence in
them. Therefore it was necessary,that some
workes might be effected , which should
transgresse the bounds of nature,least otherwise

wise men might thinke, that there were
no power aboue the nature and condition
of corporall things: for by reason of the exorbitancy and the vnaccustomednes of such
stupendious euents, men are often stirred vp
to thinke of the Authour of them, and to
prosecute him with true religion, reuerece,
and honour. *Secondly*, Miracles are effected
to the end, that men may be confirmed in
other poynts of religion, giuing a full assent
therto without any hesitation or doubtful-
nes, and making vse of them with all due
reuerence. *Thirdly*, that the doctrine and lyues of those who worke miracles, may hereby be fully warranted, and so with greater certainty of truth may be commended to
vs. For miracles are certaine diuyne testimonyes both of the infallibility of doctryue,
and of sanctity of life; especially where the
life is conformable to the doctrine. *Fourthly*,
that by this meanes the seruants of God may
be honoured: for there is nothing, which
maketh holy men more celebrious and famous throughout the whole world, and
which more incyteth the mynds of others
to loue, worship, and imitate thē then the
exhibiting of miracles. For as God wil haue
himselfe belieued of Men aboue all things,
and our neighbours not aboue al things, but
euery one in his degree: so doth he expect
himselfe

himfelfe to be worfhiped aboue all things ;
to wit as the firft efficient, & laft final caufe
of all things ; and his feruants not to be honoured after this fupreme manner , but in
their peculiar degree, and in that refpect ,
which they beare towards God ; that is , as
they are his adoptiue fonnes , partakers of
his kingdome, and his moft deare friends.
Thus from hence it appeareth , that there is
no feare of Idolatry in honouring here Gods
Saints; for where there is Idolatry committed , there is fupreme honour giuen , by the
which a Creature is worfhipped , as the
Creatour and firft beginning, but no worfhip is afcribed to the Saints in this fort .

Fiftly , 'Miracles are wrought, that men
through occafion of corporall benefits obtained therby , may the fooner be ftirred vp to
repentance & amendment of life: for where
miracles are wrought , there is to that place
(for the moft part) a great confluence and
concourfe of many theufads of grieuous finners, who being afore contaminated with al
kynds of vices , and hauing conceaued a remorfe of their former licentious lyues , do
vndertake an amendment & change of their
former courfes; and thus by this meanes it
hapneth, that the foules of many thoufands
are faued , which otherwife had perifhed e-
uerlaftingly . *To conclude* this poynt, by miracles

racles all men are ſtirred vp to reuerence &
praiſe of God to the giuing of thankes, &
ſpirituall ioy and exultation, and the minds
of all are raiſed vp to a confident & erected
hope , as conceauing the expectation of the
like help in their future calamityes and afflictions.

CHAP. XII.

I Heere call propheſying, a prediction
of things to come, which do depend of
the liberty of mans freewill. This prediction is a manifeſt ſigne of a *Deity* or *Diuinity*;
for that Mynd , which through its owne
ſtrength & power knoweth things future,
muſt alſo(*à fortiori*) know all things preſent
and paſt ; and conſequently muſt know all
things abſolutly ; I meane all thoſe things ,
which are intelligible and may be vnderſtood . Now that Mynd, which knoweth
omnia intelligibilia , knoweth alſo *omnia poſſi-
bilia*, all things which are poſſible; & therupon muſt be omniſcient(or know al things)
and omnipotent . For here the knowledge,
Idea , or Notion of things is the cauſe of
things;therfore what of it ſelt hath al know-
M   ledge,

ledge, must needs be omnipotent. For who
is prescient and knoweth thinges to come,
doth herein far exceed the faculty of al mortall men according to that saying of *Pindarus:*
ἰῶν μελλόντων φρᾶδαι ἐτύφλωνται, that is, *Humane
mindes are blind in thinges to come* . Therfore
there is an *inuisible intelligence* far more noble
and worthy , then mans mynd , to which
euen through its owne proper force this
prenotion and foreknowledge agreeth ; and
this is *God*. Which poynt is the more true ,
seeing this prenotion is so sublime , high ,
and difficult , as that it seemeth to exact an
infinite power of vnderstanding: for things
future do neither exist , or terminate in theselues , nor in their causes , neither is there
any reason, from whence it may be certainly gathered , that they rather are to be, then
that they are not to be . How then is that
Intelligence, or *Mind* able determinatly and
certainly to foresee what is to come , and
what is not ; but that its intuitiue power &
sight is so perfect,& the efficacy of its light
so great , as that it is able to extend it selfe
to all things future , as they shalbe in themselues in their due tyme ;& this as certainly
as if they did now really exist , or had exi-
sted from all eternity ?

Now it is requisite, that this power be
infinite , both because there cannot be imagined

gined a greater & worthyer manner of seeing; as also in that it stretcheth it selfe forth
to all future things (seing there is the same
reason, manner, and height of knowing
all things.) From which it followeth, that
euen in this respect, that if an Intelligence
by its owne peculiar force knoweth one
thing to come, it knoweth all things. Therfore this prenotion and fortelling of future
things is an euident signe of a *Diuinity*, and
for that cause this kynd of prediction is called *Diuination*; as if to tell what euents are
to happen, were a proper signe of a *Diuinity*
or *deity*: and therefore vpon this ground the
Gods of the Gentils are refuted by *Isay*, in
that they had not the ability to foretell future euets; for thus he saith: *Annunciate quæ*
vētura sunt &c. Shew the things, that are to come
hereafter, that we may know that you are Gods.

That there is a prenotion of future things
is clearly proued from innumerable predictions, which from their euents are found
to be most true, for prediction or foretelling euer presupposeth prenotion and foreknowledge. This prenotion the Prophets
had not from themselues, and from their
owne industry or perspicacity and clearnes
of iudgment (since prenotion far transcendeth mans capacity) but they receaued it
from some superiour power, which hath it

by

by its owne vertue, from it ſelte, and not from another. Now many of theſe predicti-ons are contained in the holy Scripture; out of the which I will alledge ſome, which to haue bene accompliſhed, is moſt euident .

Firſt then , *Geneſis 3* . it is foretold, that the *ſeed* (meaning the of-ſpringe of the woman, ſhould cruſh the head of the Ser-pent ; that is, ſhall ouerthrow the power domination , and rule of the Diuell ; which prophecy is accompliſhed partly already by Chriſt, aboliſhing in moſt places the wor-ſhip of Diuels, wherin the world afore did lye plunged; and partly reſteth to be further fulfilled by Chriſt at the day of iudgment ; when the power and ſway of the Diuell & the wicked ſhalbe vtterly extinguiſhed. In *Geneſ.* alſo c. 18. and 22. it is propheſyed , that *a Child ſhalbe borne to Abraam by the benefit of whom all nations ſhall obtaine benediction and felicity*, which is euidently performed in Chriſt, throgh whom the world is with-drawne from Idolatry and pernicious er-rours , to the worſhip & knowledge of the true God , and ſhall by him obtayne the hope of eternall ſaluation. Againe in the 40. chapter of the ſaid booke, there is a wō-derfull prediction of *Ioſeph* , which was to be fulfilled within three dayes ; as alſo in interpretation of certaine moſt obſcure dre-
ames

ames touching three stocks of a vyne, and
three baskets; and c. 41. an exposition of
Pharoes dreame, touching the twyce seauen
beasts, & twice seauen ears of corne. Where
we are to consider now expeditely, and
with what cōfidence are expounded all the
particulers of thē according to their euents.
Now those dreames being presages and signes of things to come, cannot proceed, but
only from a *diuine Power*, from whose prouidence all humane matters receiue their
disposall; neither can the true meaning &
construction of them be obtained, but only
by reuelation of the same *diuyne Power*. A-
gaine c. 49. *Iacob* the Patriarch immediatly
before his death, did prophesy to euery one
of his sonnes, what should happen to their
posterity; especially so far forth, as concer-
ned their offspring, their riches, and the diuision of the land of *Promise*; which all particulers were after a long deuolutiō of yeares fulfilled, as appeareth out of the sacred
Scripture. But among other things, that is
very memorable and notorious, which is
there said. *Non auferetur sceptrum de Iuda &c.*
The scepter shall not depart from Iuda, nor a
Lawgiuer from betweene his feete, till he come
who is to be sent; and he shalbe the expectation
of the Gentils. In which words three things
are foretould. First that regall principality

M 3   shalbe

ſhalbe in the tribe of *Iuda*; which was accō-
pliſhed, when it was tranſlated vpon *Dauid*,
in whoſe family and race it continued 520.
yeares . Secondly , that this Soueraingty
ſhould continue in the tribe of *Iuda* , till the
comming of *Chriſt* , which poynt was alſo
accompliſhed, for it continued in that tribe
till it was transferred vpon *Herod Aſcalonites*
(who was no Iew) in the tyme of whoſe
reigne *Chriſt* was borne . Thirdly , that
Chriſt was to be reiected by the Iewes , &
receaued by the Gentils ; who for that reſpect is there called *Expectatio gentium* , *the*
expectation of the Gentils. In the 24. of the
booke of *Numbers* , *Balaam* being poſſeſſed
with a diuyne fury, foretelleth many things
and among the reſt, theſe three . Firſt, that
the King of *Iſrael* was to be taken away by
reaſon of *Agag* King of *Amalec* ; where we
ſee, that the name of that King is expreſſed ,
who was to be borne ſome foure ages after,
and for whoſe cauſe *Saul* was to be depriued of his kingdome , which is fulfilled in
the firſt booke of the Kings c. 15. Secondly
that a King ſhould riſe out of *Iſrael* who
(like a glorious ſtar) was to enlighten the
whole world , and to haue dominion ouer
all men , which was performed in *Chriſt* .
Thirdly, that the Romanes were to come
with their gallies, and ſhould ouercome the
Iewes

Iewes : and this was effected vnder *Titus &*
Vespasian, more then a thousand yeares after
the said prediction.

In the 18. of *Deuteronomy, Moyses* prophesyeth, that God would raise out of the Iewes, a Prophet like to himselfe; whom all
ought to heare, & such as would not, were
to be seuerely punished by God, where in
expresse words he prophesyeth of the comming of Christ, and doth intimate his function, the incredulity of the Iewes, & their
ouerthrow. Now *Christ* was like to *Moyses,*
as the body is to the shadow, the truth to
the figure, and the Exemplar, or Sample to
the image, in that *Moyses* was a type and figure of *Christ.* For *Moyses* deliuered the people from the seruitude of Egypt; Christ the
world from the thraldome of the Diuell.
Moyses brought them safe from the red sea ,
the Egiptians being there drowned ; Christ
saued his Belieuers through Baptisme
(which deriueth al its vertue frō the bloud
of Christ) with the submersion and drowning of all their sinnes, *Moyses* gaue to them
the old law, Christ giueth to the world the
new and Euangelicall law. *Moyses* fed the
people in the desert with *Manna* from heauen, and gaue them to drinke of the rock.
Christ feedeth his seruants in the Church
with his owne celestiall body and bloud ;
for

for he is the bread, that defcended from heauen, and the hidden *Manna*; he is the Rock
of eternall faluation, which giueth drinke.
The *people* by the endeauour of *Moyfes* ouercame their enemyes, comming at the length
to the land of *Promife*, wee by the mediatiō
of Chrift vanquifh our foules aduerfaries, &
are brought to heauen. Thus by reafon of
thefe and other fuch comparifons, *Chrift* is
called a Prophet like vnto *Moyfes*.

In the 28. 29. 30. 31. and 32. of *Deuteronomy* the Idolatry of the Iewes, their fins
and diuers calamityes, which were to fall
vpon them for the fame caufe, are prophefyed: and in the 33. of *Deuteronomy Moyfes*
foretelleth the particuler lot to euery trybe,
and diuers euents, which *Iacob* had not ex-
preffed in his benediction.

In like fort, that Prediction which is
related in the third booke of the Kings c.
13. is moft wonderfull, where when *Ieroboam* incenfed frankinfence to the Idols, a
certaine Prophet thus exclaymed forth.
Altare, Altare, &c. *O Altar, Altar, thus
faith the Lord. behold a child shalbe borne vnto the
houfe of Dauid Iofias by name, & vpon thee shal
he facrifice the Priefts of the high pl aces, that burne
incenfe vpon thee, and they shall burne bones vpon
thee.* All which things were accomplifhed
after, as appeareth out of the fourth of the
Kings.

Kings c. 23 . and this some 301. yeares after ; for as *Iosephus* wryteth in the tenth
booke of his *Antiquities* c. 5. so many yeares
passed betwene that prediction, and the ac-
complishment of it .

In the 45. chapter of *Isay* , the kingdome
of *Cyrus* (who was to be borne some two
hundred yeares after) is prophesyed , his
name being expresly set downe , as also his
power , warres , victories , spoyles , riches ,
and his beneficence towards the Iewes are
insinuated ; which very place of Scripture,
when the Iewes had shewed to *Cyrus* , he
wonderfully admyred the diuination of the
Prophet ; and being incensed with the desire of performing such things , as he had
there read , conferred great benefits vpon
the Iewes , as *Iosephus* recorderh in his eleuenth booke of *Antiquities* c . 1. I omit innumerable other prophesyes , which are to be
found of *Isay* .

In *Daniel* we synd , many stupendious
predictions, and interpretations of most difficult things . In the second chapter, wheras
a certaine strange dreame was shewed to
the King of the *Chaldeans*; and the King for-
getting the same , *Daniel* distinctly opened
the vision to him; to wit, that there appeared to the King in his sleepe a great & terrible *statua* or Image , whose head was

made

made of gold, his breaſt and armes of ſiluer, his belly and thighes of braſſe, his
legs of Iron, ending in feet which were
partly of clay, and partly of iron. Furthermore he told the King, that he ſaw a ſtone
cut out of a mountaine without hands; and
that it did ſtrike the *ſtatua* vpon the feete ;
which being broken and ſhiuered aſunder,
the *ſtatua* fell downe, and was turned into
duſt: and that the ſtone did increaſe into a
great mountaine, which filled the whole
earth. This being thus expreſſed, *Daniel*
further gaue the interpretation thereof; to
wit, that by the *ſtatua* were figured foure
Monarchies, of the which the firſt was thē
in being, the other three ſhould ſucceed one
after other in their due reuolution of tymes.
For the head of gold did ſignify the Empyre
of the *Chaldeans*, which thē was moſt ample
opulent, and rich. The breaſt of ſiluer de-
ſigned the monarchy of the *Perſians* and *the
Medes*, which ſucceeded the former, conſiſting of two kingdomes, as of two legs.
The belly and thighes of braſſe did ſpecify
the monarchy of the *Grecians* : the legs of I-
ron did prefigure the moſt powerfull mo-
narcy of the *Romanes*, diuided into the Empire of the Eaſt and the weſt. The feete being made partly of clay, and partly of Iron,
did ſignify the monarchy of the *Romanes* to
be

be partly ftrong, and partly weake . The ftone cut out of the mountaine without the help of handes, did demonftrate *Chrift* our Lord, who without any endeauour of man was borne of the moft holy, pure, and immaculate Virgin, and proceeded from the progeny of *Abraham* ; & who increafed into a great mountaine; in that his kingdome was to replenifh & poffeffe the whole earth & who in the end of the world was to deftroy all other kingdomes, himfelfe only poffeffing an eternall kingdome . Now in fhewing and interpreting of this dreame, the power, wifedome and prouidence of God fo clearly fhyned, that the proud King proftrated himfelfe vpon his face before *Daniel* his feruant, and worfhipped him, and openly confeffed the maiefty & power of God .

The forefaid foure Monarchyes (which were to fucceed in order) and the conditions, ftates, and proprieties of euery one of them were forefhewed to *Daniel* by another wonderful vifion in the feauenth Chapter, vnder the forme and fhew of foure beafts ; & then after was fignifyed to him the kingdome of the Saints, which (after all the kingdomes of the world were extinguifhed) fhould continue and florifh eternally. For thus doth the Angell interprete this

vifion

viſion vnto *Daniel* : *Ha quatuor beſtia &c.*
Theſe foure great oraſts are ſoure Kingdomes ,
*which ſhalt ariſe out of the earth , and they ſhall
take the kingdom of the Saints of the moſt higheſt,
and they ſhall poſſeſſe the kingdome for euer, euen
for euer and euer;* that is, for all eternity . And
now ſeing we haue obſerued by experience
all thoſe things to be accompliſhed concerning the foure Monarchyes , which were
ſhewed to *Daniel* in the former viſion; we
therefore ought to aſſure our ſelues, and not
to fluctuate in any vncertainty of beliefe ,
but ſuch things, as there were propheſyed
to him of the kingdome , of the Saints, ſhal
alſo be fulfilled in their due tyme .

Againe in the eight Chapter, as yet the
monarchy of the *Chaldeans* floriſhing, that
other monarchyes ſhould ſucced to the former, was alſo foreſhewed to the ſaid *Daniel*:
to wit the monarchy of the *Medes* and *Perſiās*
vnder the forme of a Ram with two hornes ; the monarchy of the *Grecians* alſo, of a
goat with one horne; as alſo was foreſhewed the manner , how the firſt Monarch
was to be deſtroyed by this other ; and that
this, after the firſt king thereof, ſhould be
deuided among foure kings ; out of the po-
ſterity of which kings one ſhall come (to
wit *Antiochus Epiphanes*) who (from a ſmall
ſtate becoming great) ſhall after perſecute
                                                    and

and afflict the Iewes , shall profane the sanctuary, shal take away the daily sacrifice, and shall force al vnto Idolatry for the space of 2300. dayes, which is for six yeares , three moneths , and twenty dayes ; & who in the end (without any machination or endeauour of Man) shall , euen by Gods reuenge only , be extinguished. All which particulers to be fulfilled in the persecutiō of *Antiochus* is euidēt euen out of the bookes of the *Machabees,* at least 400. and eight yeares after this prediction of *Daniel* , as *Iosephus Antiquit.* c. 11. relateth, who in his 11. booke c. 8. further sheweth , that this prophecy of *Daniel* (touching the King of the *Grecians,* ouerthrowing the Empire of the *Persians*) was related by the Prophets to *Alexander* then being in *Ierusalem* ; and that *Alexander* reioyced much therat , as interpreting this was to be performed by himselfe ; to wit , that he was that *Grecian* King (as indeed he was) who should arryue to the Empyre of the *Persians.*

In the eleuenth chapter of *Daniel* many things are in like sort prophesyed , first the progresse and good successe of the *Persian* Empire . Secondly the expedition of *Xerxes* against the *Grecians.* Thirdly , that the empyre of *Alexander* the great should succed the *Persian* empyre : fourthly the diuision of the

Grecian

Grecian Empyre into foure kingdomes .
Fiftly , that moſt bloudly warres ſhould fal
out betwene two ſucceſſours of *Alexander* ;
to wit betwene the kings of *Syria* and *Egipt*,
during which violent conflict, *Iudaa* (as
being ſeated betwene them both) ſhould
be moſt miſerably afflicted . Moreouer in
the foreſaid chapter are foreſhewed the a-
mityes , mariages , deceites, proditions,and
diuers other euents , which were to happē
betwene the ſaid kings ; in ſo much that it
ſeemeth to the reader rather a hiſtory then a
propheſy . Sixtly , the perſecution of *Antiochus Epiphanes* againſt the Iewes . Seuently ,
through occaſion of this perſecution, he paſ-
ſeth ouer to the perſecutiō of *Antichriſt* prefigured by that of *Antiochus*. Now that all
theſe (the laſt only excepted , which is to
receaue its performance in the end of the
world) are already accompliſhed, appeareth
out of the wrytinges of the Heathens , out
of *Ioſephus*, & out of the *Machabees* . Doubtleſly ſo exact , particular , and various a
propheſy of things to come was moſt admirable and ſtupendious . But it were an infinite labour to proſecute all things of this
uature; ſeing all the bookes of the Prophets
are euen fraughted and ſtored with ſuch
predictions; only now I will touch ſuch,as
concerne *Chriſt* our Lord, and are rehearſed
and

& acknowledged by the Euägelifts, which
very particulerly many ages before, were
forefeene and prophefyed.

And firft, it is infinuated in diuers places
of Scripture, but efpecially in the 3. of *Ba-*
ruch, that God was to conuerfe with men in
an humane fhape; *Hic eft Deus nofter* &c. *This*
is our Lord, and there shal none other be compared
vnto him, he hath found out the way of knowledge,
& hath giuen it vnto Iacob his feruant; & to Ifrael
his beloued; afterwards he was feene vpõ the earth
and dwelt among men; as alfo in the thirty
fiue of Ifay, of which place fee heereafter.

2. That he was to be borne of a virgin,
appeareth in Ifay c.7. *Ecce virgo concipiet* &c.
Behold. a Virgin shal beare a fonne, and she shal
cal his name Emanuel. By which name it is infinuated, that he fhalbe both God and man;
for the word *Emanuel* fignifyeth as much, as
nobifcum Deus, or, *God with vs.*

3. That he was to be borne in Bethleē,
Micheas c. 7. fayth: *Et tu Bethleem* &c. *And*
thou Bethleem Ephrathah art litle to be among
the thoufands of Iuda; yet out of thee shal come
forth a Captaine that shalbe the ruler in Ifrael,
whofe goings forth haue been from the beginning
and from euerlafting. In which wordes his
diuinity is alfo implyed.

4. The time wherin he was to come, was
foretold by Iacob in the 49. of Genefis: *Non*
auferetur

auferetur ſceptrum &c . *The ſcepter ſhal not be taken from* Iuda &c *til he come who is to be ſēt, and he ſhal be the expectation of the Gentils.* And more diſtinctly in *Daniel* c.9. of which place we ſhal hereafter ſpeake.

5.   That he ſhould haue a *precurſour*, who ſhould prepare the mynds of the people to receaue him, was prophecyed in the third of *Malachy: Ecce ego mitto Angelum* &c. *Behold I wil ſend my meſſenger, & he ſhal prepare the way before me, and the Lord whom you ſeeke ſhal ſpeedily come to his temple, the euen meſſeger of the Couenant, whom you deſire:* which very text our Lord him ſelfe in *Matth.* 11. and *Luke* 7. did teach to be vnderſtood of *S. Iohn Baptiſt* the precurſour. Againe his precurſour is alſo foretold in the 40. of *Iſay; Vox clamantis* &c *a voyce cryeth in the wildernes, prepare ye the way of our Lord, make ſtraight in the deſert a path for our Lord* Of which place ſee the third of *Matthew*, as alſo the 4. of *Luke*.

6.   The preaching of our Lord in *Iſay* 61. *Spiritus Domini.* &c *The ſpirit of the Lord is vpon me,therfore the Lord hath annointed me, he hath ſent me to preach good tydings to the poore, to bynd vp the broken harted, to preach liberty to the captiues,and to them that are bound the opening of the priſō,to preach the acceptable yeare of our Lord and the day of vengance of our God, to comfort al that mourne.* Which prophecy our Lord tea

cheth

cheth to be accoplished in himselfe, in Luke
c.4.

7.　Of the miracles of Christ in Isay 25.
*Dicite pusillanimes &c. Say vnto them that are
fearful: bee you strong, feare not: behold your God
cometh with vengeace, euen God wil come & saue
you* : then shal the eyes of the blynd be lightned,
and the eares of the deafe be opened; then shal the
lame man leape, as a Hart, and the dumbe mans
tongue shal sing &c. Which wordes our Lord
sheweth also to be vnderstood of himself, in
Mathew c.11. Where he saith: *Ite & renun-
ciate &c. Goe & shew Iohn what things you haue
heard and seene, the blynd receaue sight, and the
halt goe: the leapers are cleansed, and the deafe
heare; the dead are raised vp, and the poore receaue
the Ghospell* .

8.　The entrance of Christ in Ierusalem
in Zachary c.9. *Exulta satis filia Sion &c. Reioyce greatly O daughter Sion, shout for ioy, O
daughter Ierusalem; behold thy king cometh vnto
thee, he is iust, poore and ryding vpon an Asse, and
vpon a colt the fole of an Asse*. That this was fulfilled is euident out of Mathew c. 21.

9.　The prodition & betraying by his own
disciple, in Psal.41. *Etenim homo pacis &c. For
the familiar friend who I trusted, which did eat of
my bread, hath lifted vp the heel against me*. Which
very place Christ himself did interprete in
the 23. of Iohn, of Iudas who betrayed him.

10. That he was to be fold for thirty pieces of filuer, is in Zachary. 11. *Appēderunt mercedem &c. They weighed for my wages thirty pieces of filuer, and the Lord faid vnto me, caft it vnto the potter; a goodly price, that I was valued at of them And I tooke the thirty pence of filuer, & caft them to the potter in the houfe of the Lord.* Heere it is clearly prophecyed, that Chrift fhould be valued at thirty pieces of filuer; and that thofe thirty pieces were to be caft into the Téple, & that a field of an image-maker of earth, or Potter was to be bought therwith. All which things we fynd to be fulfilled in Mathew 27.

11. *The flight of his Difciples*, in Zachary, 13. *Percutiam paftorem &c. I will fmite the shee pheard, & the sheep shal be fcattered.* Which place our Sauiour interpreted in the approach of his Paffion. Mathew 26.

12. That he fhould fuffer diuers kinds of paines and dolours by reafō of his ftripes, his Coronation, and Croffe, is in like maner foretold in Ifay 53. *Non eſt fpecies ei &c. He hath neither forme, nor beauty; and we faw him defpifed and reieɛted of men; he is a man ful of forrowes, & hath experience of infirmities &c.*

13. That he was to fuffer for our fakes al thefe preffures and afflictions with wonderful modefty, gentlenes and patience, in Ifay 53. *Vere lāguores noſtros &c. Surely he hath*

borne

borne our *infirmities, & hath caryed our forrowes,
yet we did iuᵈ e him as plagued & fmitten of God
and humbled.* But he *was wounded for our tranfgreffions he was broken for our iniquities; the chaftifement of our peace was vpon him, and with his
ftripes we are healed. Al we like fheepe haue gone
aftray, we haue turned euery one to his owne way
and the Lord hath laid vpon him the iniquity of vs
al.* He *was oppreffed, he was afflicted yet did he not
opē his mouth. He is brought asa fheep to the flaugh
ter, and as a fheepe before the fhearer is dumbe ; fo
he opeeed not his mouth &c.* Al which particulers, that they were moft euidently fulfilled
in Chrift, appeareth out of the Euangelifts.

14.　His Crucifixiō is recorded in Pfalm
22. *Foderunt manus &c. They pierced my hands
and my feet &c.* The fame was prefigured in
the brafen ferpent being hanged a height, at
the beholding wherof al fuch as were bittē
by ferpents were cured. *Numer.* 21. as our
Lord himfelfe declareth, *Iohn* 3.

15.　That the was crucifyed betweene
two theeues, and that he was to pray to
his Father for his perfecutours, is foretold
in Ifay . 53. *Ideo difpertiam &c.* Therfore *I
wil giue him a portion with the great , and he fhall
deuide the fpoile with the ftrong, becaufe he hath
powred out his foule vnto death; and he was coūted
with the tranfgreffours , and he bare the finnes of
many, and prayed for his trefpaffers.*

　　　　16. Tho

16. The iriſions & blaſphemyes of the Iewes againſt Chriſt hanging vpon the Croſſe, in Pſalm. 21. *Ego ſum vermis &c. I am a worme, and not a man, a ſhame of men, & contempt of the people. All they that ſee me, haue me in deriſion, & make a mowe, and nod the head ſaying he truſted in the Lord, let him deliuer him, let him ſaue him, ſeeing he loued him.* Where we find almoſt the ſame words in part, in Mathew 27.

17. The diuiſion of his garments and caſting lots for the ſame, in pſalm. 21. *Diuiſerunt* &c. *They parted my garments amõg them, & did caſt lots vpon my veſture.* For, one veſtmẽt they diuided into foure parts; & for the other (becauſe it was not to be deuided) they did caſt lots. Iohn. 19.

18. That being vpõ the Croſſe, he drũke gall and vinegar, pſalm. 68. *Dederũt in eſcam* &c. *They gaue me gall in my meat, & in my thirſt they gaue me vinegar to drinke.*

19. That his bones were not to be broken. Exod. 12. and Num. 9. *Os illius* &c. *You ſhal not breake a bone thereof.* That his ſyde was to be thruſt through with a ſpeare appeareth in *Zachary* 12. *Aſpiciunt &c. They ſhal looke vpon me, whome they haue pierced,* both which places are expounded of Chriſt by S. Iohn the Euangeliſt. c. 19.

20. His Reſurrection is propheſyed in
Pſal.

Pfal. 15. *Non derelinques animã* &c. *Thou wilt not leaue my soule in hel, neither wilt thou suffer thine holy one to see corruption.* &c. which paſſage of Scripture S. Peter (inſtantly after he had receaued the holy Ghoſt, and of a rude & ignorãt fiſher, became a moſt wiſe Doctour of the whole world) interpreted of the Reſurrection of our Lord. Act. 2.

21. That he was to riſe from death the third day, Oſee. c. 6 *Viuificabis nos &c. After two daies will he reuiue vs, and the third day wil he raiſe vs vp, and we shall liue in his fight* . Of which verity *Ionas*, who was three dayes in the whales belly, & the third day came out aliue, *Ionas* c. 2. was (according to our Sauiours explication) a type and figure.

22. His Aſcenſion into heauen in Pſal. 14. *Aperite &c. Lift vp your heads you gates, and be you lifted vp you euerlaſting doores, & the King of glory shall come in.* And Pſal. 67. *Aſcendiſti &c. Thou art gone on high, thou haſt led captiuity captiue, and receaued guifts for men.* Which place in the fourth to the *Epheſians,* the Apoſtle doth thus interprete.

23. The ſending of the holy Ghoſt in Ioel. 2. *Effundam Spiritum meum* &c. *I wil power out my ſpirit vpon al flesh, and your ſonnes, & your daughters shal propheſy, your old men shal dreame dreames, and your young men shal ſee viſions :* Which propheſy was fulfilled in

the ſecond of the Acts, euē accoiding to the expoſition of S. Peter

24. The deſtruction of the Iewes for the death of Chriſt, was prophelyeu in Pſalm. 69. *Fiat menſa* &c. *Let their table be a ſnare before thē & their proſperity their ruine, Let their eyes be blinded, that they ſee not, and make their loynes alwaies to tremble: powre out thine anger vpon them, and let thy wrathful diſpleaſure take them. Let their inhabitans be void, & let none dwel in their tents; for they perſecuted him whom tvou haſt ſmitten &c.*

25. The tyme wherin al theſe things are to happen is exactly deſcribed by *Daniel* being taught herein by an Euāgelical reuelation, for thus the Angel ſpeaketh c. 9. *Tu animaduerte ſermonem &c. Vnderſtand the matter, and conſider the viſion: Seauenty weekes are determined vpon the people, & vpon thine holy Citty, to finiſh the wickednes, and to ſeale vp the viſion and propheſy, and to annoynt the moſt holy,* The ſenſe of which place is, that God appointed the ſpace of 490. yeares (for ſo many yeares do ſeauenty *Hebdomadaes,* or weekes of yeares containe) within which compaſſe of tyme (to wit towards the end therof) the Meſſias was to come, who being the authour of al holines, ſhal blot away the ſinne of mankind; ſhal recōcile man to God; ſhal bring into the world eternal iuſtice; &

as

at whofe comming the vifions & prediҫiõs
of the Prophets fhal be fulfilled . And then
he declareth , where thefe *Hebdomadaes* are
to begin,and where to end. *Scito ergo & ani-*
maduerte ab exitu fermonis &c 1. Know therfore
and vnderſtand , that from the going forth of the
commandement, and to build Ierufalem againe ,
vnto the Meſſias the prince, shalbe feauen weeks,
and threefcore, and two weekes, and that is 69.
weekes ,or 483. yeares .

Now this *Exitus fermonis* (that is the ful-
filling of the kings cõmandement touching
the building of *Ierufalem,* to wit , when the
Citty was finifhed & dedicated,as the learned do interprete and proue) is made in
the 23 . yeare of *Artaxerxes,* or as Iofephus
wryteth in his 11. Booke of *Antiquities* c.5 .
in the 28. yeare, reckoning frõ the beginning of the reigne of *Xerxes* ; that is , in the
third yeare of the 80. *Olimpiade* , which
was the feauenth yeare of *Artaxerxes* then
gouerning priuately . Furthermore from
the third yeare of the 80. *Olimpiade* to the
baptifme of Chrift , when Chrift was de-
clared by his Father to be *Dux Populi,* and
that he begun fo to fhew himfelfe in doctrine & miracles , are precifely 483. yeares.
And where in the fame chapter it is faid;(1)
And the ftreet shall be built againe , and the wall
in a troublefome tyme. This was often attemp-

Daniel .1.
9.
(1) *v.25.*

N 4   ted

ted, but twice hindred, & at the laſt perfe-
ɛ̃ted ; from the twentith yeare of *Artaxer-*
xes, til the 23. yeare, being in the 80. *Olimpi-*
ade: And (2) *after threſcore & two weeks,* which
ſh. i follow after the ſeauen firſt weekes) *the*
Meſſias ſhal be ſlaine ; that is , after 483. yeares

(2) *v.* 26. or in the 70. Weeke: *And it ſhal not be his people*
which ſhal deny him &c. that is , the people of
the Iewes ſhal not be accouted any longer

(3) *v.* 26. as the people of God . (3) *And the prince ſhal*
come and ſhal deſtroy the Citty and the ſanctuary
&c. that is, the Roman army with *Titus* and
Veſpaſian. (4) *and the end therof ſhal be with a*

(4) *v.* 26. *floud and vnto the end of the battel it ſhal be des-*
troyed by deſolations &c. To wit, which God
hath ord uned and foretold . (5) *And he ſhal*

(5) *v.* 27. *cõſirme the couenãt with many in one weeke;* that
is, Chriſt being the captaine ſhal confirme
his Euangelical law by many miracles and
many wayes in the laſt week (to wit the 70.
Weeke) for Chriſt after his baptiſme pre-
ched thrée yeares and ſome months .(6) *And*

(6) ▬ . *in the weeke , he ſhal cauſe the ſacrifice & the obla-*
tion to ceaſe &c. For Chriſt ſuffering death in
the middeſt of the laſt wéeke, the reaſon of
al the old ſacrifices ſhal ceaſe , which were
inſtituted to prefigure the ſacrifice of the

(7) *v.* 27. Croſſe . (7) *And there ſhal be in the Temple the*
abhominatiõ of deſolation &c. In which wordes
is inſinuated the deteſtable faction of the
Zelotyts ,

Zelotyts, which was the cause of the whole
desolation & ouerthrow , as *Iosephus* fheweth, *Lib.6.de bello Iudaic. cap.16. & c.4.l 7.*
Or otherwise,it is signified hereby,that the
army of the Gentils causing the desolation ,
& vastity , shal not only possesse & destroy
the citry,but also the Tеple. (8)*And the deso-
tion shal continue vntil the consumation and end of   (8)v.ibid.*
the world &c. Al which things (the last only
excepted) we see fulfilled ; and therfore we
are not to doubt , but this last also shal be
performed,seeing that the desolation & dif-
persion of the Iewes haue already cōtinued
almost 16. ages .

.26.   The conuersion of the Gentils to
the faith of Chrift is prophefyed in Genef .
18.*In semine tuo &c.In thy seed all nations shall
be bleßed* And in Pfal.22.*Reminifcetur &c. Al
the ends of the world shal remember, and turne to
the Lord and al the kinreds of the nations shall
worship before thee,for the kingdome is the Lords,
and he ruleth ouer nations.&c.* The fame is prophefyed alfo in Ifay .49. *Parum eft &c . It is
a fmal thing that thou shouldeft be my feruant
to raife vp the tribes of Iacob , and to reftore the
defolatiōs of Ifrael, I wil giue thee for a light of the
Gentils, that thou maift be my health vnto the end
of the world .* And in c. 66 *I will fend thofe ,
that haue efcaped of them , vnto the nations of Af-
fricke , Lydia, Italy , and Greece , and vnto the*

N 5   *Ifles*

Iſles a far of, that haue not heard my fame , nor haue ſeene my glory; and they ſhall declare my glory among the Gentils, and from all nations they ſhall bring an offering vnto God .

Theſe and many other were foretold of our Lord by the Prophets many yeares before his incarnation , which we fynd to be already accompliſhed . But our Lord himſelfe , as preſcious, and foreknowing of all things , deliuered alſo wonderfull predictions, in which he manifeſted his diuinity , of which I will relate ſome . For he foretold moſt particularly, and in order all the ſeuerall paſſages of his Paſſion; as in Matth. 20. *Ecce Aſcendimus &c . Behold we goe vp to Ieruſalem , and the ſonne of man ſhalbe deliuered vnto the chiefe Prieſts , and vnto the Scribes ; and they ſhall condemne him vnto death , and ſhall deliuer him vnto the Gentils to be mocked , and to be ſcourged, and the third day he ſhall riſe againe .* Which is ofté els where inſinuated in Math. c. 16. 17. and 26. Marke. 9. Luke . 10. Iohn. 3.

2. The abnegation and denyall of *Peter,* in Marke 14. For thus ſaith our Lord to him . *Amen dico tibi &c. Amen I ſay vnto thee, this day, euen in this night ,before the Cock crow twice , thou ſhalt deny me thrice .* Doubtleſly this ſo particular and preciſe a prediction was moſt ſtrange , eſpecially ſeing that at the

the fpeaking of thefe words *Peter* feemed
moft conftant and firme , and that the tyme
of this euen: was fo fhort , and that his pre-
monition might haue bene a fufficient fore-
warning vnto *Peter*. From which former
words of Chrift , we may not only gather,
that he knew this thing fo to come to paſſe,
but alfo knew , that telling *Peter* aforehand
of it , fhould not in any fort hinder & preuent the euent .

3.   His prodition or betraying of *Iudas*,
and the flight of his difciples in Math. 26.
Marke 14. Luke 22. Iohn. 13.

4.   The meeting of the man carrying a
veſſell of water was prophecyed, in Marke
14. and Luke 22. *Mittit duos &c* . *He fent two*
of his difciples , and faid vnto them . Goe into the
ci ty , and there shall a man meete you bearing a
pitcher of water. Follow him , and whither foeuer
he goeth in . fay to the Maister of the houfe : Our
maifter faith , where is the refectory , where I
shal eate the Pafche with my difciples ? And he shal
shew you a great chamber adorned , there prepare
for vs . So his difciples went forth, and came to the
citty , and found as he had faid vnto them .

5.   The like prediction of the foale of
the Aſſe is in Luke 19. and Math .12. touching the coyne of filuer in the mouth of the
fifh , which was firft to be taken , we haue
it foretold in Math .17. *Vt autem non fcanda-*
lizemus

lizemus eos &c. And that we may not ſcandalize them , goe to the ſea , and caſt in a hooke , and take the firſt fiſh that commeth vp ; and when thou haſt opened his mouth , thou ſhalt fynd a peece of twenty pence; that take , and giue it to them for me , and thee . In which words he ſheweth himſelfe not only to foreknow things to come , but alſo to be the Lord both of the ſea and fiſhes , as hauing in his power all things , though they be abſent & far diſtant from him .

6.   Laſtly , touching the euerſion and finall deſtruction of the Iewes , we read it foreſhewed in Math .c. 24. *Videtis hæc omnia? Do you ſee all theſe things ?* Amen I ſay vnto you; there ſhall not be heere left a ſtone vpon a ſtone , which ſhall not be deſtroyed . As alſo in Luke c. 19. *Videns ciuitatem fleuit &c.* He beheld the Citty , and wept vpon it, ſaying: Becauſe if thou hadſt knowne , and that in this thy day, the things which appertaine to thy peace ; but now are they hid from thine eyes ; for the daies ſhall come vpon thee, that thine enemies ſhall compaſſe thee with a trench, and encloſe thee about , and ſtraiten thee on euery ſide , and ſhall beat thee flat to the groũd, and thy children which are in thee ; and they ſhall not leaue in thee a ſtone vpon a ſtone , becauſe thou haſt not knowne the tyme of thy viſitation . The ſame matter is alſo related , as prophecyed by Chriſt in 21. of Luke . *Cùm videritis cir-*
                                                    cumdari

cumdari &c. When you shall *see Ierusalem com-passed about with an army*, then *know that the desolation thereof is at hand.* Then let *them, which are in Iudæa*, *flie to the mountaines; and let them which are in the middest thereof*, *depart out, and let not them*, *which are in the Country enter into it*, *for these are the daies of vengeance*, *that all things may be fulfilled*, *that are written &c.* they *shall fall by the edge of the sword*, *and shalbe led captiue into all nations* &c. All which, that it is already accomplished, is euidēt out of the history of *Iosephus* the *Iew*. I omit many other predictious of our Lord, as of the preaching and miracles of the Apostles, of their persecution, of the crucifixion of *Peter*, of the stay of *Iohn*, of the conuersions of the Gentils, of the preaching of the Gospell throughout the whole earth, of the continuance of the Church till the end of the world, and the like. I omit in like sort the innumerable predictiōs of al the holy men, which haue liued in the ages since Christ, & being assisted with the holy Ghost, haue foretold future euents, and haue reuealed many matters kept afore in great secret.

Now out of all these things, which are here said, we may gather three poynts, as most true and infallible. First, that there is a *diuyne Power*, who is priuy to all future euents, and to the secretest things that are, **and**

and by whome all humane matters are gouerned; and that he reuealeth to diuers of
such, which truly serue and worship him,
those future euents, whereof there are no
determinate causes. Secondly, that *Christ*
is the true and only *Sauiour of the world*; since
all his actions and doings were foretold by
his Prophets so many ages before, and since
himselfe was so eminent and admirable for
his birth, works, predictions, doctrine,
life, end, and resurrection. Thirdly, that the
faith of Christ is necessary to saluation; for
no man can with any shew of reason call
these three poynts into question, who hath
with iudgment and maturity of discourse
expended and waighed the forerehearsed
predictions, and Prophesyes.

THE ELEAVENTH REASON, TAKEN from the being of Spirits.

CHAP. XIII.

IT is euident euen by infinite example
and long experience, that there are *Spirits*; that is, certaine inuisible substances
indued with an vnderstanding, and penetrating all things through their subtility of
nature, and which do far transcend, and
exceed all humane power, wisedome, and
industry. This

This is manifeſt, *firſt* from Oracles and anſweres, which were accuſtomed to be giuen by Idols in all countryes, to ſuch as came to take counſell from them. For thoſe ſtatuaes or Images(wanting altogether life and ſenſe) could not returne any anſwere, but it was ſpirits or deuils entring into the ſaid ſtatuaes, which ſo anſwered . In ſome places theſe anſweres were giuē by Idolatrous Prieſts; who with certaine Ceremonies calling vpō the Diuel, were ſo poſſeſſed by them, as if they had been ſtirred vp by ſome diuine power; theſe powred out Oracles and anſweres, the Diuel ſpeaking through their mouths, or belly, or Nauill, or ſome other part of their body. Herupon ſome were called ἐγγαϲρίμυθοι, or *ventriloqui*; to wit, *ſpeaking through their belly* . Theſe things may not only be proued from the ſacred Scripture, but alſo from prophane hiſtory : for the Oracle of *Apollo at Delphos*, and of *Iupiter* of *Ammon*, and diuers others were moſt famous for many ages. The Diuels(ſeconded by this impoſture and deceit) did propagate and ſpread Idolatry, procuring themſelues by this meanes to be worſhiped as Gods, or diuyne powers in their images throughout the whole world, for diuers ages together. And euen at this day they are ſo honoured in *India*, *China*, *Iapon*, *Tartary*,

tary, *Braſil*, *Perù* , & ſeuerall other countries.
So as we ſee , it was truly ſaid of the Prophet Pſalm. 95 *Quoniam omnes dij &c.* For al
the Gods of the Gentils are Idols , *but the Lord
made the heauens* . *Secondly* , the ſame is made
demonſtrable from the doctrine and practiſe of *Nigromanticks* , and *Magi* , or Wiſards,
which are found in all places . For theſe
through certaine ceremonies and verſes are
able to call vp the Diuels, & do cauſe, that
they not only ſhew ſtrange effects (which
neceſſarily imply their preſence) but alſo
make them to appeare in a viſible forme ,
and to conuerſe familiarly and talke with
men. The forme of this raiſing vp of ſpirits
is deſcribed by (1) *Homer,* where *Vliſſes* calleth vp *Tireſias*,and the ſpirits of *Orcus*, que-
ſtioning of them touching his returne . The
like Negromantical euocatiō to be made by
Scipio, is read in *Siluius*, by *Tireſias* in *Statius*,
by *Oeſon* in *Flaccus* , by *Canidia* in *Horace*, &
by *Ericthon* in *Lucane* : from all which it is
moſt cleare , that this thing was much vſed
in thoſe former times ; yea that it is moſt
ancyent. appeareth from Gods ſacred writ,
which ſpeaketh of the Wiſemē (2) of *Pharao*,
and of the *Pythoniſſa* ; and the ſame is made
moſt plaine euen in this our age (I meane
touching the commerſe , aſſociation , and
confederacy of ſorcerers and witches with
the

the Diuell) from the iudiciall censures a-
gainst such persons, and the great and daily
experience had herein. *Thirdly* this verity is
further confirmed by those, which are ob-
sessed, which are called *Energumeni*: for two
things appeareth in them, which are aboue
humane power. One, that such as are possessed, do speake strange tongs, which thē-
selues neither vnderstand, nor euer did learne. The other, that they discouer things
secret, or do relate things done in great distance of place, as if they saw them openly.
Both these two things afford an euident demonstration of a certaine superiour inuisible
nature, by the power wherof they are performed. To conclude this point of the beeing of spirits, is euicted from the many apparitions of spirits, which are affirmed to
haue beene from the testimony of diuers
most probable histories.

From all these proofs then it may be concluded, that there are in the world spirits,
and that in a wonderfull great number.
Since in all places, and from all antiquity
they haue most ofte manifested themselues.
In so much as there is no kingdome, no prouince, no citty, no village, but there remaineth some memory of their apparitions.
Pythagoras was of opinion (as *Laertius* wryteth) that all the ayre was full of spirits or

O   soules;

foules ; And this alfo was the iudgement of
many of other ancients , who taught, that
euery one had his *genius*, or fpirit affigned by
God . Thus did *Hefiode* , *Homer* , *Menander* ,
Trifmegiftus , *Plato*, and the *Stoickes* affirme.
Now if there be many fpirits , then it ineuitably may be concluded, that there is one
fupreme fpirit , to the which all the reft are
fubiect, and at whofe command they are
gouerned : for euery multitude of things
(except there be a dependency and fubor-
dination to one moft high)begetteth diforder and confufion. And hence it is, that euen
among bodies , there is a fuperiority and
predominacy of one aboue all the reft , at
whofe command all the others do moue or
reft quyet. Now then by force of this reafo,
there ought much more to be the like order
among fpirits , fo as all are (in regard of fo-
ueraignty ouer them) to be reduced to one
fupreme fpirit : for by how much any thing
is more excellent, by fo much it ought to
enioy a more perfect order in the world :
but fpirits are far more worthy in nature ,
then corporall things ; therefore among the
there ought to be the perfecteft order, to
wit, of fubiection and domination. For it
were moft abfurd to grant an ἀταξία and
confufion in the nobleft ranke of Creatures;
feeing we fynd the loweft and moft inferiour

our degree of things, to be so orderly disposed and distributed .

This poynt is further confirmed from the
most dangerous and imminent inconueniences accompanying the contrary doctrine;
for if among spirits there were no order, &
that the rest should not be subiect vnto one,
at the command wherof the power of them
were to be restrained ; then might euery
one of them trouble and afflict the world at
its owne pleasure , might take away mens
goods, burne and destroy all things, might
infest mens bodyes with griefes, diseases &
death , to be briefe might destroy and ouerthrow all mankynd ; neither could any re-
dresse be found to the contrary, seing there
were no supreme spirit, to the which this
other did stand subiect , and so the world
could not in any sort long consist. For how
prone wicked spirits are to hurt and afflict
men , appeareth both frō the history of *Iob*,
(all whose substance the Diuell destroyed,
killed his sonnes and daughters, infected his
body with most grieuous vlcers) as also frō
the innumerable sacrifices of the heathens,
in the which the malignant spirits commāded that mens bodyes should be sacrificed
vnto thē; still making choyce of that, which
was most deare to the sacrificer, as his sonne,
his daughter , or one who was in great estimation

mation in the Common wealth ; finally frō
the warres and tumults, to the which the
Diuels vnder the ſhew of diuyne and celeſtiall powers, haue ſtirred men. Now if
they are thus cruell and merciles towards
men, God but giuing them in ſome ſort the
bridle for the offences of men, what would
they not do, & with what calamities would
they not afflict men, and what honours &
worſhips would they not extort at our
hands, if they were at their owne power
and liberty, receauing from no ſuperiour
ſpirit any reſtraint or inhibition? Yea amōg
themſelues, warres, emulations & diſſētiōs
would grow, if there were not one, that
could impoſe a command ouer them. For as
among Princes, who acknowledge no ſuperiour, oftētimes wars are ſtirred vp (with
the which the world is miſerably afflicted)
becauſe there is none, to whoſe ſouerainty
they ſtand ſubiect, and who is of power to
compaſe the riſing controuerſies among
them ; Euen ſo among ſpirits there would
grow repinings, contentions & wars, (with
the which the world would be vtterly extinguiſhed) if they ſtood not in ſubiection
to ſome one ſupreme power: for euery one
of them would ſeeke to aduance himſelfe,
and labour to draw all things to his owne
pleaſure and deſire : wherfore *Homer* moſt
truly

truly did leaue it regiftred: Οὐκ ἀγαθὴ πολυκοι.
ρανίη ἡς κοίρανος ἔςω, ἡς βασιλεὺς: that is, *It is not
good, that there be many Princes in one kingdome:
let one Prince, one King be* . And anſwerably
hereto *Aristotle* (as borrowing it out of *Homer*)thus writeth in the twelth booke of his
Metaphiſickes c. vlt. Τὰ γαρ ὄντα οὐ βούλεται πο-
λιτεύεσθαι κακῶς that is, *Things in nature do not
couet to be gouerned in an euill fort and manner* .

To conclude , feeing there are many
ſpirits (as is fhewed aboue) I would here
demand , from whence this multitude had
its begining? Or who brought thé into the
world ? They proceed not from bodies , in
that they are of a more excellent and eminent nature , then bodyes are;as alſo in that
bodyes do bring forth only bodies. Neither
is one of them ingendred of another (as we
fee liuing creatures are propagated) feeing
this kind of generation is peculiar to things,
which are ſubiect to corruptiõ, to wit , that
by this meanes, the *ſpecies* & kinds of things
may be perpetuated , whiles the nature ,
being extinct in the parent, is conſerued in
the iſſue. Neither can it be faid , that euery
one of thefe ſpirits haue their being from
themfelues , fo as they depend of no other
caufe,granting,that any thing receaueth its
exiftence and being from it felfe , it is far
more probable, that this fo taking it exiſtéce

ſhould

should be but one, not many. For it is much more fitting, that there should be one certaine *Nature* independent of any, in the which the whole fulnes of beeing resteth *eminenter,* and vnitedly; & from which one nature, the beeing of all things is deriued, according to the degree of euery such thing thē to maintaine, that there are many *Natures,* which depend not of one supreme *nature*. For where there is a multitude of seuerall *species*, or *Indiuidua*, and particuler things, there is also a limitation and imperfection; seeing those many things are altogither distinct and seuerall; neither do one comprehend the perfection and vertue of another. And hence it ryseth, that none of those is for it selfe, but for another, and all together conspyre and meet in one, and are (as it were) parts of one entyre *whole,* which riseth out of them. Thus do many bodies make the world, many men a Common wealth, many spirits one kingdome or cō-mon wealth of spirits; but what is of it self, ought to be altogether perfect, and sufficiēt to it selfe, needing not the support & help of any other thing. And what may be the reason thereof? Euen this, that what is of it selfe, is also for it selfe, according to that :
Quod caret principio effectiué, caret etiam fine .
What wanteth an efficient cause, wanteth also a
                                                                    finall

finall cause ; and therefore it felfe becomes
the end to it felfe, not feeking out of it felfe
any ayde, light, truth, ioy or beatitude; but
hauing all thefe things in it felfe, and from
it felfe. Therefore that, which is of it felfe,
and independent of another, muft needes
be but one, not many; to wit a primordiall
or illimitable effence, fufficient by it felfe,
being the fountaine of euery thing, and of
each limitable nature. We may ad hereto,
that to grant a being of many fpirits independent of any, is to introduce a πολυθεια
or confufed company of Gods, and many
firft beginnings, as blynd Gentility was
accuftomed to do, affigning proper and peculiar Gods to euery particuler bufines &
affaires of man; who fhould be the authours
directours, and vpon whome that kind of
particuler negotiation fhould be peculiarly
incumbét. So they made *Venus* the goddeffe
of loue and luft, *Diana* of *hunting*, *Ceres* of
fruyte, *Mercury* of *negotiation*, *Efculapius* of
curing difeafes, *Mars* of warre, *Pallas* of wifedome, *Apollo* and the Mufes of Poetry,
Fortune, of cafuall euents, and the like in diuers other things, but all this with a ftráge
blindnes of iudgment; as if one fupreme &
diuine powet were not able to vndertake
the charge of fo great a multitude of affaires,
or had not fufficient power and wifedome

O 4   to

to direct and moderate them all, without
any tedious molestatiõ, saying herein with
*Pliny: Fraile and laborious mortalsty hath diuided
all these thinges into parts, being conscious to it self
of its owne weaknes, that euery one should attend
to that, which chiefly is needfull.*

Now from all this it is (I hope) sufficiently demonstrated, that there is one *supreme spirit*, to the which all other spirits are
subiect, and at whose command they rest
obedyent, and of whome they are all procreated and made, and this supreme spirit
we call *God.*

THE TVVELFTH REASON, TAKEN FROM the absurdities rising from the contrary doctrine.

CHAP. XIIII.

IF there were no diuine *Power*, nor any
Prouidence, by the which mens affaires
and negotiations are to be gouerned, thē
many absurdities and irremediable inconueniences, and such as do mainly crosse all
true iudgment and reason, would follow,
which points do euidently conuince the fal-
sity of this supposed doctrine.

And first (supposing that there is no
celestiall power or Prouidence) it would
from

from hence follow, that the first & supreme *truth* (to wit, that there is no such Prouidence) should open the sluce to men to all impurity of life, to all wickednes, iniustice, pryde, arrogancy, tyranny, and briefly to all perfidy, periury, sacriledge, and any other villany whatsoeuer. For nothing is so facinorous, heinous, or wicked, which (taking away all feare of diuine power) ma would not vndertake and do, according to that of the Psalmist: (f) *Dixit insipiens &c. The foole said in his hart, there is no God: they are corrupted, and haue done abhominable wickednes &c.*

(f) *Psf.* 51

See heere the fruite and successe of this doctrine and perswasion, to wit, all turpitude & abhominable enormity of wickednes. That this is true, is most euident: for, as granting that there is a diuine power, then the first and supreme truth is this, *That there is a God, who gouerneth the world*; so one the contrary part, supposing that there is no such power, the first & chiefest verity *is, that there is not a God, which gouerneth the world.* For that must be acknowledged for a truth, which is apprehended and taken by all me for the first highest principle of all things. Now this truth (supposing it for such) would extinguish and cancel in mens minds all feare and reuerence. Which reuerence

O 5 and

and feare being loſt, the way lyes open to all wickednes. But what can be ſaid or cō-ceaued, more abſurd, then that the primi-tiue and *ſupreme Truth*, and the chieteſt ſe-cret & miſtery of all (being acknowledged and apprehended of all men) ſhould giue paſſage to all neſarious and wicked courſes whatſoeuer, making men to exceed in all vice and impurity? Secondly, it followeth, that, that which is in it ſelfe falſe, impoſſible and a mere *Chimera* or *imagination*, ſhouldbe the cauſe of all religion, piety, iuſtice, tem-perance, modeſty, benignity, patience, & briefly of all vertue and honeſty, as alſo of all tranquillity in a Common wealth, & of all goodnes in mankynd.

An im-poſſible figment cannot be the cauſe of al vertue

For a perſwaſion, that there is a God, & a loue & feare of him produceth all theſe effects, and by how much this perſwaſion and feare is greater and more vehement, by ſo much it worketh more eminent and re-markable effects of vertue and goodnes in the ſoules of men, and in a politicall ſtate. And hence it riſeth, that there was neuer common wealth well and peaceably go-uerned, in the which Religion, and a per-ſwaſion of a *diuine Prouidence* was not well and ſoundly planted in the minds of men; and the more that any one was priuatly de-uoted to Religion, and to the reuerencing

of

of a *diuine Spirit*, the more illustrious and famous he became in all innocency & probity of life : as also on the contray , how much the more any one became irreligious, by so much he also became more wicked & detestable in conuersation, as appeareth frō the testimonies of all sacred and prophane histories . Now what madnes were it to belieue , that there should be in a false & impossible fiction or imagination , so great a power to the procuring of all vertue ; and in a solid and vndoubted truth, so great an incytement and prouocation to the perpetrating and performing of al flagitious outrages , and wicked attempts ?

Thirdly, it followeth , that the chiefest and most true Wisedome extinguisheth all vertue , and maketh men most vicious : & that on the contrary part , the chiefest Errour stirreth them to vertue , and causeth them to become holy men . For if there be *no diuine power or deity* , then the greatest errour that can be , is to belieue , that there is *a deity* or *Prouidence*; and the greatest wisedome to thinke that there is no such celestiall power at all ; but all what is deliuered thereof , is but the fictions and figments of men . In like sort it followeth from the said ground, that truth and wisedome are to be concealed , as being that, which impoyso-
neth

If there be no God, thē should Wisedome extinguish all vertue & Errour increase vertue.

neth mens mynds, and euery common wealth ; but Errour is to be aduanced by all
meanes, as the fountaine of all vertue and
goodnes; finally that the chiefeſt light of
the vnderſtanding, begetteth the greateſt
darknes in the mynd, and will, touching
maners; & the chiefeſt darkenes of the vnderſtanding ingendreth the greateſt light,
ſplendour, and beauty of vertue in the wil
and mind; all which to affirme and maintaine were no leſſe, then incredible madnes.

Fourthly it followeth, that all thoſe,
who haue bene eminent and remarkable
for wiſedome, ſanctity of life, prophetiall
ſpirit, and working of miracles, haue bene
deceaued in the chiefeſt matter of all, as not
belieuing aright touching the being, or not
being of a God; ſince they al acknowledged
a deity & a prouidence, and honoured the
ſame : but ſuch as euer were moſt infamous
for impiety & turpitude of life & all other
wickednes, haue only apprehended truly
this myſtery & ſecret; for al ſuch haue bene
euer contemners of God, and his Prouidence, therefore from this principle it may
be inferred, that the wiſeſt men of all haue
bene for manners the worſt men of all; &
the moſt ſimple, ignorant, and erroneous
haue

Vpõ the foreſaid principle the beſt Men ſhould be the moſt foliſh; & the worſt the moſt wiſe.

haue bene the beſt, and the moſt vertuous.

Fiftly it followeth, that to loue God,
to feare reuenge, to honour the ſupreme
power with due praiſes & laudes, to keepe
an oath, and the like, are not in themſelues
good, but vaine, fooliſh, wicked, and aduerſe to true reaſon; that to do theſe things
are indeed but to loue, feare, worſhip and
adore a mere *Chimera,* or a plaine fiction of
mans braine; for if all Diuinity be but a fiction (as a *Chimera* is) thē is it manifeſt, that
we ought to beare no more reuerence and
reſpect to it, then to a *Chimera.* Sixtly it
followeth, that to be wicked, ſacrilegious
blaſphemous, and a contemner of all diuine and ſupernaturall power, is not euil in
it ſelfe, nor repugnant to the true vſe of reaſon; but that theſe things are good & praiſe
worthy, as being agreable to the ttue
doctrine of the being, and not being of a
Deity. For if there be no ſupreme or celeſtiall power, then all theſe acts, by the which
he is contemned and ignominiouſly trea-
ted, are good; both becauſe they are certaine proteſtations of an infallible and ſecret truth; as alſo in that they fitly ſerue &
are of force to take away from mens mynds
the falſe perſwaſion of the being of a God,
and his Prouidence; no otherwiſe then, as

Vpon the
former
ground
Blaſphe-
myes
ſhould
not be
euill.

Contu-

Contumelyes and difgraces committed a-
gainft the Idols of the Gentils are laudable
and good, becaufe by thofe actions, we
teftify no true diuinity to be in thofe Idols,
for nothing is more cotemptible, then that
which neither is, nor *cannot be.* Seauenthly,
it might feeme to follow, that the world
were, as a fhip floating on the fea without
any Maft or Pylot; or as a mighty Commonwealth confifting of all kynds of men,
in the which there is no lawes, no Iudge,
no gouernour, nor any Procurer of tranquillity, peace and common good. And if
it be fo, how then can the world continue,
efpecially feing it confifteth of fo different,
contrary and repugnant things ? For as a
fhip without a directour is violently toffed
to and fro, till it fall vpon fome Rock, or
fands, or be ouerwhelmed with flouds ; or
as a Commonwealth wanting a magiftrate
and ruler, wafteth it felfe away with inteftine, feditious, murthers, and other calamities ; fo muft the world be moft exor-
bitantly and inordinatly menaged, and in
the end be diffolued through a colluctation
and fight of contraries, if there be no power, which is to fterne the fame, and to
procure a fimpathy and accord amog thofe
contraries.

Eightly it followeth, that all this *vni-*
uerfe,

uerſe, and diſpoſition; and framing of the
parts thereof exiſteth thus by *chance.* For if
there be no *diuyne power*, which framed the
parts of it, digeſting them into this forme,
which now we ſee, then is it neceſſarily to
be acknowledged, that it hath its being by
chance, according to the opinion of *Democri-*
tus, who maintained, that all things were
firſt framed of a caſual force & concourſe of
Atomi, or ſmal indiuiſible bodyes. But what
is this, but mere doting madnes, and want
of reaſō? for how can it be, that that, whoſe
frame and making exiſteth with ſo great
reaſon, prouidence and iudgement, ſhould
haue its being by *chance*? One ſeeth a moſt
ſumptuous building, framed with all art &
skill; all Architects admire the ſtructure of
it; queſtion being asked, who made this
curious edifice? It is anſweared, that it is
made by no body; but that there was long
ſince a mountaine in the ſame place, ſtored
with trees, & that it falling aſüder through
an Earth quake, the parts of this mountaine
being thus ſhiuered, did through meanes
of this colliſion and fall, caſt and frame thē-
ſelues caſually into this curious forme of a
pallace. Now who is ſo ſimple, that would
belieue this? And yet ſuch is the like caſe in
the ſtupēdious ſabrick of the whole world,
maintayned not to be made by the hand of
                                          any

any diuine Power.

These, and many other like absurdities, incongruences and impossibilities do rise and result from the foresaid deniall of a *Deity*, & *a Prouidence*; all which how aduerse they are to all shew of truth, how repugnant to the very light of reason; & how fearefull and dreadfull to be but spoken in words, who seeth not? Wherefore it followeth, that that principle, which is the fountaine of such pudled aud stinking waters, must of necessity be most far distant & estranged from all truth. But heere some may reply, that euen a false perswasion in matters of religion conduceth much to the deterring and withdrawing man from wickednes; and to the perswading and inuiting them to probity, iustice, and other vertues. For the Heathens, who belieued diuers Gods, to be according to the multitude and diuersity of humane affaires, and that their negotiations & businesses were guyded by the prouidence of the said Gods, & that they rewarded and chastised men according to their different deserts (al which things were false and impossible) did notwithstanding from this strong & setled cōceyt of theirs, abstaine from many iniuries, offences, and enormities; as thinking the Gods to be offended therewith, and that themselues

themselues should be punished by them for
the same, either in this world, or in the
world to come. I answere hereto and say,
that this perswasion of the heathens was
false in particuler (to wit in thinking, that
there was such a multiplicity of Gods, as
also in thinking that such, and, such were
Gods, *as Iupiter, Saturne, Pallas &c.* & the
like) and that they had the charge of mens
affaires ; but their persuasion was true in
generall, that is in thinking that there was
a diuyne power, that mens affaires were
subiect to his prouidence, and that he ex-
acted an account of them.

Wherefore when the Heathens either
abstained from euill, or did good through
feare of offending their Gods, or desire of
pleasing them, they were moued thereto,
not through any perswasion, as it was
false in respect of such a God, but as it was
true in generall. Only they did erre in the
Obiect, to wit, in ascribing a diuinity and
Prouidence to those, to whome they ought
not, and in worshipping it in them. Therefore they did not take away, or deny the
true and *formall reason* of a deity and of Prouidence; but they affirmed and maintayned
it, and therefore retayned after a certaine
manner the true foundation of Politicall
iustice. But if there were no *diuine Power,*

P   nor

nor any *Prouidence*, then were this foundation of theirs moſt fictious and falſe, euen
in generall; and conſequently it could haue
no force towards vertue and probity of má-
ners ; or if it hath any (as by experience we
find it to haue) then followeth it euidētly,
that it is not a thing forged and inuented,
but moſt true and vndoubted.

THE 13 REASON, DRAVVNE FROM
the Immortality of the Soule.

CHAP. XV.

IF it be ſo ordayned, that the *reaſonable*
ſoule ſhall not be extinguiſhed with the
body, but after the death of the body it
ſhall liue and be immortall ; then there can
be no reaſon pretented for the denying of a
diuine power, & *a Prouidence*: for if the loweſt
ſpirit be incorporeall, intelligent, and immortall, why ſhould not then there be a
ſupreme ſpirit, endued with the ſame proprietyes ? Since, where there are feuerall
degrees of natures, it is as neceſſary, that
there be found one ſupreme degree, as
well as the loweſt and midle degrees. Now
it is ſhewed aboue, that there are certaine
degrees of ſpirits far more excellent then
mans ſoule ; but vnder the ſoule of man,
there

there is no lower degree, for it selfe is the lowest; seing that it is manifest, that the soules of beasts do dye with their bodies. Furthermore, if mans soule be immortall, then can we not doubt, but there must be after this life a retribution of deeds & actions; to wit, reward for vertue and punishment for vyce: for it is most absurd to affirme, that those Soules, which while they were here inuested with their bodies, did liue wickedly in al affluence and abundāce of riches and pleasures, and in committing of wrongs, and which (before their departure from hence) made no recompence for the same, should after this life be equall in state to those, who wrongfully haue suffred many tribulations, and yet liued very vertuously; and that there is to be had no account for things committed here; therefore it followeth, that there ought to be a *Prouidence,* which is to giue a retributiō answerable to euery ones deserts. And hence it is, that all Philosophers and all religions (who maintayned the soule to liue after the body) did withall maintaine, that there were future rewards and punishments, and did confesse a Prouidence of a *supreme spirit,* by the which these rewards & punishmēts are iustly dispensed. S. *Chrysostome* in his fourth sermon *de Prouidentia,* handleth this

P 2   point

point elegantly in these wordes . *If nothing
be to follow after this life, then is there no God; for
granting that there is a God , that God must needs
be iust , and if he be iust , then doth he recompence
euery one according to his deseruings ; And if nothing be after this life , then where shall euery one
be rewarded according to his deserts ? Many wicked men do liue here in all pleasure and honour, as
also many vertuous suffer great pressures and afflictions . If therefore nothing be to follow hereafter , the iust shall finally depart , remaining still
wronged, and the vniust with vndeserued felicity.
If then this should be so , where is iustice ? For if
Man do not receaue retaliation for such things , as
he hath done , then is God not iust ; and if not iust,
then he is not God &c. But that there is a God, all
Creatures do preach it; therefore it followeth that
that God is iust : and if he be iust , then dispen-
seth he iustice to euery one . And if he giueth what
is iust to euery man , then followeth it , that there
must be a tyme after this life , in the which al shal
receaue, answerably to their liues and actions .*
Thus far this Father . Therefore once grā-
ting the immortality of the Soule, it neces-
farily is to be inferred , that there is a God ,
and that he exerciseth his prouidence vpon
all mens affaires : as also on the other side
taking away and denying the Soules immortality, then is all Iustice and Prouidéce
of God , yea God himselfe is taken away , &
flatly

flatly denyed to be. Therfore it resteth vpon to proue and demonstrate the immortality of it; but becaufe this point requireth a more long and prolixe difcourfe, it fhalbe handled largely in the fecond booke here following fepofed, and appointed only to that end.

THE 14. REASON TAKEN FROM DIuers examples of diuine reuenge, and benignity.

CHAP. XVI.

ALTHOVGH the chiefeft punifhmēt of finne be referued to bee inflicted in the world to come, when there fhalbe made to all a iuft recompenfation for their demerits; neuertheles euen in this world ofte tymes there are fhewed diuers examples, to put men in mind, that God doth not fleepe, but that he watcheth and obferueth mens actions; and to intimate vnto them, how feuere punifhments do attend wicked men after this life. Therefore though the bridle and liberty of liuing according to ech mans will and mind be giuen in this life; and that diuers things may be thoght to be carried fo troublefomly & confufedly; as that for the time no Prouidence of any diuyne power may ſeeme to be in mens affaires, the wicked doing all things according to their ſenſuality, and the vertuous being miſerably oppreſſed and afflicted; Notwithſtanding, if *Man* will take into his conſideratiõ the paſſages of all tymes, he ſhall ſee, that *Gods prouidence* is not ſo quyet, ſtill, and ſilent, but for the moſt part after ſome tyme paſſed (the meaſure of the ſins being once complete and filled vp in any one Country) it diſcouereth & bewrayeth it ſelfe by taking reuenge of the ſaid coũtry with ſome heauy and notable puniſhment; of which point there are many examples extant both in the ſacred Scripture, as alſo in prophane Authours; the ſtore whereof being ſo great, we will inſiſt in ſome of the moſt remarkable of them.

The firſt then may be the *generall deluge*, in the which al mankind (except eight perſons) was vtterly extinguiſhed for their enormious liues. The great Prophet *Moyſes* hath diſcribed moſt elegantly this heauy puniſhment with al its due circumſtances in the 6. 7. and 8. of *Geneſis*, in the procedure whereof, the *diuine Prouidence* hath ſeuerall wayes diſplayed it ſelfe. Firſt in decreeing the aboliſhment and death of mankind in reuenge of their ſinnes, and in foretelling

it

it to *Noe* a hundred and twenty yeares before it came to paſſe. Secondly, in that God for a new increaſe of the world, cauſed an *Arke* to be made in that preſcribed forme & meaſure, which might contayne the kinds of all liuing Creatures both vpon earth, & ſuch as did fly, and might reſerue thē from deſtruction; to wit, it being 300. cubits in length, fifty in breadth, & thirty in height: which meaſure and largenes, that it was ſufficient for the receite not only of all liuing Creatures, but alſo for meat for them for one yeare, may eaſily be demonſtrated, and hath already bene made euident by learned men: ſo as it is cleare that this proportion or quantity was appointed not by mās aduiſe, but through the ſpeciall direction of the diuine Wiſedome.

Thirdly, becauſe it proceeded from the foreſaid Prouidence of God, that at the beginning of the deluge euery kind of liuing Creature ſhould reſort to the Arke, & take its fitting manſion. Fourthly, in that the globe of the water with the increaſe of the raine, which fell continually for the ſpace of forty daies and forty nights, was ſo great, as that it exceeded in height the higheſt hils fifteene cubits. Now that ſo much raine could cauſe ſo great an inundation & ouerflowing of water, may be made iuſti-

fyable

fyable partly by reaſon, and partly by experience. Fiftly, *the prouidence of God* was
further manifeſted, in that both ſo much
water could fall vpon the earth, and yet
after could be exhaled vp in vapours and
clouds, & all this in the ſpace of one yeare;
for at the end of forty dayes the floud was
come to its height, and ſo continued durnig
a hundred and fifty dayes, the reſt of that
yeare (to wit 175. dayes) it was ſo waſted
away & diſſipated & diſſolued into clouds
that the laſt day of the yeare, the earth being become dry, *Noe* with his whole family and the liuing Creatures came out of
the Arke: therefore he continued in the
Arke a whole yeare meaſured by the courſe
of the Sunne (that is 365. dayes) for he entred into the Arke, the ſix hundreth yeare
of his life, in the ſecond moneth, & 17. day;
and he came out in the 601. yeare, the ſecond moneth, and 27. day; ſo as he continued therein twelue moneths of the moone
and eleuen dayes, which make preciſely
one *ſolare* yeare. Sixtly, in giuing to thoſe
miſerable men ſpace of repentance through
the length and ſlownes of their puniſhmét,
for it cannot be doubted, but that innumerable perſons (feeling the dreadfull hand of
God in ſo horrible a caſtigation) had true
penitency and remorſe of their Sinnes, and
obtayned

obtayned mercy and pardon for the fame :
As the like is accuftomed to fal out in dágers
of fhipwrack , where many moft wicked
men flie to God with great fhew of piety ;
who conceauing a deepe remorfe of their
former iniquities , and promifing an améd-
ment , do purchafe their foules faluation ,
by the loffe of their bodyes . All heathen
hiftoriographers make mentió of this floud
and the *Arke* , as witneffeth *Iofephus* in his
firft booke of *Antiquities* , c. 4. where he addeth , that euen in his tyme the remnants
and broken peeces of the *Arke* were accuftomed to be fhewed amongft the *Arme-
nians.*

The fecond example of diuine reuenge
may be the ouerthrow of *Sodome,* and thofe
other adioining cittyes, when God deftroyed all that region with their inhabitants for
their abhominable wickednes with a fho-
wer of brimftone fent from heauen. This
inexplicable calamity *Moyfes* thus defcry-
beth , *Genef.*19. *Sol egreffus eft &c. The Sunne
did rife vpó the earth , whé Lot entred into Zoar,
then the Lord rayned vpon Sodome, and vpon Go-
morrha brimftone , and fyar from the Lord out of
heauen , and ouerthrew thofe Cities, and all the
plaine , and all the inhabitants of the Cittyes,and
that , that grew vpon the earth .* There had
fcarcely paffed foure hundred yeares from

the flouds, whē this hapned, by the which they were made leſſe excuſable; who not-withſtanding the late and freſh memory of ſo great a chaſtiſment, would ingurgitate themſelues into all kind of wickednes, & chiefly into moſt filthy and beaſtly luſts, which was indeed the chiefeſt cauſe of the foreſaid inundation. Certainly both the mercy & iuſtice of God did ſhine moſt wō-derfully in this worke; His mercy in that God (at the praiers of *Abrahā*) ſhewed him-ſelfe moſt ready to ſpare *Sodome*, if therein could be found, but ten iuſt perſons. Now what greater benignity and fauour can be conceaued, then to ſpare ten thouſands wi-cked perſons for the ſakes of ten holy men liuing among them? So preciable and eſti-mable is the life of vertuous men in the eye of God. His iuſtice in like ſort appeared, ſeeing that ſo vnexpectedly, as not fearing any ſuch matter, and in ſo ſhorr a tyme of repentance, God oppreſſed them with ſo cruell and dreadfull a torment: for what is more terrible, then an impetuous precipatiō and falling downe from heauen of burning ſulphur or brimſtone in ſo great abundáce? The waters all round about became ſo bit-ter hereby that no liuing thing remained in them; yea the neighbour places alſo by reaſon of the filthy ſtench thereof were made

made sterill and barren; so as euen to this day, they bring forth nothing, but certaine aples full of a stinking dust, seruing only as signes and remembrance of Gods ire & indignation . For God was willing by this example to manifest vnto sinners, what they were to expect after this life, to wit, sulphureous fyer, and eternall vastity, or destruction .

The third example may be that manifold castigation of *Pharao*, and the *Egiptians* for not dismissing and setting at liberty the people of God . *Moyses* describeth this most euidently, who was not only present among them, but also an arbitratour or gouernour, whome God vsed as his instrumēt both in inflicting, continuing, and ceasing those punishments. First, God conuerted all the waters in *Egipt* (whether riuers, lakes, or welsprings) into bloud , & this thus continued for the space of seauen dayes. Secondly, he brought into *Egipt* such an abundance of frogs, as that they filled all the houses of the *Egiptians* , infecting all things with a loathsome smell. *Thirdly* , next after the frogs, the *Cimises* succeeded ; all the dust in *Egipt* being suddenly conuerted into thē. These *Cimises* were a small kind of Gnats armed with a very sharpe sting in the forhead , pricking the skin of a mās body with

                              payne,

Exod .7.
c. 9.

payne, and fucking bloud ; though *Iofephus*
l. 2. c. 5. is of opinion, that they were lyce
breading among fo great a multitude of the
Egiptians, & feeding vpon their flefh. Fourthly , all thefe feuerall plagues ceafing at
the earneft prayer of *Moyfes*, and *Pharao* notwithftanding perfifting in his former con-
tumacy , God did fend whole fwarmes of
flies, with the which the *Egiptians* were
wonderfully molefted . Fiftly , after the
flies , came a general infection of the beafts,
by meanes whereof all the Horfes, Affes,
Camels, fheep, Oxen and Kyne throughout all *Egipt* , (thofe only preferued, which
belōged to the children of *Ifrael*)did perifh.
Sixtly, after this plague prefently followed
the fcab or fcuruy extremely exulcerating
and afflicting the bodies of men and beafts
yet remaining. Seuenthly , enfued a moft
cruell haile, mixted with thunder (the like
whereto was neuer feene in *Egipt* before)
through the impetuous violence whereof
all liuing Creatures (which were abroad
in the fields) were killed , as alfo all
groues, and vndergroaths , and the like
were pulled vp, and ouerthrowne .
Eightly , followed a huge number of Lo-
cufts, thefe deuoured euery thing, that the
hayle and thunder had fpared; in like fort
they wonderfully afflicted mens bodyes
with

with their bytings, sharp nayles, beating
of their winges, filthy excrements & smel.
Ninthly, this chastisement at the interces-
fion of *Moyses* also ceased : but when as
Pharao would not stand to his promises, succeeded most horrible darknes throughout
all Ægypt (that place where the Israelites
inhabited, only excepted:) this continued
three dayes, it being such, that no man
could see another, neither durst any through
feare moue out of the place, wherein afore
they were . Tenthly, after the light was
restored, and the King continuing stil ob-
stinate, there fell out a great destruction, to
wit, in the midest of night in the compasse
of one houre, there were slayne by an Angell all the first borne of men, and beasts ;
so as no house or family was without griefe
and lamentation, as being depriued of that,
which was most worthy and deare to thē .
This plague hapned in the fourtēth moone
of the first moneth . The memory of this is
yet so markable amōg the Iewes, that they
euen to this day do celebrate it with peculiar ceremonies, to wit, with the sacrifice
of the *Paschall Lambe*, the vse of their *Azimes,*
and the oblation of their first borne of any
thing .

    The *Egiptians* being consumed and
wasted with such diuersity of calamities, at
length

length gaue liberty to the Iſraelites to depart away ; but a little after repenting thē-
ſelues of their former graunt , they followed the Iſraelites with a mighty army thereby to bring them backe againe into their
ſeruitude ; but they being almoſt ouerta-
ken by the other betweene the ſea, and the
mountaines, and when there was no hope
to eſcape; God ſuddenly opened the ſea, ſo
as a very broad dry way (and great inough
for the twift paſſage of an army) was made
in the chanoel from one ſhore to the other
on the contrary ſide , through which the
Iſraelites ſecurely paſſed ouer : but the Æ-
gyptians purſuing them in haſt, and being
all in the middeſt of the ſayd dry chánel,
God looſed his hand, and *Moyſes* at his command ſtricking the water , all thoſe huge
hills (as it were) of waters , which being
thus reſtrained, and ſerued as wals on both
ſides, fell downe with a frightfull noyſe, &
running into their wonted chanel , ſo ouer
whelmed the Ægyptiás with their horſes,
chariots , and other prouiſion, as that not
one of them eſcaped. Theſe calamities of
the Ægyptians (perſecuting the people of
God) are (as it were) a certaine type and a-
dumbration of the tormentes , wherewith
the wicked after the end of the world(whē
God ſhall free and deliuer his ſeruants from
the

the tyranny of the reprobate) shalbe punished . For after he shall send to them diuers
afflictions, thereby that they may reclayme
themselues frō their enormities and sinnes;
and if notwithstanding they will persist
in their former courses , then shall they all
in the end (the whole world being in a generall conflagration of feare) be vtterly &
eternally extinguished .

Fourthly , there do occurre diuers examples of the *diuyne prouidence* (especially
of Gods benignity and feuerity) shewed to
the *Israelites* , whyles they were in the desart. For when as he had brought into a
vast desart so many of them , as amounted
to twenty hundred thousand persons; and
that the meates , which they had caryed
with them from *Egipt,* were spent; then after a new and vnheard manner he prouided sustenance for them: for euery day(the
Sabbaoth only excepted) there did rayne
downe from heauen vpon them (1) *Manna* ,
being a substance like vnto a small hayle ,
wherwith for the space of forty yeares they
were nourished. (2) Next , when the waters were salty and bitter , God presently
made them sweet and potable .

3.   The fiftith day from their departure out of *Egipt* , he gaue a law in the sight
and hearing of thē all , making himselfe in
a sort

(1) *Exod.*
16.

(2) *Ibid.*
c. 15.

a ſort viſible to all their eyes, in the hieght of the mountaine *Sinay*, in the ſhew of a mighty fyar, and a darke cloud, with the ſound of trumpets and great thunder; the earth it ſelfe trembling, & the mountaine ſomewhat mouing and leaping.

(3) *Exod.* 40.

4.   For the ſpace (3) of forty yeares, he exhibited his preſence to them continually in the day tyme, by defending their campes or tents from the heat of the ſunne, in the forme of a great cloudy pillar; by night, by lightning their tents with the ſaid pillar in forme of fyre; when the Camps were to be remoued from place to place, this pillar did lift it ſelfe high in the ayre, going before them, with a ſlow pace, that they might know, what way they were to goe, and ſtaying when, & where, they were to reſt; in ſo much that all the profection, or going, and ſtaying of their camps depended only vpon the prouidence *of the higheſt power*.

(4) *Ibid.*

5.   *Moyſes* (by (4) the commandement of God) did build in the firſt yeare of his egreſſe out of *Egipt* a Tabernacle, and in the ſecond yeare, the firſt moneth and firſt day therof, erected it in the middeſt of the cāpe, the which was no ſooner ſet vp, but that inſtātly the foreſaid pillar cōtinually ſtood ouer the tabernacle, as it were couering it; excepting the tabernacle were to remoue, and

and then the pillar aduancing it selfe on
high, went afore (as is fayd) to shew whither they were to goe, and when to stay.
When (5) *Moyses* entred into the tabernacle
to pray vnto God, then God in the sight of (5) *Exod.*
all the people descended downe vpon the 33.
Tabernacle vnder that cloud, & the prayer
being ended, the cloud ascended vp againe
into his accustomed place.

6. When the people of Israel (6) were
afflicted with the extremity of thirst in the (6)*Exod.*
eleuenth mansion in *Raphidim*, *Moyses* by di- 17.
uine commandement did strike with his *Num.* 20.
rod a dry Rocke, out of which presently
gushed great store of water; the same also
was done in their thirtith three stay in *Ca-
des*. At which place *Moyses* somewhat doubted (in regard of the Israelites incredulity)
whether God would giue them water or
no, and was therefore chastised with this
punishment from God, to wit, Thou shalt
not bring the people into the Land of promise; for thou shalt dye before that tyme.

7. When the children of Israel desired to
feed vpon flesh, and for that cause, coueting
after the pots of *Egipt*, murmured against
Moyses; God (though offended therewith)
promised them flesh, and therupon the day
after did send into their camps such a multitude of quayles, as that they serued them all

Q   for

for a whole moneth after. It might be probably thought, that there were scarce to be found in the whole world so great abūdance of this kynd of birds. But God (7) presently punished this their inordinate desire of eating flesh, with the death of many of them, and thereupon the place, where they were buryed was called, *Sepulchra Concupiscentiæ.*

8. The spyes being returned (which were sent by the Isralites abroad) and extolling the strength of their Enemies, and calūniating & debasing the land of promise, the people through teare shewed great diffidence in Gods promises; in so much, that they disclaymed from al interest in the land of Promise, & desyred to returne into *Egipt*; For which cause our Lord being angry, condemned to death all those, who were twenty yeares of age or aboue (which number came to 63. thousands of Men, and fiue hundred) two only excepted, to wit, *Caleb* and *Iosue*, which trusting in the assistance of God, much animated the people; for he decreed, that none of them should enter into the land of Promise, but that they all (as being murmurers against his diuine prouidence) should dye in the wildernes, for which cause he detained them fourty yeares in the desart, leading them now hither

(7) *Num.* 11.

ther, now thither vntill they were all confumed and wafted away. Yet their chil-
dren, (8) which arriued not to the years of *(8) Num.*
twenty, were referued aliue, & fubftitu- **26.**
ted in their parents places. Whereupon it
followed, that although in the fortith yeare
(when the land of Promife was to be pof-
feffed by them) all the murmurers were
dead, yet in regard of the many thoufands
proceeding from their children, and thofe
of the tribe of *Leui* (which amounted to **23.**
thoufand) there were then more to enter
into the land of Promife, then were in the
firft yeare.

9. *Core*, *Dathan*, and *Abiron* being the
chiefeft men among the Ifraelites (fecon-
ded by two hundred & fifty of the nobleft
among them) rayfed a fedition againft *Moy-*
fes and *Aaron*; and thus the mindes of the
people were auerted from perfoming their *Num. 16.*
obedience, as if *Moyfes* and *Aaron* had ambi- *& 28.*
tioufly fought the Principality and Ponti-
ficality, and did not vndertake it at the cō-
mandement of God. Therefore for the indignity of the matter, *Moyfes* appealed to
the iudgment of God heerein, who decy-
ded the caufe by inflicting a moft horrible
chaftifement vpon them, in the eye of all
the reft; for *Moyfes* had fcarce made an end
of his cōminations and threats, but the earth
vnder-

vnderneath them began to tremble, and (as a Sea) to floate to and fro. And then gaping with a vast opennes, & mighty fragour and noyse, it did absorpe and swallow downe *Core, Dathan,* and *Abiron,* with all their tabernacles and goodes, and after closed it selfe togeather, not leauing any print or shew of its former opening; and as touching the other two hundred and fifty, being their associates in rebelling, a huge fire from heauen rushed vpon them, & consumed them, so as no parcels of their bodies remayned. The day after, when as the people began another insurrection against *Moyses* and *Aaron,* as esteming them the authours of the former destruction, and that God (for their sakes) punished with death (as they thought) innocent men, at which God was so highly offended, that he sent a fyar among them, with the which fourteene thousand and seauen hundred were instantly burned to death.

(9) *Num.*
10.

10.   Another tyme in like sort, the people (through the tedious wearisomnes of their iourney) murmuring against God, he againe sent a fyar among them, which deuoured (9) and consumed the vttermost parts of their camps, and tents; & had wasted further therein, if *Moyses* had not prayed to the contrary; at whose prayers the earth
opening

opening, the fyar defcended downewards, and fo ceafed.

11. Not long after this, the people a-gaine murmuring againſt the diuine Maieſty, by reafon of the length of their tra-uell, God fent among them certaine fiery (10) ſerpetns, at whofe ſtingings and by-tings, many of the people fubmitted them-felues to *Moyſes*, with acknowledgment of their finne. Thereupon *Moyſes* (by the cō-mandement of God) erected the *brazen ſer-pent*, hanging it vpon a high Pole, or forke, at the beholding only whereof, all thofe were cured, that were afore wounded by the forefaid dangerous ferpents. This (11) was a moſt illuſtrious and cleare type or fi-gure of *Chriſt* our *Lord* hanging vpon the Croſſe, in the beliefe and faith of whome alone, the wounds of the old ferpent are cured, and eternall faluation is purchafed.

(10) *vbi ſupra c. 21*

(11) *Ioan 3.*

12. To conclude, during thofe forty yeares of the *Iſraelites* ſtay in the wildernes neither their clothes, nor their ſhoes be-came worfe, or old with wearing; Gods good prouidence fo preferuing them, in that they had not there conuenient meanes of procuring of new. Add to all thefe former, fo many helpes and furtherances in their warrs, fo many famous victories obtained through Gods particuler affiftance, fo many

of

of their enemies ſlaine either with no loſſe
or with very ſmall on the Iſraelites ſide ;
we read that the Army (12) of *Amalec* was
(12) *Exo.* ouercome by the Iſraelites , through the
17. prayers of *Moyſes*; for during all that tyme
that *Moyſes* was litting vp his hands to God,
Iſraell ouęrcame, and when he ſuffered his
hands to fall downe , *Amalec* vanquiſhed :
which point no doubt ſerued , as a great
miſtery. The riuer of (13) *Iordan* did de-
(13) *Ioſue* uide it ſelfe in the preſence of the *Arke*, to
3. wit, the higher part of it ſwelling , as a
mountaine , and the lower part altogether
dry , and gaue paſſages to all the people .
The (14)walles of *Iericho* being moſt ſtrõg,
(4) *Ibid.* fell downe to the ground only at the ſound
cap.6. of the trumpets, & voice or clamour of the
(15) *Ibid.* people . Many of the army of the fiue kings
cap. 10. of the (15) *Amortheans* being diſcomfited by
the Iſraelites , and flying away ; were in
their flight killed by haile ſtones ſent from
heauen . The Sunne and the Moone at the
commandement of *Ioſue* (God yealding to
his petition) for the ſpace of ten or twelue
houres ſtayed their motions , vntill he had
vanquiſhed his enemyes . I omit many o-
ther fauours granted to the people of Iſrael
for their obtaining of the land of Promiſe ;
all which do euidently demonſtrate the peculiar prouidence & aſſiſtance of God. Now
all

all thefe euents ferued , but as figures and
types of fuch things , as fhould happen in
the Church during the tyme of the new
teftament; alfo they are of force to fecure vs
now in tyme of grace , of Gods prouidence
(befides in freeing his feruantes from the
bondage of the Diuel) for our entrance into
the heauenly country .

Fiftly, thofe things are to be confidered,
which chanced to the *Ifraelites*, when they
were gouerned by *Iudges*, and after they
entred into the land of Promife; for as ofté
as (after the cuftome of other countries)
they fell to the worfhip of Idols, they were
moft grieuoufly afflicted by God , as being
brought vnder the yoke and feruitude of
their enemyes, but whenfoeuer they grew
truly penitent of fuch their Idolatry, returning vnto God with a contrite and fincere
mind , then God (being at hand ready to
commiferate the diftreffed) raifed vnto thé
a Captaine or leader , which did vindicate
and free them from their thraldome and
oppreffion , and did reduce thé to their former liberty . For feauen feuerall tymes (a
thing moft ftrange and wonderfull) while
they were gouerned by captaines this hapned ; for as often they relapfed into Idolatry , fo often they were deliuered into the
hands of their enemies; and fo often, flying

with

with true penitency vnto God, they were
ſuccoured. And firſt *Ioſue* and others of the
more ancient, being dead, (who were
behoulders of the wonderfull workes of
God, and contained the people in the true
religion) they left God, (16) mancipating
and ſubiecting themſelues to the worſhipping of the Idols of *Baalim* and *Aſtaroth.* For
which ſinne God deliuered them into the
hands of *Chuſan Rathaſaim* King of *Meſopota-*
mia, whome they ſerued eight yeares. Now
this ſubiection ſeeming in the end very
heauy vnto them, and they (through the
admonition of holy men) acknowledging
it to be inflicted by God for their ſinne of I-
dolatry, & being penitent for it, earneſtly
beſeeched mercy and helpe; therefore our
Lord taking mercy of them ſent them *Otho-*
niell, who gathering forces, ouerthrew the
King of *Meſopotamia,* and freed the people
from their bondage. After the death of *O-*
thoniell, the people againe (forgetful of Gods
benefits and commandements, & led with
the cuſtome of other countries) returned to
Idolatry; for the puniſhment of which their
ſinne, our Lord ſtirred vp *Eglon* King of
Moab, with the *Amalites* and *Amalacites,* by
whome they (17) were badly intreated for
the ſpace of eighteene yeares; but they after
loathing their former ſinnes, and flying
vnto

(16) *Iud.*
cap. 3.

(17) *Iud.*
cap. 3.

vnto God for pardon, God sent them *Aod*,
who with the death of the King and destruction of the army of the *Moabites*, set the
people at liberty. *Aod* being dead, they returned againe to (18) Idolatry, in reuenge (18) *Iud.*
of which wickednes, our Lord deliuered *cap.* 4.
them vp vnto the power of *Iabin* King of
Chanaan, who afflicted them twenty yeares together; but tribulation giuing them
againe vnderstāding, they grieued for their
sinnes, and supplicated Gods mercy, who
moued therewith raysed vp *Debora* a pro-
phetesse, & *Barac* a man of armes, who gathering an army, vanquished the forces of
the King of *Iabin*, with the death of *Sisara*
his captaine, by the hands of a woman called *Iahel*.

The people of Israel enioying peace,
and quiet, fell againe to idolatry, and be- (19) *Iud.*
came therefore subiect to the (19) *Madianits*, *cap.* 6.
by whome during seauen yeares they were
grieuously oppressed. But they being in
this calamity, repented and prayed help frō
God, whereupon they were first sharply
rebuked by a Prophet, because they being
so often deliuered out of the handes of their
enemies by God, and hauing receaued so
many benefits from his diuine bounty, did
neuertheles so often depart from his seruice
and worship. But when they were most

Q 5   impor-

importunate and inſtant with God in their prayers for their deliuery, he rayſed *Gedeon,* to whome an Angell was ſent in mans forme, encouraging him to ſo great a worke; who when he was aſſured by pregnant ſignes from heauen of the victory, he alone with three hundred vnarmed men, furniſhed only with a trumpet, and a veſſell of earth containing in it a firebrand, vndertooke ſo great an enterpriſe. Theſe ſounding the trumpet in three places of the army, there inſtantly did ryſe ſo great a tumult amõg the enemies, as that they being ſtroken with a ſudden fury, partly by killing one another with their owne ſwords, and partly by being ſlaine in the purſuit, there were dead of them more then a hundred thouſand. *Gedeon* being dead, they relapſed againe to Idolatry (20.) for which cauſe our Lord deliuered thẽ to the power of the Philiſtians and the Ammonites, from whoſe hands they receaued great afflictiõs and preſſures, during the tyme of eighteene yeares: they returning againe to our Lord, & asking pardon of him, obtained for their captaine *Iephte,* who being prouided of an army fought with the enemies, and got at one tyme twenty of the *Ammonites* citties, reſtoring the Iſraelites to their former liberty.

(20) *Iud.* 10.

Scar-

Scarcely had fiue and twenty yeares
passed from the death of *Iepthe*, but the I-
fraelites returned againe to their old vomit
by abandoning of God (of whose benefites
they had before so often tasted) plunging
themselues anew into Idolatry, the chiefe
cause of all their miseries, and therfore they
were made againe subiect vnder the yoke
of the (21) *Philistians* during the space of for- (21) *Iud.*
ty yeares; but in the end God being moued *c. 14. 15.*
with mercy, sent them *Sampson*, whose *16.*
strength of body was such (seconded with
the peculiar force of God) as nothing was
able to withstand him, for he toare asunder
with his handes a Lyon, that came fiercely
vpon him, and carryed vpon his shoulders
the gate doores of the citty *Gaza*, within
which, being besieged by his enemyes, he
was shut; in like sort, he being vnarmed,
inuaded the whole army of many armed
souldiers oly with the Iawbone of an Asse,
wherewith he killed a thousand, & droue
the rest into flight. Againe he ouerthrew
the house of *Dagon*, two of the chiefe pillars
therof, being shaken downe by the strength
of his arme; many thousandes of the Phili-
stiás (who were present) being killed with
the fall. Which afflictions gaue to the I-
fraelites some breathing tyme of ease and
rest: but they againe enioying a long peace
and

and increaſing the mount of their former
ſinnes, with the acceſſe of more, they were
once more caſt into the handes of Philiſtians, by whome there were ſlaine 34. thouſand Iſraelites: beſides the Arke was taken,
& the keepers of it (to wit *Ophni* & *Phinees*,
two principall Prieſts) were killed, as God
foretould by *Samuel* , that the ſame ſhould
come to paſſe . This calamity happened in
the fortith yeare of *Heli.* Yet heere were
the Iſraelites (though ouercome) ſo puniſhed, as that the Philiſtians (though con-
querours) were afflicted with farre more
grieuous miſeries; for when they offered
the Arke of God to their Idol (as a ſpoyle to
to the Victour) God in reuenge of ſo great
an indignity, puniſhed them ſeueral waies:
for the Idol did not only fall twice downe
before the Arke, the head and handes of it
being maymed and broken ; but alſo the
bodies of the Philiſtians throughout all the
citties were ſtroken with a moſt ioathſome
diſeaſe, to wit , their hindermoſt inteſtine
or gut became putrifyed, & ſtood farre out,
ſo as innumerable dyed thereof. Beſides al
their fruites of the earth & their yeares prouiſion aforehand were eaten & conſumed
with abundance of myce, comming out of
the fieldes and villages . Doubtleſly theſe
tribulations were farre more heauy , then
                                                            if

if they had beene brought vnder the yoake of the Israelites. Therefore the Philistians were in the end enforced to confesse the power of God of Israel, and honourably to send backe the Arke, with all its dowryes, and guifts, euen by thofe men, who were witnesses of the calamities inflicted by God vpon them. All this is at large set downe in the bookes of the *Iudges.*

1. Sixthly, thofe thinges are to be taken in our confideration, which chanced to the Israelits being vnder the gouerment of the Kinges. Firft (22) *Saul* after a wonder-full manner, and by the fpeciall fauour of God (to wit by diuine election, and alfo by lot) was aduanced to the kingdome, who when he would not obey Gods command-ments, was with all his pofterity depriued by God of all regall authority, and in the end his army being vanquifhed, and the kingdome transferred vpon *Dauid,* himfelf with his eldeft fonne was flaine in the warre.

(22) 1. Re 13. & 15.

2. *Dauid* (although a great worfhipper of God) had his finnes (to wit the one of his adultery, and the other of his homicide) moft feuerely punifhed of God euen after his repentance: for his Sonne (to his great griefe) was depriued of life, and the faireft of his daughters was violated, and defaced with

with an infamous inceſt by his eldeſt ſon,
and the ſayd ſonne was afterwardes trea-
cherouſly ſlaine by his owne brother, and
Dauid himſelfe was contumeliouſly caſtout
of the Kingdome by his owne ſonne, and
his wiues were conſtuprated & abuſed by
his ſonne. All which aduerſities, that they
ſhould fall to him in puniſhment of his a-
dultery & homicide, were foretold by *Na-*
than the Prophet.

3. Againe, when *Dauid* ſinned through
elation (24) & pride of mind, in numbring
the people, God in puniſhment thereof, by
his Prophet *Gad*, ſent to him, gaue him
choyce of one of theſe three chaſtiſements,
to wit, whether his kingdome ſhould be
afflicted with famine for ſeauen yeares; or
himſelfe ſhould bè ouercome by his enemies for three moneths; or ſhould be infected with peſtilence for three dayes. Wherupon *Dauid* ſeing himſelfe brought into
theſe ſtraights, thus anſwered: *Coarctor ni-*
mis &c. I am ſtraitned ouermuch, but it is better,
that I fall into the hands ef God (for many are his
mercyes) then iuto the hands of men. And anſwerably hereto, he made choyce of peſtilence, with the which being ſuddenly ſent
from God, there dyed ſeauenty thouſand
men in three dayes; but after ſacrifice being
offered vp for the appeaſing of Gods iuſtice,
the

(24) 3.
Reg. 2.4.

the plague inſtantly ceaſed.

4.   *Salomon* ſucceeded *Dauid*, whŏ being
indued from God with a greater meaſure
of wiſdome, then any other man, and enioying more riches, honour, glory, and a
longer peace, then any of the former Kings
of that people, at length being giuen ouer
to the loue of women, was ſo abſorpt with
the pleaſure of them, as that for their ſakes
he was content to worſhip Idols: In reuége
of which ſo great an offence, God preſently
after his death diuided & ſhared his Kingdome, ten trybes wherof were transferred
vpon *Ierobam*; and the other two only left
to the ſonne of *Salomon*; with which point
Salomon in his life tyme was threatned certainly. The *prouidence of God* appeared wŏ-
derfully in the execution of this diuiſion, as
is to be ſeene in the third book of the Kings,
cap. 11. and 12.

5.   *Ieroboam* aduanced from a meane eſtate to the Kingdome, was mainly bent to
fortify & ſettle himſelfe by al meanes whatſoeuer; he fearing then, that if the People
went yearely to *Ieruſalem*, to ſacrifice in the
Temple of the Lord, that his Kingdome
might be loſt, the people turning theſelues
to *Roboam* King of *Iuda*; therefore for the
better preuention hereof, he cauſed two
golden calues to be erected vp as Gods, and
diuulged

diuulged an Edict, whereby the people
were commanded not to go to *Ieruſalem*,
but to ſacrifice to thoſe two Idols. This
proceeding might (perhaps) ſeeme much
conducing to the preſeruation of his poli-
ticke ſtate; and yet in a mature conſideration of the matter, nothing could be inuented more ſorting & fitting to the vtter ſub-
uerſion thereof; for it is ſaid in the third of
the Kings cap. 13. *For this cauſe the houſe of*
Ieroboam is ouerthrowne, and blotted out of the
roundnes of the earth. He raigned 2 2. yeares,
not without great troubles and moleſtati-
ons; who being dead, his ſonne *Nadab* ſucceeded; but he ſcarce gouerned two yeares,
being depriued both of his life and Kingdome by his ſeruant *Baaſa*, who inſtantly
ſo extinguiſhed the race and family of *Iero-*
boam, as that there was not left one thereof.
And this very thing was threatned to him
by the Prophet. But ſuch (for the moſt part)
are the Counſels and proiects of Polititians
(of whome this *Ieroboam* may ſerue for an
example) who make religion to be ſubiect
and ſeruiceable to policy, & who imbrace
that profeſſion of faith, which beſt ſorteth
eyther to the obtayning, or keeping, or en-
creaſing of their States, and other ſuch humane reſpects: for although their ſubtle machinations and plots ſeeme at the firſt to be
ſpecious,

specious, fayre, and conuenient; yet in pro-
cesse of tyme they commonly inuolue and
intangle the Actours, with great difficul-
ties, & such as in the end do occasion their
destruction; all which proceedeth from the
disposall of the diuine Prouidence, which
euer hath a predominancy and ouerruling
ouer mens actions and determinations.

6.   After the death of *Ieroboam* and his
sonne, the Empyre of the Israelites, was
houlden by *Baasa*, whose indiscretion and
madnes was wonderfull : for though he
knew, that *Ieroboam* with his whole family
was vtterly extinct for committing of Idolatry, notwithstanding himselfe did not for-
sake it, wherefore the like finall destruction
was denounced against him by the Prophet
Iehu ; the execution whereof was not long
delayed. For when he had raigned two &
twenty yeares (as *Ieroboam* did) & that his
sonne *Ela* succeeded him, euen in the secōd
yeare of *Ela*, one of his Captaines by name
Zamri, did ryse vp against him, who being
killed, *Zamri* inuaded the kingdome, and
presently by death did extirpate all the family of *Baasa*.

Some few yeares after, the same fortune happened to King *Achab*, and to his
impious wife *Iesabel*; for *Achab* himselfe after he had tasted of many calamities, was

R   slaine

slaine in warre againſt the Syrians, and after his death *Iehu* (appointed by God captaine or leader of the warre) killed *Ochozias*
the ſonne of *Achab*, and ſucceſſour of the
Kingdome, as alſo all his progeny; and cauſed *Iefabel* the Queen to be caſt frō a height
headlong downe, to be deuoured of dogs.
Al which miſeries God by his Prophets did
foretell to fall vnto them, by reaſon of their
idolatry, and their other ſinnes.

8. At the length, ſeeing the Kings of
Iſrael, and the people would neuer ceaſe
from ſinning, and particulerly from worſhipping of Idols (notwithſtanding ſo many comminations and threats, ſo many ad-
monitions and increpations, and ſo many
chaſtiſements inflicted by God for this their
offence) they were in the end depriued of
their Kingdome, Citties, houſes, grounds,
poſſeſſions, and liberty, themſelues being
carryed away into *Aſſyria* to liue in perpetuall bondage and ſlauery. Iuſt after this
manner, the prouidence of God carryed it
ſelfe towardes the Kinges of *Iuda*, and that
people; for as often as they yielded to the
committing of Idolatry, they were worne
out with diuers warres and calamities, till
they became penitēt of their former ſinnes;
but when they worſhipped God truly and
religiouſly, then they enioyed great proſperity,

perity, and were honoured with many victoryes, as alfo flowed in all opulency and wealth, as it falled out in *Abia*, *Afa*, *Iofaphat*, and *Ezechias*. For againft *Abia* (25) King of *Iuda*, *Ieroboam* came with fourefcore thoufand men: but *Abia* finding himfelfe much inferiour in forces, put his fole confidence in his prayers to God, befeeching his help and ayde; whereupon God fending a terrour into the army of *Ieroboam*, forced it to flight, the which *Abia* following, killed fifty thoufand of his men, and tooke many of his citties. But *Afa* (26) had a farre more famous victory; for *Zara* the Ethiopian, with a huge army confifting of ten hundred thoufand armed men, made warre vpon *Afa*, who though farre inferiour in force, yet putting his truft in our Lord, met him in the field, and vpon his humble prayers made to him, the Ethiopians were fuddenly affrighted and difmayed, and thereupon began to fly, but *Afa* following them, killed moft of the army, and returned enriched with infinite fpoiles of the enemy.

Neither was leffe wonderfull that victory of (27) *Iofaphat*, who only with his prayers, vertue, and affured hope of Gods affiftance, without any weapons at all ouercame a mighty army, which was gathered of three very populous nations, to wit,

R 2   the

(25) 2.
Paralip.
c. 13.

(26) 2.
Paralip.
c. 14

(27) Ibidem. 20.

the *Ammonites*, *Moabites*, and the *Idumeans*. For his ſmall forces being drawne out a-gainſt the enemy, he commanded his Qui-riſters, who did ſing diuine ſeruice & lau-des, to go before his ſouldiers, ſinging; at which ſight the Enemies were by Gods ſpeciall prouidence poſſeſſed with ſuch a fury, as that they killed one another, lea-uing a great valew of ſpoyles to the Ie-wes.

(28) 4.   To the former may worthily be adioined
Reg. 19. the victory of (28) *Ezechias*, who as being
& 2. Pa- brought to great extremities by the Aſſy-
ralip. 32. rians, made his recourſe to God by prayer, who hearing him, ſent an Angell to aſſiſt him, who in one night killed one hundred fourſcore and fiue thouſand Aſſiryans.

I omit the captiuity of *Babilon*, the hiſto-ry of *Eſther*, the hiſtory of *Iudith*, the hiſtory of *Tobias*, the warres of the *Machabees*, the beſieging of the *Romans*, and the vtter ouer-throw of the Iewes; in all which the *pro-uidence of God* hath wonderfully appeared. It were an infinite labour to ſet downe all thoſe examples, in which the *Diuine Pro-uidence* hath helped, ſuccoured and extolled the godly and vertuous; and on the other ſide hath depreſſed, humbled, chaſtiſed, & puniſhed the impious and wicked. For in-deed the chiefeſt ſubiect of the holy Scrip-

ture

ture is this; feeing all their narrations doe
tend to this end, to wit, to inftruct men,
that profperity and aduerfity do depend of
the prouidence of God; and that both thefe
feuerall fortunes are allotted vnto men, according to the quality of their workes;nei-
ther can any one decline & auoid the power of the fayd Prouidence. In which point
the facred Write of God differeth from all
prophane hiftories; for that being written
by the peculiar incumbency and direction
of the holy Ghoft, relateth humane matters
as they are gouerned by diuine prouidence.
Whereas thefe other,as penned by a human
fpirit, make narration of them, as they proceed only from mans prudence and induftry. Therfore that former teacheth diuine
wifedome, by the which, man with a godly worfhip of him, adhereth vnto God:
thefe later humane wifdome., and certaine
fmall trifling cautions and obferuations inuented, through the wit and induftry of
man; which for the moft part are but of
little power, yet often are accompanyed
with danger and deftruction. Wherefore it
may be iuftly concluded, that nothing is
more agreable to the education & framing
of Princes, then the reading of facred and
diuine hiftories; efpecially of the bookes of
the Kinges; for there they fhalbe inftru-

ſted, that the foundation & ground-worke
of a kingdome and of true policy , is ſeated
in true religion and iuſtice, without which
any Chriſtian ſtate cannot expect any fir-
menes or tranquility . This very point was
moſt profitable to *Charles* the fiſt, vnto whō
Adrianus his Schoolemaſter did read the
bookes of the *Kings*, from whence he tooke
thoſe principles , miſteries, and documents
of gouernemet, which made him not only
vertuous , but alſo a moſt great, potent, and
fortunate prince . Now that theſe bookes
are to be altogether credited, as being written by the concurrency and direction of
the holy ghoſt , is aboue made moſt cleare
and euident .

THE 15. REASON TAKEN FROM THE *ſecret puniſhing of Blaſphemy , Periury, and Sacriledge .*

C H A P.   X V I I.

THESE ſinnes of *blaſphemy , periury*
and *ſacriledge* are directly againſt the
reuerence of a *Deity* and *diuine power*;
wherefore ſeing it is euident from the experience and obſeruation of diuers exāples,
that theſe are more ſeuerely puniſhed by
Gods inuiſible hand , then other ſinnes are,
we

we therefore may infallibly conclude , that there is a *Deity* and *a diuine Power* , which hath a sense and feeling of these iniuries & indignities cōmitted against it . For if there were no *diuine power* , then were these former actions no siunes , as it is no sinne to speake cōtemptuously of a *chimera* , or imaginary thing , or to sweare by it , or to cō-culcate, & with disgrace to tread the signe of it vnder our feete . Againe if these former things be no sinnes, thē is there due to them no castigation or punishment ; But the contrary to this is euident by many examples . *Pharao* (the King of *Egipt*) when he misprised God, and spake of him with contempt in those words : (1) *Quis est Dominus &c* . *VVho is the Lord , that I should heare his voice, and let Israell goe? I know not the Lord, neither will I let Israel goe* : was for such his offence afflicted with many Calamityes,& in the end vtterly ouerthrowne with his whole army . (2) *Sennacherib* the King of the *Assirians* , inuading *Iudea* with a powerfull army , commanded it to be related by his captaines to *Ezechias* the King , that in vaine he reposed his trust in any *diuine power* ; for seeing (said he) the Gods of other nations were not able to defend their worshippers against the puissance and might of the King of the *Assirians* ; therefore neither

R 4   could

(1) *Exod.* 5.

(2) 4. *Reg.*19. (2) *Paralip.* 32. *Tobiæ.* 1.

could the God of *Israel*. For which horrible blasphemy God in one night destroyed almost his whole army, there being a hundred eighty fiue thousand armed men slaine by an Angell. And the King himselfe after his returne into *Niniuy* his citty, and sacrificing to his Gods (who could not defend him) was murthered by his owne sonnes.

(3) *Daniel c. 3.*
(3) *Nabuchodonosor* (King of *Chaldæa*) when in his fury he cast the three children into the burning Furnace, for that they refused to adore a *Statua* erected by him, and further blasphemed against God, in preferring his owne power before the power of God, in these words: *Quis est Deus? VVho is God, that can take you out of my hands?* did immediatly after acknowledge the contrary, and confessed *a Deity* through the sight of that stupendious miracle, by the which the children being in the middest of the flames remained vnhurt & not burned. But after when he had forgot the same, and bare himselfe with his former elation and pryde of mind, maintayning, that his power and glory stood obnoxious or subiect to none, he was suddenly punished by God; a voyce from heauen rushing vpon him, and speaking thus: *Tibi* (4) *dicitur Nabuchodono-*

(4) *Daniel 4.*
sor rex &c. O King Nabuchodonosor, to thee be it spoken:thy Kingdome shall departe from thee. And they

they shall driue thee from men, *and thy dwelling
shalbe with the beasts of the field ; They shall make
thee to eate graße, as the oxen ; And seauen tymes
shall paße ouer thee, till thou knoweſt, that
the moſt high beareth rule ouer the Kingdome of
men, and giueth it vnto whomesoeuer he will.*
Which voyce being ended, he was presently
depriued of reaſon & grew madd. Wher-
vpon being driuen from all mens society, he
begun to liue in the woods among beaſts,
and during ſeauen yeares liued after the
manner of beaſts. Which period of tyme being ended, he was reſtored to his wits and
senſes, and preſently thereupon moſt excellently confeſſed a *diuine power.* That this was
to happen vnto him, God foreſhewed it a
yeare before in a viſion, which he had,
while he dreamed; which viſion *Daniel* did
interpret.

Agrippa (5) the elder being in *Cesarea,* and
cloathed with sumptuous apparell, and ſit-
ting in a high and regall ſeat, began to make
a ſpeach to the people ; but ſome of his flat-
tters cryed out, that it was the voice of ſome
God, and not of man; which words being
gratefull vnto him, (who could be willing
to aſſume diuine honour to himſelfe) he was
ſuddenly ſtroken with an Angell, and ſo
his fleſh and bowels putrifying, he was conſumed with lice.

The

(5) *Acts*
12. *Ioseph.*
l. 19. *An-*
tiquit. c. 7.

The (6) *Syrians* being ouercome in warre by the *Iſraelites* in certaine mountanous places, aſcribed their ouerthrow to the Gods of the mountaines, who (they ſayd) did fauour the *Iſraelites* : Therefore they would fight with the *Iſraelites* in the vallies, where they thought the God of *Iſrael* was not intereſſed; vpon which cauſe, God by his Prophet thus ſpake to the King of *Iſrael* ; *Quia dixerunt Syri &c. Becauſe the Syrians ſayd, the Lord is God of the mountaines, and not God of the vallies, I will giue all this great multitude in thy hand, and you ſhall know, that I am the Lord.* And thereupon both their armyes ioyning battel after, the Iſraelites (though but few in number)killed in one day a hundred thouſand footmen : And there remained in a neere place twenty ſeauen thouſand Syrians, who flying into the citty, were killed with the fall of the citty wals: doubtleſly this was a manifeſt reuenge and puniſhment of the former blaſphemy.

Nicanor (7) being leader of the army of *Demetrius* the King, & intending to inuade the Iewes vpon the Sabaoth, was admoniſhed that in honour and reuerence to God (who ſeeth all things) he ſhoud forbeare that ſacred day: to the which aduiſe he thus anſwered : *Eſtne potens quiſpiam in cælo &c. Is there a Lord in heauen, that commandeth the Saboth*

(7) 2. Ma chab. 15.

both day to be kept: to whom when it was answered. *Est dominus viuus &c. There is a liuing Lord,*
which ruleth in heauen, who commanded the sea-
uenth day to be kept: he replyed; Et ego potens
&c. And I am mighty vpon earth to command
them, for to arme themselues, and to performe
the Kings busines. Vpon which occasion the
day of warre being begun, though *Nica-*
nor had a most powerfull army, furnished
with all kind of munition and armour; yet
was he ouerthrowne by very few, with
the losse of thirty fiue thousand men. His
blasphemous tongue likewise was cut of,
and by small peeces cast vnto birds; and his
hands, which he lifted vp against the Teple, were set vp in an opposite place to the
Temple.

In the 24. of *Leuiticus*, the Lord commanded, that the sonne of an Israelite woman, who had blasphemed against God,
should be stoned to death; and euen in that
place this law of stoning is established, and
two seueral tymes repeated in these words:
(8) *Qui blasphemauerit &c. He that blasphemeth*
the name of the Lord, shall bee put to death; al the
congregation shall stone him to death, aswell the
stranger, as he that is borne in the land: VVhen he
blasphemeth the name of the Lord, let him be slaine
Certainly this repetition doth intimate &
insinuate the firme and resolute will and

(8) *Leui-*
ticus, 24.

            mind

mind of the lawgiuer herein .

(9) Iudith 6.
All what tyme *Achior* (9) cōmended the power of the God of heauen , and auerred , that the Iewes were secure and safe , in that they worshiphed God religiously,at which words *Holofernes* in great indignation thus answered : *Quoniam prophetaſti &c. Becauſe thou haſt prophecyed among vs to day, that the pe-ople of Iſrael is defended by their God, I will shew thee,that there is no other God , but Nabuchodo-noſor &c* . For which blasphemy he pa ed deare , for his owne head was cut of by the hand of a woman (10) and his army being driuen to flight,a great part therof was put to the sword by the Iewes.

(10) Ibid. 13.

(11)2. Machab.
Antiochus (11) for his pryde and blasphe-my , was stroken from God with an inui-sible and incurable diseaſe ; for first sudden-ly a violent payne of his bowels inuaded him ; and then quickly after he fell out of his charriot, wounding himselfe dágerous-ly ; lastly his body putrifying with a filthy consumption , and breathing out a most loathsome smell was consumed aliue with wormes.

(12) 1. Reg. c. 6.
The *Philiſtians* (12) were oppressed with most heauy afflictions from God, in that they handled the *Arke* of the Lord vn-worthily;and except they had sent it backe againe within a short tyme, perhaps they all had

had then perished : but within seauen moneths they restored it with honour and reuerence, vpon which their so doing, the plague afore among them instantly ceased.

When the *Bethsamites* (13) behoulded the *Arke* of the Lord curiously & with smal reuerence (contrary to the diuine precept in that behalfe, expressed in the fourth booke of *Numbers*) there were slaine of the chiefest among them seauenty men, and of the common multitude fifty thousand: thus did the *Diuine Prouidence of God* punish with death that curious and irreligious sight of theirs. {13) *Ibid.* 6.

Balthazar (14) (King of the *Chaldeans*) when he commāded the holy vessels to be brought to him (which were taken out of the temple of the Lord at *Ierusalem*) and did drinke in them with his noble men and his Concubines; for such his prophaning of thē did presently feele Gods iust reuenge, for in the middest of the banquet and iollity with his guests, it is said, *Apparuerunt digiti &c. There appeared fingers of a mans hand, which wrote ouer against the candlesticke vpon the plaister of the wall of the Kings pallace.* And this appeared in the sight of all men, and with great consternation of mind and feare to the King himselfe. The words there writtē were these three : *Mane, Thecel, Phares.* Of which {14) *Da- niel* 5.

which words (according to the interpretation of *Daniel*) this was the meaning: *Mane*,
that is , *God hath numbred thy Kingdome , and
hath finished it* : *Thecel* : *thou art weighed in the
ballance, & art found too light. Phares*; *thy Kingdome is diuided, and giuen to the Medes and Perſians.* To conclude, that very night the Citty, was taken, and the King with infinite
multitude of men , & with the greateſt part
of his nobility was ſlaine . Now three obſeruations we collect from this one fact :
firſt , that there is a certaine period of tyme
giuen by God to all Kingdomes; the which
being once expired , the Kingdomes are
changed, and the Souera+inty of them tranſ-
ferred to others. Secondly, that the workes
of euery Prince and King are to be expended and weighed, and that for the moſt part
the tyme of their gouerment is appointed
by God . Thirdly , that the beginning of
principalities and Kingdomes, their deſtru-
ctions, their continuance, and tranſlations
are diſpoſed by the *Prouidence* of the Almighty.

　　3.　When *Heliodorus* (15) endeauoured
to rob the ſacred Treaſury by prophaning
the ſanctuary of the temple; the Iewes pray-
ing deuoutly to God for the preuenting
hereof, he was not only reſtrained by God
of his purpoſe; but was greatly puniſhed
　　　　　　　　　　　　　　　with

(15) 2.
Machab.
3.

with stripes for such his sacrilegious attempt; and his souldiers, which he brought with him to that end, were possessed with a great feare and dismayednes. For there appeared vnto him a horseman of a terrible aspect, and rich in apparell, whose horse comming violently vpon *Heliodorus* with his former feet, did greatly hurt him; & then there were seene two yong men of excellēt strength and beauty, who on each side inuading *Heliodorus*, did so whip him, as that he dispayred of his life. But sacrifice being offered vp for his recouery, he was presently cured. And thus much of these examples, which are taken out of the holy Scriptures: for if we should insist in all other examples of this subiect, which do occurre in prophane Histories, and other Ecclesiasticall wryters, we should find almost infinite of them: for there is no Nation, no Prouince, no citty, no village, where blasphemyes, sacriledges and periuries haue not very often beene most dreadfully punished by Gods owne hand; In so much that the very terrour and feare of his chastisements heerein hath beene sufficient to deterre many men from the perpetrating of so heinous sinnes. It may perhaps seeme strange to some, that we do often read those, who were contemners not only of one true and supreme diuine

uine power, but alſo euen of falſe Gods , to
haue been puniſhed moſt ſtrangely. Anſwerably hereto we find, that the ſouldiers
of *Zerxes*, who through hope of ſpoyle entred into the temple of the *Cabiri* in *Thebes*
(wherein *Ceres* was worſhipped) became al
preſently madd ; ſome of them caſting thé-
ſelues into the ſea , others of them hurling
themſelues precipitately downe from the
top of high rocks, as *Pauſanias* in his *Beoticu*
relateth. Againe, when *Alexander* the *Mace-
don* did take by force *Miletum* , a moſt ſtrong
citty in *Ionia* , and that ſome of the ſouldiers
burſt into the temple for the ſpoyling of it ;
ſuddenly a flame of fyre burned and blinded
the eyes of them all , as *Lactantius* wryteth
lib. 2. cap. 8. and *Valerius Maximas* lib. 1. c.
2. *Appius Claudius* the Cenſour for taking a-
way of ſacred things of the falſe Gods , was
ſtroken blind. *Fuluius* the Cenſour, in that
he tooke certaine marble tyles or plate out
of the temple of *Iuno Laſcinia* , with the
which he couered the building which he
made at Rome, called *Ædes Fortunæ Equeſtris,*
became madd , and in the end dyed through
griefe, conceaued for the loſſe of his two
ſonnes in the warrs in Greece. *Pirrhus* (King
of the *Epirots*) for robbing the treaſury of
Proſerpina Locrenſis, ſuffred ſhipwracke vpon
the ſhores neereſt to that Goddeſſe , where
there

there was after nothing to be found safe, but
the siluer, which he had taken afore. These
things are related out of ancient wryters by
Lactantius lib. 2. cap. 8. and diuers other ap-
prooued authours make mention of the like
euents in this kind. For anſwere hereto, it is
to be faid, that thefe puniſhments do not
proceed from the true God; but from the
Diuells, who are emulous of diuinity; who
that they may be accounted Gods, and that
they may the more eafily extort diuine honours, endeauour to imitate the cuſtome &
proceeding of the true God. And from hence
it rifeth, that there are fo many vifions, apparitions, and Oracles; fo many falfe and a-
dulterate miracles perfourmed by them; fo
many benefits feeming to be beſtowed by
them vpon their worfhippers; and fo many
puniſhments inflicted vpon fuch, as feeme
more negligent in their honours: for by
their preſtigious ſleights and endeauours it
was brought to paffe, that a *ſtatua* or Image
of *Iuno Veienfis* fpoke to a fouldier, that it intended to go to Rome; that the Goddeffe
Fortune was accuſtomed to denounce perill
& danger in a Womans forme or ſhow; that
a ſhip (drawne with a ſtring) did follow
the hand of *Claudia*; that Rome fhould be
freed of the plague, if a ferpent were fent
from *Epidaurus*; that *Ceres Thebana, Ceres Mi-*

S   *lefia;*

esia, Proserpina *Locrensis,* and *Iuno Lascinia* did Ireuenge themselues vpon those, who bore themielues sacrilegioufly towards them: finally, that for the same matter *Hercules* tooke punithment of *Appius,* Iupiter of *Atinius,* and *Apollo* of a fouldier of *Scipio.* But of this point fee more in *Lactantius* l. 2. c. 17.

God fuffered thefe euents both for the finnes of thofe men, who deferued to liue vnder the tiranny of the Diuells; as alfo becaufe the Heathens in committing indignities againft their falfe Gods, did either finne againft their confcience, which perfwaded them, that there was a kind of diuinity in them; or otherwife committed thefe difgraces with contempt, not only of falfe Gods but alfo of all diuine and fupernaturall power whatfoeuer. For feeing, they were ignorant of the true God, the creatour of all things, and with all did know by the light of reafon, that thofe vulgar powers, which were worfhipped of the common fort were no Gods, they might more eafily be induced to thinke, that there was no *diuine power* at all, by the which the world is gouerned; but that all things had their being and euent by a fatall neceffity, or by temerity and rafhnes of fortune. And from this ground it is, that among the *Iaponians* & the of *China,* fuch as are ignorát, are ey-

ther

ther Atheists, and open contemners of all diuinity; or at least, do greatly fluctuate & stagger in their iudgments therein.

Therfore when the Heathens (as in the examples aboue related)do commit any sacrilegious act against their false Gods, either they sinne against their conscience, in the which they belieue, that there is a certaine diuinity in those Gods; or els they sinne through a generall contempt of all diuine power; wherfore (whatsoeuer the reason is) it is not strange, if the Heathens suffer punishments for such their actions. Neither is it any preiudice to what is deliuered in this Chapter, that among blasphemous, sacrilegious, and periured men, there is a far greater number of those, who are not punished in this life; then of those who are punished; Seing this is no signe or argument of any defect or want of Prouidence, but only of the delaying of the punishment. For it doth not necessarily belong to the nature of prouidence, to punish all sinnes in this world; but to suffer actions and things for the tyme to be carryed according (for the most part) to the forces of the worker; the chiefest punishment being reserued for the tyme to come; Since otherwise, mankind would shortly be extinguished, and the offices or operations of vertue would rather

S 2   seeme

seeme to be feruilely coacted and enforced, then free, or proceeding from any ingenuous or generous lyking of vertue. It is certaine, that *Prouidence* manifesteth it selfe sufficiently, if it taketh punishment of some particular men in this world after an vnaccustomed manner; and this in the eye of the world, with admiration and astonishment of all; as acknowledging the secret hand of Gods power, and omnipotency therein.

THE ARGVMENTS ANSVVERED,
which are brought againſt the being of
a Prouidence, and a Deity.

CHAP. XVIII.

THE firſt argument againſt a diuine Prouidence may be this: Yf the world be gouerned by the Prouidence of some supernatural power, then would not impiety & wickednes so much preuaile and predominate, nor haue such prosperous euents againſt vertue and innocency : for it may seeme chiefly to belong to the prouidence of a gouernour, not to giue the bridle of liuing loosely to the wicked, but to curbe them, and force them to better courses ; and on the other side to defend and cherish the pious, and to aduance them to honours

and

and riches. Yf in any great Citty the most licentious and prophane persons should continually gouerne and sterne all matters, wronging with all impunity others; and the vertuous should euer rest thus afflicted; who would say, that this Citty were gouerned by a prouident & iust Ruler? Wherfore seeing in the world we may obserue such a perturbation of Order, as that a greater can hardly be conceaued; to wit, the wicked ruling and doing euery thing to their owne sensuality, and the vertuous miserably afflicted & oppressed; all which may seeme to impugne, that the world is gouerned by *one supreme Prouidence*, which iustly disposeth and measureth all things.

I answere hereto, and say, that the prophane Athists do chiefly ground themselues vpon this argument; as also that the faithful are sometimes troubled and distracted therwith, as the Prophet Dauid in his Psalme 72. insinuateth himselfe to haue bene moued herein. But the answere hereto, is obuious, facile, and easy. For as there is a double end; the one belonging to this temporal life, to wit, the tranquillity and peace of the common wealth; the other to the life to come, and this is the eternal glory in heauen: euen so we are to consider a double *Prouidence*, wherof the one disposeth the

S 3   meanes

meanes for the obtaining of the temporal
end; the other of the eternal end. The firſt is
humane and political, as reſting vpon mans
wiſdome, and tending to a political and
temporal good; this other is diuyne, as being grounded vpon diuyne wiſdome, and
directed to an eternal good or benefit.

Therfore where it is ſaid, that it belongeth to *Prouidence* to bridle the wicked, not
to ſuffer them to afflict the vertuous without controule, and the like; this is true, if
we ſpeake of politicall prouidence, and of
temporall coercion and conſtraint; for ſeing
this Prouidence is ordained to obtaine temporall peace and reſt, the function of it is to
hinder (what in it lyeth) all wickednes and
ſinnes, wherby the temporall peace may be
diſturbed. Wherfore it may be truly granted, that in what Commonwealth ſoeuer
outrages are committed without any feare
of puniſhment; the ſame either wanteth a
gouernour, or at leaſt the magiſtrate thereof
is vniuſt, partiall, and tyrannous.

But if we ſpeake of that *Supreme Prouidence* (afore mentioned) then is it falſe to
affirme, that it belongeth to its function, not
to ſuffer the impious to gouerne and rule
temporally; ſince indeed, the contrary rather appertaineth to it, to wit, to ſuffer all
things (as they are heere furniſhed with
their

their owne faculties and abilities) for the tyme to take and enioy their proceedings and desires; and this for many causes.

First, that we may spontaneously and voluntarily be carried to the exercise of vertue, & not be compelled thereto through any necessity: for vertue coacted and forced, is not vertue, but rather a bondage of the mind; since true vertue exerciseth it selfe not through any seruile feare of punishmēt, but through loue of honesty: therfore to the end, that true vertue and perfect desert may haue their due place, it was necessary, that the *Diuine Prouidence* should not constraine men thereto, but should leaue euery man to his free choice and liberty herein.

VVhy diuine Prouidence suffereth the courses of she wicked in this VVorld.

Secondly, because the dignity and worth of eternall reward is so great, that if it be duely considered, it is abundantly sufficient to inflame our desires to the loue of it, and to excite vs to all vertue and sanctity; therfore it should much impugne the excellency of so inestimable a felicity, if men through compulsion were driuen to the seeking of it.

Thirdly, if eternall punishments be maturely expended and considered, they are fully preuailing to deterre men from all flagitious and impious attempts. Wherupon if God should not chastice men in this world,

S 4   yet

yet were they not deſtitute of his Prouidence; for it is ſufficient, that he promiſeth
rewards, & threatneth puniſhments for the
tyme to come.

Fourthly, if by Gods diſpoſall & his prouidence, wickednes ſhould euer receaue its
retaliation and recompence in this world
(as we ſee, politicall Prouidence inflicteth
the ſame) then would the world be in a
ſhort tyme extinguiſhed and ended; wherupon it would follow, that there ſhould be
few imbracers of vertue, and the meanes for
the wicked to their ſaluation ſhould be re-
cluded and ſhut vp.

Fiftly, the malignity of the wicked is
not in vaine permitted by God, ſeeing by
reaſon therof the vertue of the iuſt is often
more ſtirred vp and exerciſed, and appeareth more worthily; as alſo there is giuen
them thereby an occaſion of a greater me-
rit, and a more glorious crowne. For take
away the ſeuerity of tyrants, and then there
ſhalbe no glory of Martyrs; take away the
wrongs proferred by euill men, and there
ſhall not appeare the patience or longanimity of the iuſt and vertuous; briefly, the
world would be depriued of an infinite
ſeed of goodnes, if God ſhould euer reſtraine
and curbe the wicked in this world. The
ſame malignity ſerueth to puniſh as wel
the

he sinnes of the iust, as of the impious (as is euident out of the holy Scripture.) So God diuers tymes vsed the malice and ambition of the *Assyrians*, *Chaldeans*, *Persians*, *Egiptians*, & *Romanes*, as a meanes, wherwith to chastice the *Israelites* & other nations; suffering them according to a limited proportion of tymes, places, persons, calamities, and punishments, to afflict and molest the people of God, and otheer countries; and this order God hath obserued in all ages, and will obserue it till the consummation of the world.

Sixtly, we are furthermore instructed from this Prouidence, that temporall benefits are not much to be esteemed; since both the vertuous, and the vicious do promiscuously participate of them; and in the which the wicked do commonly more increase, then the pious and the iust. Which point being so, then how great are those benefits, which God hath promised and prepared for his seruants? For if he doth not giue these temporall commodities (so much prized) to such as daily dishonour him with their bad liues, then what, and how great are those rewards, which he hath reserued only for such, as do truly feare and serue him? To be briefe, this temperature of Gods prruidence doth greatly commend and magnify the wonderfull benignity & clemency of God, which

which while it flowly proceedeth to reuenge, it daily expecteth the conuerfion of
finners. And yet it proceedeth in fuch fort, as
that it is not altogeather voyde of iuſtice &
feuerity ; becaufe often by vnaccuſtomed
meanes euen in this life, it puniſheth finnes,
to fhow that God doth not fleepe , but ſhat
he will in due tyme exact an account of all
men. From all which, it appeareth, that this
Prouidence, which fuffereth fo great a perturbation in humane and temporall things,
is perfect and grounded vpon moſt forcible
reafon; fince the wrong of the vertuous is
temporall & momentary, and is to be changed hereafter for eternall reſt and beatitude.
He that diligently weigheth this point, wil
not only , not be fcandalized at the vneuen
difpenfation of thefe humane things ; but
will greatly admire & prayfe the Prouidence of God , who vpon fo iuſt motiues
permitteth the fame.

THE SECOND ARGVMENT AGAINST
the diuine Prouidence , anſwered.

CHAP. XIX.

EXPERIENCE inſtructeth vs,
that mens negotiations and bufines
haue (for the moſt part) euents and
fuccefſe,

succeſſe. anſwerable to the induſtry & care
vſed by them therein, and not according to
the right or equity of the cauſe; wherupon
it often falleth out, that who maintaineth
the moſt iniuſt cauſes, doth preuaile in thē;
which conſideration may ſeeme to inſinuate, that each man is to be left to his owne
Prouidence, without diſquiſition or ſearch
of any other Prouidence. Accordingly hereto it is to be remembred, that a great Generall or Leader in the warres (who had
gotten diuers worthy victoryes, and had
taken a Prince priſoner) diſcourſing with
him of the *Prouidence of God*, in matters of
warres, & laying his hand vpon his ſword,
ſaid, That (& no other) was the Prouidēce,
wherupon he was to reſt and depend.

I anſwere, that the ſolution of this argument much relyeth vpon the former; for
Mens affayres for the moſt part do ſucceed
according to their labour, care and ſolicitude vſed therein, in that *the diuine* and *ſupreme Prouidence* hath decreed to ſuffer, that
matters (during the ſeaſon and tyme of this
world) ſhalbe carryed according to their
owne peculiar motions and forces, the
reynes of working thus, or not thus, being
freely granted to mans nature. Therefore
where greater induſtry or power is found
(though leſſe iuſtice or equity) there it is
commonly

commonly accōpanyed with more happy and fortunate euents. The reaſons of Gods permiſſion herein are aboue ſet downe and vnfoulded. Ad hereto, that though the endeauours of the wicked may (for the tyme) be ouer preuailing, yet there is no perpetuity or continuance thereof; for this proſperity is for the moſt part tempered, or rather ouer ballanced with many aduerſities and afflictions. Seing many there are, who either in their firſt beginnings, or in their progreſſe (at what tyme they hould themſelues moſt free from all ſudden conuulſiōs of miſery and infelicity) are vtterly ouerthrowne. This appeareth firſt in the moſt celebrious & famous Monarchies that euer haue flouriſhed: for we read, that the Monarchy of the *Aſſyrians* was ouerthrowne by the *Chaldeans*; that of the Chaldeans by the *Perſians* and the *Medes*; this of the *Perſians* by the *Grecians*; & the monarchy of the *Grecians* by the *Romans*, which is at this preſēt much obſcured of its former honour, and brought to great ſtraits. Againe the ſame point is alſo made cleare in the perſōs of the Monarchs themſelues, if we but cōſider the calamityes and miſeryes, which the moſt powerfull and moſt formidable among them haue ſuſtained - For *Nabuchodonezor* being placed vpon the higheſt pinacle

of

of profperity, and after the ouerthrow of fo
many Countries and nations, was fuddely
ftroken with a fentence from heauen, and
compelled to liue in defart places after the
manner of beafts. *Baltafar* (nephew to the
former) being deuoted and giuen to epicu-
rifme and fenfuality, was flaine in that very
night, when his Citty was taken. *Cyrus*,
when he had obtained the honour of fo
many victories, was (with the lofle of his
army) pittifully maffacred by the *Scithians.*
Xerxes, with his forces, confifting of three
hundred thoufand fighting men, was fhá-
fully ouercome by the Grecians, & almoft
extinguifhed. *Alexander* the great after the
diffolution of the Perfian Empire, and fub-
iugation of diuers other kingdomes to his
command, dyed without any heires, and
left his kingdomes to be fhared by his
Generals and Leaders, who after through
mutuall and inward afflictions fo weakned
and impouerifhed themfelues, as that in the
end they were brought vnder the yoake of
the Romans. Now for the Romans, with
what fweating, paynes, and labours did
they rife and grow dreadfull? With what
calamityes were they often worne out and
wearyed? With what inteftine and ciuill
warres were they afflicted? What exorbitant and vnaccuftomed crueltyes fuffered
they

they of their Generals and Emperours? Finally how many of their Generals and Emperours after their inceffant and indefatigable paines vndertaketor the honour of their countries, were ignominioufly and bafely handled, and in the end cruelly butchered? Certainly it were an infinite labour to infift in all the particulars of this kind. For if a man will but perufe either the ancient, or moderne, and later hiftoryes, he fhall find many in euery age, whofe vnlawfull attempts and labours (though they were extraordinarily furnifhed and enabled with power & forces) had moft vnfortunate and deplorable fuccefles : the *Prouidence of God* interpofing it felfe, and difturbing al their wicked motions & endeauours, according to that of the Pfalme 32. *Dominus diffipat cō-filia gentium &c* .

THE THIRD ARGVMENT.

CHAP. XX.

VVE fee, that all naturall things do euer proceed after one and the fame manner, and do retayne one courfe and order . As the Sunne (for exaple)we obferue to ryfe, to fet, to runne, or renew his circles, and

to make with his approach and departure
the accustomed seasons of the yeare. In like
sort all sublunary bodyes to grow & decay
and one to be procreated and generated of
another (without end) to the perpetuity
or continuance of it *species* or kind. Now all
this procedure and carriage of things riseth
from the force of nature , which is accustomed to hold so perfect & constant an order.
And therefore (saith the Atheist) no other
Prouidence or Deity (besides nature) is to
be sought after, neither any rewards or punishments are to be expected . I answere; &
first say , that the Atheists of these dayes do
chiefly support themselues with this argument , as *S. Peter* prophecyed in his second
epistle c. 7. *Venient in nouissimis diebus &c.*

To the which point himselfe doth answere: to wit , that the promises of God by
the which he hath promised his etetnall
kingdome, are not to be accounted as vaine,
because they seeme to be deferred, for a long
tyme; since what is long in tyme to vs, is
most short to God : for a thousand yeares to
him (who comprehendeth *Eternity* it selfe)
is but as one day , or rather as a moment of
tyme . Againe all that procrastination and
delay proceedeth fro the benignity of God
by the which he expecteth each mans saluation . Furthermore, they erre, who affirme

me the world euer to continue in one , &
the same state ; for long since it was ouerflowed with water, and hereafter it shalbe
consumed with fyar , & then there shalbe
created new heauens and a new earth. Besides , all such things , as may seeme to proceed by force of nature , are indeed the
workes of an intelligent mynd and of Prouidence ; for these two do not impugne the
one the other ; for the motion of the heauens , the situation of the stars , the disposal
of the earth, mountaines , riuers, and seas,
the formes of liuing Creatures and plants,
as also their beginnings , increase , & propagation are the works of *Prouidence* (as a-
boue we haue fully demonstrated.)Neither
is the constancy of things incompatible or
repugnant to *Prouidence*,seing this constācy
is assigned to things by an intellectuall *Prouidence* , that they may the more commodi-
ously serue mankind , vntill the end of this
world,appointed and determined by God,
be come.

THE FOVRTH ARGVMENT.

CHAP. XXI.

THE fourth argument is taken from the
similitude of being borne, of growing,
                              increasing ,

increasing, waxing old, and dying (which
is indifferenly common to men with beasts)
as also from the conformity of corporeall
members in them both. From which consideration the Atheist argueth, that men are
absolutely & vtterly extinguished by death,
as well as vnreasonable creatures. I answere, that this illation is most inconsequēt,
for although man, in respect of his affections or passions of the mind, be like to beasts;
yet with referēce to the nature of his soule,
he is infinitly more excellent, then they are.
In which consideration man approacheth
more neere to God and incorporeall spirits,
then to beasts; And therefore it is no won-
der, if the body being corrupted, the soule
remayneth immortall. But this argument
rather belōgeth to the second booke, wherof the subiect is, touching the Immortality
of the soule; though secondarily and by way
of consequence only, it impugneth the nature of Prouidence.

THE FIFTH ARGVMENT.

CHAP. XXII.

I F there be a *Diuine Power*, it is credible,
that it doth not intermeddle with humane affaires; but being happy and blessed

T   in

in it felfe, is content to enioy its owne *Eterni-*
ty, and to be freed from the cares of men.
This may be probably coniectured, both
becaufe it may feeme vnworthy of fuch a
maiefty to defcend to fo bafe and vile matters; as alfo in that he being bleffed in himfelfe, feeth nothing out of it felfe; and laftly
becaufe the vndertaking the charge of any
fuch matters cannot be aduantageous or beneficiall vnto him.

I anfwere, that in this fort, *Epicurus,*
Lucretius, *Pliny*, and fome others of the ancients did difpute, who meafured God by
the narrow ftraits of their owne vnderftan-
dings. And certainly, if the *Supreme Intelli-*
gence, or *God* were a limited and bounded
nature, and had not an infinit power of vnderftanding, this former reafon might feeme
probable. For then it would follow, that it
were better for God not to attend to humane affaires; both becaufe he could not
without moleftation and diftraction performe the charge, *tam multiplicis & triftis mi-*
niftery, (as Pliny faith) *of fo multiplicious, and*
vngratefull a miniftery, *or function* ; as alfo
in that this labour would call him from
better and more pleafing bufines: but this
conceite of God is ouer groffe and dull; and
vnworthy of him : for as the *Diuine Effence*
is infinite, in whome euery thing is contayned

ned *eminenter*, after an eminent and peculiar manner; fo his vnderftanding is infinite, extending it felfe to euery intelligible
thing, and this without labour, or paine,
but only by the neceffity of his owne nature. Neither doth the multiplicity of bufines hinder his attention to particulars; for
he as perfectly confidereth euery particular
thing, as if it only were propofed vnto him;
feing to euery fuch particular he fendeth
forth an infinite beame or light of vnderftanding. The holy Scripture infinuateth
this point moft excellently in many places,
and efpecially in the 23. of *Ecclefiafticus* in
thefe words: *Oculi domini decies millies &c.*
The eyes of the Lord are 10000. *tymes brighter,*
then the Sunne, beholding all the wayes of men,
and confidering the moft fecret parts. That is, all
things whatfoeuer which lye hid & latent
in the moft fecret corners of the Heart.

Therefore this confideration or care of
fmall things is not vnworthy the *Diuine Ma-*
iefty, but very worthy, or rather it is neceffary; fince otherwife it would follow, that
God fhould be ignorant of many things.
And though fuch things, and diuers of mans
actions be but bafe, fordid, and vyle, yet the
vnderftanding and iudgment of them is not
bafe and vyle, neither is the reafon or nature of **Iuftice** vile, by the which a fitting

T 2   retri-

retribution or reward is allotted vnto them.

Neither is it preiudiciall, that God is in himſelfe moſt fully bleſſed; ſince this only proueth, that he taketh not the care of things to the end, that he might become more bleſſed or happy thereby, or that he might reape ſome benefit by ſuch his doing; but it proueth not abſolutly, that he endeauoureth nothing out of himſelfe. For becauſe he is *Summum bonum*, and the fulnes of all goodnes, as containing in himſelfe *eminenter* all goodnes wharſoeuer; it was moſt conuenient, that he ſhould not keepe this fountaine of goodnes ſhut vp within himſelfe; but ſhould ſuffer it to flow into his creatures, according to the ſeuerall degrees & kinds of things, and the meaſure of the capacity of euery one, by creating, framing, conſeruing, and directing ech thing to its peculiar end. For that ſaying is moſt true: *Bonum eſt ſui diffuſiuum. Goodnes is of a ſpreading and dilating nature.* Therefore no want, nor expectation of any priuate benefit, inuited God to create and preſerue things, but only Gods owne ſupereminent goodnes: to wit, that his goodnes might be diffuſed into things created, according to the nature of euery one of them, and might be communicated with them. To conclude this point, it is fully and copiouſly proued aboue, that, God

God hath a knowledge and care of the least creatures that are, as of mice, gnats, wormes and the like; then with how much more reason is he to shroud man vnder the wings of his Prouidence, who in regard of his Soule beareth a great conformity & resemblance with God?

It may be heere replyed, That God knoweth (indeed) what men do, thinke, or say, but yet he taketh no care of these things; Like vnto potent and mighty Princes, who in regard of the security of their state, little respect, what the Communalty speake of them. But in answere hereof, I say, this is most absurdly spoken : for seeing man is the worke of God, in whose soule he hath implanted the lawes of Iustice, and of all vertue, it is a charge (euen in reason) peculiarly incumbent and belonging to him, to see, that man liueth according to those lawes; for the workeman ought euer to be most solicitous and carefull, that his worke be perfect; the Lawgiuer, that the lawes prescribed may be obserued by his subiects; And finally, the Parents, how the children do beare and carry themselues. Now, God is the parent and Father of all.

No man will commend that architect, who leaueth a pallace builded by himselfe ynfinished and neglected, so as it cannot be

seruiceable

ſeruiceable for dwelling : Neither is that Lawgiuer to be prayſed, who (though he hath ſet downe many wholeſome lawes) is careleſſe of the execution of them, permitting all things at the freedome and liberty of the ſubiects. Finally, that father is much to be reprehended, who taketh no care for the education and bringing vp of his children. How much leſſe then are the proceedings of that God to be approued, who ſhould ſhew a dereliction, and open neglect of ſo worthy a worke made by himſelfe, and ſhould free himſelfe of al care of humane affaires; eſpecially ſeing with great facility, & without any labour he could gouerne and ſterne them? To conclude, what Prince is he, who is indifferét how his ſubiects beare themſelues in his ſight and preſence, what they ſpeake, or what they do, whether they obſerue or violate his lawes, whether they affect him with honour or contumely, with praiſes or conuitious and railing inuectiues? Yea what priuate man is ſo rude and brutiſh who is not ſenſible of honours & diſgraces? But now God is euery where preſent, heareth all things, ſeeth all things, penetrateth into all the ſecrets of the heart; for all things whatſoeuer are done in his eye ſight & preſence. Therfore it is madnes to thinke, that God is not touched, offended, and delighsed ted with the words, deedes, & thoughts of men: for by how much his maiesty, wisdome, and power is greater, and how much more worthy are his benefits bestowed vpon vs; so much the more sharpely and feelingly he considereth all iniuryes and transgressions of his lawes, and will in due time take iust reuenge for the same.

Thus farre I haue disputed of the *Prouidence of a supreme and diuine power*, and of the being of the said power. And heere this first booke shall end. The second followeth, which is of the *Immortality of the Soule.*

THE

THE SECOND
BOOKE.
WHEREIN

Is proued the Immortality of the Soule.

CHAP. I.

N the former booke we haue demonstrated, that there is a *God*, and a *diuine Prouidence*; In this second the *Immortality of the soule* is to be proued. For these two Articles are in themselues so linked together, as that they do reciprocally presuppose the one the other; for admitting the one for true, the other doth ineuitably follow. For if there be a *God* and a *Prouidence*, it is necessary, that the Soule after

ter this life be *immortal*, that it may be rewarded according to its merits; and if the Soule doth liue after death, it then muſt needes be, that there is a *God*, and a *Prouidence*, which is to diſpenſe to euery one anſwerably to the deſerts of ech mans life, as incidétally we haue ſhewed out of *Chryſoſtome*. Againe, ſuppoſing that there is no Prouidence or deity, then is the immortality of the Soule taken away; and ſuppoſing no immortality of the ſoule, then is the being of a Deity denyed; of which point we ſhall heereafter ſpeake. Now becauſe this ſentence of the *Soules Immortality* may be fortifyed and ſtrengthned with many other reaſons; and that there are not few, who do doubt thereof, although perhaps they may ſeeme, not altogether to doubt of a *deity*, or of a *Prouidence*; I hould it worthy the labour to diſcuſſe this point more elaborately and particulerly.

And here we diſpute of the Soule of mã, not of beaſts, for it is euident, that this is mortall and corruptible, ſince it deſireth nothing, nor repoſeth its delight in any thing, but what belongeth to the benefit and pleaſure of the body. Therefore that the ſoule of man (which as it is endued with vnderſtanding and freewill, is called *Animus*, or *Mens*) is immortall, may be demonſtrated

monſtrated by many arguments, which we
will here briefly and clearly ſet downe.

And firſt, if authority ſhould ſway or de-
termyne the point herein, it is certaine, that
whoſoeuer haue bene at any tyme noted
for eminency of wiſedome, haue belieued
the ſoule of man to be immortall : to wit
the *Sagi*, and wiſemen among the Hebre-
wes or Iewes, among the *Chaldeans*, the
Egiptians with their *Triſmegiſtus Mercurius*,
among the *Indians*, the *Gaules* (whom they
called *Druides*) In like ſort the *Pithagorians*,
the *Platonicks* (with their firſt Maiſters) &
the *Stoicks* vnanimouſly maintayned the
Soules Immortality, though diuers of them
were deceaued in this, that they thought al
the Soules of men to be certaine partes or
particles taken frō *Anima mūdi*, or the Soule
of the world (which they ſaid was God) &
that they were to be diſſolued in the conflagration and burning of the world, and
being then diſſolued they were to returne
to their ſimple forme, to wit, into the *ſoule
of the world* ; like as mixted bodies are reſolued into the Elements, of which they are
framed. What *Ariſtotle* thought herein is
ſomewhat doubtfull, becauſe he ſpeaketh
variouſly and vncertainly ; yet in his ſecōd
booke de *ortu animalium* c. 3. he thus writeth : *Solam mentem* &c. *Only the ſoule of Man
entreth*

entreth into the body from without , and it only is
a certaine diuine thing ; and the reason hereof is ,
because the operation or working of the body doth
not communicate it selfe , with the operation of
the Soule . Now the soules of other liuing
Creatures he affirmeth to be ingendred in
the matter through the force of the seed , in
that all their operations depend vpon the
body. Now heere he euidently teacheth ,
that mans Soule doth not depend of the
body ; and therefore it is not ingendred by
the vertue of the seed , but proceedeth from
without . Vpon which ground or reason
diuers followers of *Aristotle* do ascrybe the
sentence of the Soules immortality to *Ari-*
stotle. To conclude all men whosoeuer ,
that haue bene illustricus and markable either for sanctity of life, the guift of Prophecy , or working of miracles , haue euidetly
and indubiously houlden the Soules Immortality ; and who haue denyed the
same , were for the most part most impious
and wicked men, as the Epicureans, & the
Atheists.

Now if this point should be discussed by
Philosophicall reasons, the aduerse opinion
would tynd small firmnes therin ; seing that
reason, wherupon it chiefly grounds it selfe
is most weake. This reason is taken from
the similitude of bodyes , which is found
betwene

The ar-
gument
of the
Contra-
ry opini-
on .

betwene Man and Beaſt. For we ſee (ſay the Patrons of this heatheniſh opiniō) that men and beaſts are conceaued, formed, borne, nouriſhed, do alſo increaſe, grow old, and dye after one and the ſame máner. In like ſort they conſiſt of the like parts of the body, both internall and externall, which like parts haue the like vſes in them both; Therefore (conclude they) that whē a beaſt dyeth and breatheth out his laſt, the Soule vaniſheth & euapourateth it ſelfe into nothing, nor any thing of it remaineth after life; ſo alſo it may ſeeme to be ſaid, that man dying, his ſoule alſo dyeth, and turneth into nothing.

But this reaſon is moſt feeble, and of no force, for though there be a great affinity betwene the ſoule of Man (as it is endued with reaſon, & is called *Mens*) & the ſoule of beaſts, the difference is infinite; frō the which great diſparity, we may deſeruedly gather, that the Soule of man, as being of a high and diuine order or nature, dyeth not; though that of beaſts is abſolutly extinguiſhed euen with the body. For beaſts do not perceaue in any ſort thoſe things, which belong to men; neither is there any communication or commerce of buſines or deliberation betwene man and them. As for example, dogs, and horſes know not
　　　　　　　　　　　　　whether

whether their maister be rich, or poore,
noble or ignoble, old or young, healthful
or diseased, maryed or vnmaryed, vertuous
or wicked, an *Italian* or a *Germane*. None
of these (i say) do beasts vnderstád or make
difference of, whereupon it folioweth, that
they neither conceaue griefe, nor ioy of
those thinges, which happen to men.
Againe they see the Sunne, the Moone,
trees, houses, cittyes and villages, but they
know not, nor thinke what they are ; to
what end they are directed, or from whéce
& how they proceed. All their knowledge
is restrayned to few things; to wit, to those
things, as are pleasing, or displeasing to
their nature. Of these only they iudge, and
this after a confused and brutish manner,
conceauing them vnder the shew and title
of being profitable or disprofitable, conue-
nyent or inconuenyent; for they loue not
their maister for any other respect, but because by the help of their phantasy they
apprehend him vnder the shew of profit,
in that he giueth them meat, or the like. In
like sort on the contrary part the sheepe
flyeth the wolfe, for no other cause, but by
reason that by instinct of nature he conceaueth him as his enemy.

Therfore seing beasts haue a knowledge
so imperfect and limited, and apprehend
nothing,

nothing, but what appertaineth to the cõ-
seruation of their bodyes and lyues, nor are
delighted, or grieue at any thing, but in
respect as that thing affecteth their body
well or euill; it hereupon manifestly followeth, that the Soule of beasts doth perish
together with their body.

For if the soule of a beast cannot eleuate
it selfe (in knowing and apprehending) to
some thing, which is aboue the body and
which properly belongeth to a spirituall
nature; it is euident, that that soule is not
spirituall, nor eleuated aboue its body, but
altogether immersed and drowned in a
corporeall and bodily nature. For the substance of any thing is knowne from it, operation; and the operation from the obiect,
about which it is conuersant, or busied.
Therefore seeing this Obiect, and its *ratio
formalis*, or the true & natiue reason(which
is the profit or hurt comming to the body)
doth only respect the body; it must of necessity be granted, that the substance of the
soule in beasts is tyed and restrayned to the
body. But this point is farre otherwise in
Man.

THE

THE FIRST REASON, PROVING THE
Soules Immortality.

CHAP. II.

THE firſt reaſon may bee, in that the *knowledge of the Soule* is altogether illimitable. For it conceaueth and apprehendeth all kinds of things, all degrees of natures; neither doth it apprehéd only things, which are, but alſo things, which are not; for it forgeth in the vnderſtanding any thing, and frameth therein new worlds. It alſo conceaueth the vniuerſall reaſons of things, as they are abſtracted from particulars, from ſenſible matter, from place and tyme, and contemplateth the ſame, as they are in themſelues. It ſearcheth into the reaſons, cauſes, effectes, and proprietyes of al things, and finally iudgeth of all things. Al which conſiderations are manifeſt arguments, that the Soule of Man is not immerſed in the body, but that it is a ſpirituall ſubſtance ſeparable from the body: ſince all theſe actions and operations beare no reference to the benefit or profit of the body; but are ornaments only of the mind. In like ſort the very Obiects of the former operations are not apprehended, as they are advantagious

The knowledge of man is illimitable.

vantagious to the body or ſenſe (to wit of
taſt & feeling)but they are apprehended according to their proper reaſons; as they are
true and conformable to vniuerſall and e-
ternall principles or reaſons, in which reſpect, they belong only to the mind, or
ſoule, and not in any ſort to the body.

THE SECOND REASON,
Proouing the ſame.

CHAP. III.

TH E ſecond reaſon may be taken from
Mans deſire, which is in like ſort infinite
and boundleſſe; for the ſoule doth not only
deſire ſuch things, as belong to the body, to
wit, to ſatisfy their ſenſe of taſting and feeling (as beaſts do) but it ſtretcheth it ſelfe
forth to euery truth, deſiring the knowledge and contemplation of euery verity.
Neither is it enlarged only to ech truth,
but alſo to euery thing that is good; to the
which goodnes the appetite and loue of all
things, is finally directed. For all particular
things whatſoeuer do affect and loue (after
a certaine manner) that, which is beſt ſorting, and agreable to their natures. Now
man comprehendeth al thoſe things within
his loue, ſeeing he deſireth not only thoſe
things,

things, which are profitable to himselfe, but
wisheth to euery thing, whatsoeuer is best
fitting to it, and (as much as in him lyeth)
procureth the same. Therefore he coueteth
both to himselfe and al other things besides,
what is best agreable to them: to himselfe
he wisheth those things in knowledge, or as
the Philosophers do speake, in *esse cognito*; to
all other particular things in *esse reali*, that
they may really and truly enioy them. Here
then appeareth how much the power of de-
siring in man is eleuated & aduanced aboue
the matter & condition of his body.

THE THIRD REASON.

CHAP. IIII.

THE same point is further confirmed
from the *delights and pleasures*, wherewith the Soule solaceth her selfe. For she is
delighted chiefly with the contemplation
of truth, and with truth it selfe: She is delighted with the pulchritude and beauty of
all things, and in admyring the art & skill,
which appeareth in euery thing; She is delighted with proportions and mathemati-
call disciplines; She is delighted with the
workes of Religion, Piety, Iustice, and the
exercise of other vertues; Finally she is de-

lighted

lighted with fame, honour, glory, rule and domination: All thefe are proper goods of the Soule, and are fo efteemed by man, as that in compare hereof he contemneth and vilifyeth al profits & pleafures of the body.

Therefore feeing the capacity and the largenes of the foule of man is fo ample and great, that it comprehendeth all things, and compaffeth about (as it were) all the latitude, altitude, and profundity of *Ens* in generall, containing it within it felfe; feing alfo the foule hath her proper motions or knowledge, her defires, loues, delights and peculiar ornaments; none of all which belongeth to the benefit of the body, but all are touching fpirituall obiects, or at leaft concerning fuch things, which are eftranged from the benefits or pleafures of the body; and laftly feeing the Soule efteemeth all thefe things farre more then any corporall goods; It is therefore moft perfpicuous and euident, that the Soule is of a farre higher & more worthy difpofition, then the body; & of fuch a diuine nature, as that it dependeth not at all of the commerfe, or entercourfe, which fhe hath with the flefh.

THE

THE FOVRTH REASON.

CHAP. V.

THis verity is also warranted from the dominion which the Soule hath ouer the body, and from the soules enioying of *Freewill.* For the Soule doth so direct, gouerne and ouerrule the body in her affections and passions, as that neither the expectation of rewards, nor the feare of torments can force the body to say, or do any thing, then what the Soule willeth; which point is euident both from many examples, as also from the testimony of *Iosephus* in his small worke or booke bearing this title: *Quod ratio affectuum sit Domina*; Now of this matter no other reason can be assigned, but because the Soule doth not depend of the body, but is *sui iuris*, of its owne freedome, liberty, and and finall determination; wherupon it riseth, that the soule so valueth those things, which appertaine to the body, as if they did not belong vnto her; she being contented and fully satisfyed with her owne proper goods and delights: but the contrary falleth out in beasts, for seing their Soule is altogeather mancipated and enthralled to the body, depending of it in regard of her owne

essence,

essence, she is necessarily (and as it were violently) carryed to such things, as are pleasing and beneficiall to the body, and flyeth
all those things, which seeme aduerse and
distastfull to it; and hence it is that the Soule
in beasts hath neyther her passions nor externall motions in her owne power, and at
her owne command.

THE FIFTH REASON.

CHAP. VI.

IF the the Soule should haue all her dependance of the body, & could not consist, the body being once extinct; then should
she haue against nothing, a greater horrour
and auersion, then against *Death*; nor would
she prize any thing at so high a rate, which
willingly she would not loose for the preuenting of *Death*; for *Death* of the body, de-
priuing the soule (supposing it to be mortal)
of all good, should become her chiefest infelicity and euill, and present life her greatest
good and happynesse. And therefore it followeth, that the soule should feare nothing
so much as *Death*, and on the other side affect, desire, and defend nothing, so much,
as present life. But now daily experience
teacheth the contrary: for many do make so
                                              small

ſmall an eſtimate of life, (though abounding
with all the goods of fortune) as that they
willingly ſpend it for prayſe, fame, liberty,
auoyding of reproach and diſhonour, and for
the exerciſe of vertue. Yea ſome there are,
who for the declyning and ſhuning of diſgrace, or griefe and affliction of mynd, or
for the purchaſing of a very little reputation, ſticke not to become their owne parri-
cides & murtherers. So much more do thoſe
things, which belong to the ſoule or mind,
preponderate & ouerballance al that, which
appertaines to the body.

THE SIXTH REASON.

CHAP. VII.

SO great is the capacity and largneſſe of
the ſoule or mind, as that no riches, no
dignities, no Kingdomes, not the Empire
of the whole world, no pleaſures, briefly
no finite and limitable good can quench her
inſatiable thirſt and deſire; but to this end it is
needfull, that ſhe enioy ſome one immenſe,
infinite, and boundleſſe good, and ſuch as
containeth in it ſelfe by way of eminency
or preheminécy the fulnes of all good whatſoeuer. This the Prophet *Dauid* inſinuateth
Pſalm. 16. when he ſaith: *Satiabor cùm &c.*

I shalbe satisfye! and filled, when thy glory shall
appeare, as if he would say, no other thing
can giue me full contentment, except the
manifestation of thy glory, which is an infinite and illimitable good. And to the same
end (1) S. *Austin saith: Fecisti nos &c. Thou hast*
made vs like vnto thee, and our hart is vnquyet,
till it rest in thee. Now if the Soule were restrained to the narrownes of the body, it
should not be capable of an infinite good,
neither should her desire be extended to a-
ny thing, but what were conducing and accommodated to a corporall life; as it appeareth in other liuing creatures. For the Body
and the matter doth restraine the appetite,
desire, and capacity of the forme. From
whence it proceedeth, that by how much
the forme of any body is more materiall, by
so much it is more narrow and lesse capable;
but the more spirituall and more eleuated
the forme is, the more ample and the more
enlarged it is, and extendeth it selfe to more
things, thereby the better to perfect it selfe.
For bodyes wanting life (as stones and metals) as also their formes, because they are
materiall and grosse in the highest degree,
do desire nothing out of themselues, neither
do they endeauour any thing to further
their perfection, but rest in themselues quiet
and dead. But **Plants** (because their forme is
more

(1) Lib. 1.
Confess. c.
1.

more pure and perfect) do couet (after their manner) nourishment, and do attract it from without, as also they change it, distributing it through the whole body, and conuerting it into their owne substance: Besides they send forth flowers, fruits, and seedes; & so they continue dayly working to the augmentation, conseruation, perfection, & propagation of themselues; but because they haue no sense or feeling of their nourishment, they therfore receaue neither pleasure nor griefe thereby.

Liuing Creatures (in that their forme is in a higher degree) do not only performe all those operations, which plants do; but with all they haue knowledge and sense of their nourishment; yea they mooue themselues to it, they seeke it, from the vse of it they take pleasure, and from the want of it they receaue griefe and molestation. Notwithstanding all their knowledge, and affection or liking, is limited within certaine narrow bounds; for it only extendeth it selfe to the profit or hurt of their bodyes; so as they apprehend no other thing, they couet and fly no other thing, they are delighted and grieue at no other thing; which is a manifest demonstration, that their Soule depends only of their body: for their soule therfore perceaues and desires nothing, but

V 4 what

what conduceth to the reft & good of their
corporall life, becaufe their foule dependeth
of the felicity of their body. Aboue all other
liuing Creatures, is man indued with a reafonable foule or mind, whofe knowledge &
affection is not limited to things belonging
to the body, but is altogeather illimitable,
extending it felfe to euery truth & to euery
kind of good, (as is aboue faid) both which
beare no reference or refpect to the body;
And from hence it followeth, that the Souls
capacity or ability either in knowing, defi-
ring, or in taking delight is infinite; no o-
therwife then the ability of fpirits or celeftiall Intelligences, which is an vnanfwerable
argument that the foule of man is not wholly depending of the body, and necefarily
tyed to the fame.

This point is further thus confirmed :
Subftantiæ feparatæ (as they are called) that is
incorporeall fubftances, do therfore enioy
the force of vnderftanding, and do extend
themfelues *ad totum ens*, to euery thing; and
ad totum verum & bonum, to euery verity &
goodnes, becaufe they are fimple formes e-
leuated aboue all matter, & not depending
Ariftotle of the fame, as Philofophy teacheth. And
12. Meta- hence it is, that there is no fpirituall fub-
phyf. c. 9. ftance, but euen in that refpect it is intelligent and vnderftanding. Therfore feing the
Soule

Soule of man is endued with the faculty of vnderstanding, and is in her selfe of that expansion and largnes, as that she stretcheth her selfe to the whole latitude of *Ens* in generall; that is, to euery truth, and euery thing that is good (by vnderstanding what is true, and affecting and louing what is good) no otherwise then spirituall and separated substances do; it followeth, that the soule doth not depend vpon any matter or bodily substance. For where there is *effectus adæquatus,* there is also *causa adæquata;* that is, where there is a proper and peculiar effect, there also is to be found a proper and peculiar cause, from whence the effect riseth. But in the Soule of Man the effect is found, to wit, the force of vnderstanding, and the capacity of euery truth and euery good; therefore the cause also is to be found, that is, a spirituall nature independent of matter or of a body.

THE SEAVENTH REASON.

CHAP. VIII.

THere are in the nature of things some liuing formes, which are separated from all matter both in their essence and manner of existence, with the Philosophers

do cal *Intelligences,* or *subſtantias ſeparatas,* ſeparated ſubſtances, and Chriſtians tearme
them *Spirits,* or *Angels.* There are alſo ſome
others, which both in their Eſſence and
exiſtence are altogether tyed and immerſed
in the matter, wherin they are, and ſuch
are the Soules of beaſts. Therfore there
ought to be ſome other formes betwene the
former two; which in regard of their Eſſence, may not depend of their body, that
ſo they may be like vnto ſpirits or Angels;
yet for their exiſtence (that is, that they
may exiſt after a conuenient maner) they
are to haue a body, that therin they may a-
gree with the ſoules of beaſts, and theſe are
the ſoules of men. This argument is confirmed from analogy and proportion; in that
this degree of things ſeemeth to be beſt ſit-
ting, leaſt otherwiſe we ſhould paſſe from
one extreme to another without a meane;
to wit, from a nature abſolutly mortal &
drowned in a body, to a nature abſolutly
immortal and ſeparated from a body; therfore betwene theſe two, there is to be a nature, partly mortal, and partly immortal:
mortall according to the body, and immortal according to the Soule: And the very
Soule it ſelfe according to its Eſſence is to
be immortal, and to be ranged with ſpitits;
though according to the manner of its exiſtence,

ftence, and as informing a mortal body, it
is to be like the foules of beafts. For the v-
nion of the Soule of man with the body, as
alfo the informing and the viuification (as
I may tearme it) of the whole body decayeth no leffe, then in beafts. And thus it
falleth out, that man containeth in himfelfe
the powers and faculties of both the ex-
tremes, I meane of fpirits and beafts; being
for the body and fenfe, like vnto beaftes; for
the foule, to fpirits or intelligences. Vpon
which occafion the Platonicks do cal man
the *Horizon* of the whole *Vniuerfe* of things
created. For feing the vniuerfe of things
doth confift (as it were) of two *Hemifpheres,*
to wit of a fpiritual nature, and a corporal
nature; Man partaking of both thefe ex-
tremes, doth ioyne the fpiritual nature (being the higher *Hemifphere*) with the corporal nature, the lower *Hemifphere.* For
this very fame reafon alfo, Man is called
μικροκόσμος, that is, the leffer world, as cō-
prehending within himfelfe al the degrees
of the *vniuerfe,* no otherwife, then the grea-
er world containeth.

T H E

THE EIGHT REASON

CHAP. IX.

FOR the more acceſſion of reaſons in this point, it may be alledged, that there is a greater aſſociation and affinity in nature betwene the Soule of man and ſpirits, or Angels, then betwene man and beaſts: For as ſpirits or Angels haue their knowledge and deſire circumſcribed, or encompaſſed with no limits, and are delighted with the beauty of truth and vertue; in like ſort is the ſoule or mynd of man; In ſo much that in this reſpect there is no diſparity betwene a ſoule and a ſpirit, though there be a difference in the perfection of the operations, proceeding from the vnderſtanding and the will in them both. Now the ſenſe, knowledge, and affection or deſire of beaſts is reſtrained to their feeding, and to venery. Furthermore the Soule of man hath ſociety and familiarity with ſpirits, conuerſeth with them, intreateth help and ayde from them, diſcourſeth, diſputeth, and iudgeth of their ſtates, and wiſheth her ſelfe to be like in dignity to them: But no like affinity is diſcerned betweene man and beaſts; for beaſts can neither apprehend nor deſire the

ſtate

ſtate of man, neither is there any communication of Counſell or aduiſe betweene thē. Therefore ſo farre forth, as belongeth to the condition of Mortality and Immortality, it is not to be wondred, if mans Soule doth rather follow the condition and nature of ſpirits (betweene whome there is ſo great a ſimilitude and reſemblance) then of beaſts from whome the Soule doth ſo infinitely differ.

THE NINTH REASON.

CHAP. X.

I F the Soule could not conſiſt without the body, then ſhould the ſoules chiefeſt felicity be placed in a corporall life & pleaſures of the body, and her greateſt miſery in the affliction and death of the body; vpon the force of which inference the Sect of *Epicures* and others (who did hold the ſoule to be vtterly extinguiſhed with the body) taught the chiefeſt good to reſt in the pleaſures of the body. This is further made euident from the teſtimonyes of thoſe, who in the ſecond of the booke of *VViſdome* conclude, that during the tyme of this life, we are to giue our ſelues wholly to pleaſure, holding this to be mans felicity, in that no-

 thing

thing remaineth (ſay they) after this life ; as
alſo irō the like ſetēce of others , who in the
22. of Eſay ſay : *Comedamus & bibamus &c. Let
vs eate & drinke, for to morrow we ſhall dye.* But
if this ſtation were true , then were it laudable in a man to indulge and pamper his
belly , and ſtudiouſly to affect and ſeeke after , whatſoeuer may conduce to the ſame
end ; and the warrant hereof ſhould be, becauſe it is moſt laudable (for all things) and
particularly for man to follow its moſt ſupreme good or felicity, and to enioy it at all
tymes.

But now iuſt contrary hereto , we
find , that this coporall ſenſuality of eating and drinking , and the like , is holden as a thing diſhonourable in man ,
and vnworthy his nature , as alſo that
thoſe , who abandon themſelues wholly to
their corporall pleaſure, are ranged among
brute beaſts : for nothing draweth more
neere to the nature of beaſts , then the pleaſure of the body conſiſting in the ſenſes of
taſt and feeling. And therfore as *Tully* witneſſeth in his booke *de ſeneĉute, Architas Ta-
rentinus* was accuſtomed thus to ſay : *Nullam
capitaliorem peſtem, quàm corporis voluptatem à
natura hominibus eſſe datam : That Nature had
not giuen to man a more capitall plague , then the
pleaſure of the body.*

Againe ;

Againe, if the chiefe felicity of man did belong to our corporall life; then were it lawfull for the auoyding of death and torments (at the commanding and forcing of a tyrant) to commit periury, and blasphemy, to worship Idols, and finally to relinquish and shake hands with all piety, iustice, vertue and truth: for it is the law of nature, and of it selfe ingrafted in al men, that nothing is to be preferred before *Summum bonum,* or the chiefest felicity, and that is to be imbraced before all other things; & that on the other side, nothing is more to be auoyded, then *Summum malum,* the chiefest infelicity. From which position or ground it riseth, that in euery euent, wherin is necessarily endágered the losse of our greatest good, or of some other lesser good, we are taught euen by nature and reason, that euery inferiour good whatsoeuer, is to be willingly lost, for the retaining of the chiefest good; and euery lesser euil to be endured, for the auoyding of the greatest euil. But now what thing can be imagined more absurd in it selfe, or more vnworthy a man, then that for the preuenting of death any flagitious or heynous wickednes whatsoeuer may and ought to be committed?

THE TENTH REASON.

CHAP. XI.

ANATVRE which is intelligent, and indued with an vnderſtanding is the worthieſt nature of all others, which are in the world; this is proued, in that, ſuch a nature is capable of all natures; for it comprehendeth them all, it vſeth them al, and applyeth them to its owne benefit; for it taketh profit not only from terrene and earthly things, but alſo frō celeſtial things, as from the light, darkenes, day, night, wynds, ſhowers, heates, coldes, and from the foure Elements themſelues. Therefore a nature enioying a mind, reaſon, and vnderſtanding, is in this world, as in its owne houſe, furniſhed with al kind of prouiſion, moſt fitting either for vſe, benefit, or delight. Hence it is gathered, that it is an abſurd opinion, to maintayne this nature vtterly to periſh and to be mortall; ſince ſo it ſhould follow, that what is moſt excellēt in this world, and what hath ſole dominiō ouer other things, and to whome all other things, are ſubiect and ſerucieable, ſhould dye and become abſolutly extinct; an infe-

rence

is warranted with no fhew, or colour of reafon; for if the earth, fea, and ftarres (al which were created for the vfe of this reafonable or intelligent nature) do neuer decay, but continue eternall, and for euer permament, the with what tecture or pretext of reafon, can it be auerred, that this intelligent nature, which is the end, fcope, and miftreffe of the former, fhould become mortall and paffible? If the Soule of man (which is this intelligent Nature) be fo worthy in it felfe, that thofe things (which neuer fhall decay, and be ruined) were created for its feruice; then how can it ftand with any probability, that it felfe fhall perifh and refolue to nothing? Certainly it is altogether vniuft and vnlawful to affirme, that nature to be mortall, to the which, things, that are immortall, become feruiceable.

THE ELEVENTH REASON.

CHAP. XII.

THE nature of man (according to his Soule) is infinitly more worthy, then all other Creatures; for it is of a higher degree, then they are, and extendeth it felfe to infinite things, (as appeareth out of the
X   former

former considerations;) therefore it followeth , that the *Summum bonum* or chiefe felicity of Mans nature ought to be infinitely more excellent, then the *summum bonum* of beasts . In like fort the action of Más foule , by the which it apprehendeth and feeleth its felicity , and the pleasure , that it taketh from thence , ought infinitly to excell the action and pleasure of beasts in the fruition of their felicity . For such ought the proportion to be betweene the obiects , betweene the operations , & betweene the pleasures, which is betweene the natures and the facultyes, by the which the obiects are apprehended and perceaued . But now if the Soule of man be extinguished together with the body , then nothing is attended on with greater calamity , then Mans nature , since almost all the kinds of beasts would be more happy then Man. For in this life mans nature stands obnoxious and subiect to innumerable afflictions , from which beasts are most free . For it is incessantly solicited with cares, vexed with feares, pyneth away through enuy, worne out with griefe , burned with desires, alwayes anxious , sorrowing and complaining, neuer content with its owne state, nor enioying any true tranquility of mind. Besides it often endureth pouerty , banishments, prisons,

fons, feruitude, infamy, the yoake of Ma-
trimony, bringing vp of children, the loſſe
of temporall goodes, a repentance of actiõs
paſt, a ſolicitude and care of things to come;
many labours and paines taking, that the
poore fleſh may be maintained, and that it
may be defended from the iniuryes of the
ayre and weather; to conclude it is encompaſſed with ſo many ſuſpitions, frauds, ca-
lumnyes, diſeaſes, languors and ſickneſſes,
as that it was worthily ſaid of one ;

——— ἀκ ἔϛιν ἀ θὶν δεινὸν ἀ̓δὲ συμφορὰ
H᾿ς ἀκ ἀς φέϱοιῆ ἄχθ⊙ ἀνθϱάπων γέν⊙ . That is,

  Nothing is ſo grieuous, and full of calamity,
  The weight wherof mans nature cãnot beare.

But now beaſts are freed and deliuered
almoſt from all theſe former calamityes, &
liue in great peace, quyetnes, and liberty:
for they are not vexed with any cares, with
any feares of future euill, or with any diſ-
contents through aduerſe fortune; Neither
are they ſolicitous of things to come, nor
repent them of actions paſt, nor diſmayed
at any imminent dangers; They are not
moued with ambition or enuy, but reſt
quyet & peaceable in the enioying of their
owne ſtates.

Beſides nature doth prouide them of all
things neceſſary for their lyues, without
any labour or toyle on their part. Yf we

      X 3   conſider

confider the length of their age, we find that many liuing creatures liue a longer tyme, then Man; as *Harts*, *Elephants*, & *Crowes*. If, the place or Region wherein they liue, what may be more defired, then to liue in a high and eminent place farre diftant from the durt or myre of the earth, and to paffe through a great part of the ayre by flying in a moft fhort tyme? If the habit or cloathing of the body, it is farre more commodious to be couered with haire or feathers (which are no hinderance to the agility of the body) then to be oppreffed with the weight of outward veftments: fiually if the pleafures of the body be compa-red, it is certaine, that beafts do vfe them more daily and freely, then Man; fince they are giuen to their feeding by the fpace of whole dayes, & more frequently exercife the act of copulation, and this without fe-are or fhame: from all which it is moft cle-arly gathered, that other liuing Creatures are far more happy then man, if the Soule of man doth prefently dye vpon the diffolutiõ of the body from it.

THE TVVEFTH REASON.

CHAP. XIII.

It would not only follow from the former reason, that all other liuing Creatures should be more happy, then Man; but it also would follow, that among men themselues, those should be more happy, who were more wicked, and more giuen ouer and addicted to the flesh and to sensuality; and those more vnfortunate, who contemning the pleasures of the body, do imbrace vertue and iustice ; yea the best and most holy mē should be the most miserable; who most estranging themselues from the pleasures of the body, do afflict & punish their flesh feuerall wayes. Whereupon the Apostle in the first to the Corinthians c. 15. *Si in hac vita &c. If in this life only we haue hope in Christ* (that is , if nothing remayneth after this life) *wee are of all men the most miserable*; and the reason hereof must be (according to the Apostles mind) because we are depriued of the goods & pleasure both of this life, and of the next, and further we do endure daily labours and sharpe persecutions.

THE

THE XIII. REASON.

CHAP. XIIII.

VVE see, that things are brought to that perfection, whereof they are capable; for example, Plants and all other kinds of liuing Creatures do by little and little increase, and are strengthened so farre forth, as belong both to their body, and to all the facultyes of the vegetatiue or sensitiue soule, that so at the length they may come to that height of perfection, whereof each kind of them is capable. Therfore it must needes be expected, that mans Soule should in like sort arriue and ascend to the highest top of its owne perfection: for seing these inferiour and most vyle creatures do obtaine the perfection of their owne nature, why should not then that, which is most pretious and most worthy among them all, in the end gaine the same? But this the Soule of man cannot possibly performe, except it continueth after this life, immortall. Now the perfection of Mans Soule consisteth in wisdome & vertue, with the which her chiefest powers are beautifyed & adorned, and by meanes of which, those powers obtayne their ends & chiefe perfection: But
few

few there are, who in this life giue themselues to the obtaining of wisdome, and
therefore the greatest part of men make
small or no progresse therein ; and those
who spend their tyme in the search or pur-
chasing of it, do scarcely get the hundreth
part of that abundance of wisdome, wherof
the mynd of man is capable : for though a
man should liue a thousand yeares , yet
might he daily profit and increase therein,
& yet not obtaine it in its highest measure .
Therfore it is necessary, that the Soule of
Man doth liue after the death of the body,
that in the next life (seing in this it cannot)
it may come & arryue to its perfectiō; since
otherwise in vaine should that capacity and
extension of the Soule be giuen her; in vaine
should that vnquenchbale desire of knowledge be engrafted in her ; for that capacity
and desire is in vayne, which cannot be filled and satisfyed. Besides , it is most absurd
to say, that Nature, which in the smallest &
most despicable things neuer doth any
thing without a due purpose & end, should
in the most noble creature of all, worke and
labour so much in vaine, and to no designed
drift, or proiect.

X 4   *THE*

THE XIIII. REASON.

CHAP. XV.

IT is certaine, that the Soule of man cannot know it selfe in this life , except it be very obscurely and confusedly; (euen as he which seeth a thing farre of through a cloud perceaueth it imperfectly, as not being able to discerne the colours or lineaments of it.) Now this want of the Soules perfect knowledge of it selfe , was the cause of so many different opinions of the Philosophers, touching its owne substance, some of them teaching it to be of a fiery substance; others an ayery; and some others , that it was a substance taken from the ayre & from the soule of the world (as their phrase was.) The Soule then knoweth not , either what it selfe is, or of what quality , whether a simple or pure spirit, or consisting of a most thin body; whether it hath distinct faculties and powers in it selfe , or that it performeth all her operations immediatly by it selfe; what is the power and nature of those faculties; how they performe their functions; how the obiects do meet and associate themselues with their faculties; how the organs and instruments of the senses do concurre

curre and cooperate with the animal spirits.
In these and almost all other things belonging to her selfe, the Soule is strangely blind, and diuineth, and coniectureth of them, as it were in a dreame. Therfore if the Soule doth perish togeather with the body, she neuer knoweth her selfe, but remaines ignorant thereof, both when she is first ingendred, whyle she liueth, and after her death. But now it is most fitting both in nature and reason, that sometimes she might be able to contemplate her selfe, to see and perfectly to apprehend her owne beauty, nature, and ornaments: for as nothing more clearly belongeth to the Soule, then her owne Nature, and such things as are intrinsecall and inward to her; so no knowledge is more necessary to her, then the knowledge of her selfe, and things appertaining to her; for she is most neere and deere to her selfe. Therefore it must necessarily be granted, that she is not extinguished after this life, but that, after she is once freed of the body, and of all corporall obiects (which afore she apprehended by helpe of the externall senses) and that by meanes thereof, she enioyeth her owne simplicity, then shall she see her selfe distinctly and clearly; and shall daily esteeme those her goods & ornaments, which in this life she so smally prized. For

X 5   one

one kind of vnderſtanding agrees to her,
whiles ſhe is tyed to this mortall body; another, when by meanes of the bodyes death,
ſhe ſhal be ſet at liberty, & ſhal nakedly exiſt
by her ſelfe. For while ſhe remaynes in the
body, ſhe can know nothing perfectly, but
what is corporall , and vnder a corporall
ſhew; wherupon it followeth, that ſhe cannot ſee, or know her ſelfe; but after ſhe is
once diuorced from the body, ſhe ſhall then
take the forme and manner of vnderſtanding anſwerable to ſpirits , and then ſhall
diſcerne ſpirituall things, as now ſhe apprehendeth by her eyes corporall things. For
the manner of knowing doth euer anſwere
to the manner of exiſtence, and agreeth to
the ſtate of the thing which knoweth; ſince
euery thing worketh accotding to the manner of its owne nature.

THE XV. REASON.

CHAP. XVI.

THIS corporeall World , as alſo all
things contained therein, were made
for man (as is aboue ſhewed;) for all things
are diſpoſed in that ſort, as they may beſt
ſerue to the benefit and profit of man. Thus
the world ſeemeth nothing els , then a vaſt
house

houfe furnifhed withall things neceffary, whofe inhabitant, poffeffour, or *Fructuarius* is man. So that fuppofing man were not, then were there no vfe of the world, but it fhould be, as a defart feruing only for a denne of wild beafts, and for a wood of thornes. Therfore feeing all things are firft inftituted for man, it followeth, that man is a moft excellent thing, and created for a far greater and higher end, then it can attaine in this life; for feing fo many different feruices of things, and fo wonderfull riches are prepared for man, for his better and more eafy leading of this fhort and mortall life; how can it be thought, that no good or happynes expecteth him after his death, but that his Soule vtterly decayeth with his body? Doubtlefly, this is a great argument, that he is ordained to enioy (after his emigration & paffing out of this life) a moft noble, honourable, and admirable felicity & happines.

This point is further confirmed. If the Soule doth perifh with the body, thē it followeth, that the world, and al its admirable furniture was only framed by nature, that man for a fhort feafon and tyme might liue, eate, drinke, fleepe, ingender, and then prefently for euer decay. Thus this fhould be all the good, the end, and the fruite of fo worthy and admirable a worke. But it is

not

not likely, that to so meane & small an end
the heauens should be incessantly caryed a-
bout, with such a daily motion: That the
Sunne, Moone, and Starrs should still continue their courses; that the change of day
and night, and the vicissitude or continuall
circles of tymes and seasons, as spring, summer, autumne, and winter should be ordained. Againe, that winds should blow, the
clouds should be gathered togeather, the
showers should be powred downe; that the
earth should cause so many kinds of flowers
and fruits, & should containe within its bosome such inestimable treasure; that the Sea
should bring forth such seuerall sorts of fish,
the ayre should abound with so great store
of byrds, & Nature her selfe should so pain-
fully labour in the producing of all things;
And all this to no other end, but that man
(being a mortall creature) should for a small
tyme liue in great misery, great ignorance
& prauity of mynd, & then instantly should
returne to nothing. If there be no other
end nor fruite of so wonderfull a worke, as
the world is, then in vaine is it, & all therein created; and in vayne doth Nature labour
in all her actions. For what good doth man
reape by liuing a short tyme in so many afflictions of mynd and body? since this temporall life in it selfe is not good, nor to be
                                      wished

wished for, both in regard, that it is mixed
with so many calamities, as also in that no
corporall good or benefit is for it selfe alone
to be desired. For as the body is made for the
soule; so the corporall goods are to be referred, and finally directed to the good of
the Soule. Neither is this temporall life to
be wished, as being a meanes to a greater
good, because it is presumed by these men,
who deny the immortality of the Soule,
that no such future good remaineth after
this life. *Salomon* had a feeling vnderstanding of this point, who, after he had abundantly tasted al the pleasures of this world,
did burst out into this sentence: *Vanitas va-*
nitum, & omnia vanitas. And then after: *Vidi*
cuncta &c. I saw all things, which are vnder the
Sunne; and behold all is vanity, and affliction of
spirit. Salomon also in that his booke of *Ec-*
clesiastes, prosecuteth many other points of
this nature, but in the end he (as it were)
preacheth to al men, that al the goods of
this life, delights, riches, honours, and
pleasures are to be esteemed as of no worth
or price; to wit, as they are considered in
themselues alone, and as they conduce nothing to the life to come.

I ad further, that this temporall life hath
not only in it no true good, for the which
it should be desired, but it is also intricated

and

and intangled with ſo many euils, that it
were far better, & more conuenient for mã
neuer to haue bene, then to receaue a ſoule
lyable and ſubiect vnto death. For (beſides that man is waſted away with infinite
cares, diſeaſes, and miſeries) he doth litle
or no good, or rather in lieu thereof, he cõ-
mitteth much euill, ſpending his life (for
the moſt part) in all turpitude and baſenes
of manners and conuerſation, Now let the
euill, which he perpetrateth, be ballanced
with the good he doth, and we ſhall find,
that his wickednes by infinite degrees doth
preponderate and weigh downe his vertuous actions. If ſo, how then can it be truly
conceaued, that that creature which is the
authour of ſo great euill, and worker of ſo
ſmall good, and frõ whome no future good
can be expected, ſhould be accounted as
profitable and neceſſary to the whole vniuerſe? Yea rather (as being a thing moſt
pernicious and deſtructiue) why ſhould he
not be inſtantly exterminated and baniſhed
from thence? If in a kingdome or Commõ-
wealth there be found any ony Family,
whoſe endeauours in no ſort tend to the
common good, but only reſt in the viola-
ting and breaking of the lawes of the ſaid
ſtate; it is thought neceſſary, that the ſaid
family ſhould be vtterly extirpated & rooted

ted out, as threatning (if it fhould continue)
no fmal danger and ruine to that kingdome
or commonwealth: why then (by the fame
reafon) fhould not all mankind (which be-
trampleth the law of God and nature vnder
its feet, be exiled from al this moft ample &
large Commonwealth of the whole Vniuerfe, as a profeffed enemy to iuftice and
vertue? From thefe premifes we may further conclude, that man and the world it
felfe were not only made in vayne (fince
from thence proceedeth fo fmall good) but
alfo that Nature much erred in bringing
forth mankind. For as he deferueth euil at
that ftate, who bringeth in an improfitable
nation, contemning the inftitutions and de-
crees therof; Euē fo fhould nature be much
blamed for her producing of mankind. All
which things how far diffonant and eftrā-
ged they are from reafon, who feeth not?
Therefore for the auoyding of thefe (otherwife) ineuitable abfurdities, we muft cō-
feffe, that the Soule of man remayneth after this life immortall, and that then fhe
fhalbe partaker of moft high and ineftima-
ble rewards, or els of infupportable torments, according to her different carriage
in this world.

Thou maift heere reply, that granting
the former reafon for good and fufficient,

it

it followeth, that all wicked men should be
now borne in vaine, or rather that in reaſo
they ought not be borne ; ſince their being
in the world conferreth no good or benefit
therto , but only diſhonoureth and wrongeth the ſame , abuſing nature her ſelfe , &
all the guifts of God to their owne improbity and impiety .

Whether
wicked
Men are
made in
vayne to
liue in
the
world.

I anſwere hereto, & grant that al mē in
the world, who before their deaths ſhal not
be conuerted , but ſhall leaue this world in
a finall impenitency , may (in a certaine
manner) be ſaid to be borne in vaine; ſince
they declyne and ſwarue from that principall end , whereunto they were created: &
far better it had bene for thē, neuer to haue
bene borne , then ſo to liue and dye . Yet
from this acknowledgment, it followeth
not,that all Mankind & the whole world
it ſelf ſhould be created to no purpoſe. Firſt,
becauſe many men do here liue vertuouſly,
and ſhall hereafter be partaker of infinite remuneration and reward . Now theſe men
alone are worthy , that the world ſhould
be created to their vſe , and ſerue them for
the better gayning of ſo great a good , according as the Apoſtle ſaith : *Omnia propter*
electos &c. All things are for the elect, that they
may obtaine ſaluation.

And though the number of the reprobate
be

be imcomparably greater then of the Elect; yet this is not either so few, nor of so small importance, as that God should repēt himselfe of creating the world and mankynd: for as he, who husbandeth an Orchard, & planteth in it many trees of a strange kind, of which the greater part proue dead and fruitles, the rest do bring forth good fruyt, and sufficient for the maintaining of his houshold, cannot be iustly said to haue spent his labour in vaine, but rather solaceth himselfe at the thought of his owne paines, since the excellency of the fruite recompenceth the small number; especially seing the store is able to nourish his family. The like (by way of proportion and analogy) may be conceaued and suppofed of God, who is the workeman of the world and men, who are (as it were) his engrafted plants or seedes.

Secondly, vpon the former confession, it followeth not, that the world is made in vayne; because wicked men are not altogether in this world to no purpose. For they serue to sharpen and stir vp the vertue of the iust. For while they afflict the vertuous by seueral meanes, they minister vnto the other abundant matter of patience and humility, & giue them plentifull occasiō of more full exercise of their vertues. Since

Y

by this meanes the iuſt do learne to conte-
ne all earthly things, to follow and ſeeke
after heauenly matters, to flie to God, to
repoſe al their confidence and hope in him,
to giue almes deeds, and finally to practiſe
all kinds of good works and vertues. This
is euident euen by daily examples, & therfore S. *Auguſtine* well ſaid, vpō the Pſalme.
54. Ne putetis &c. *Do not thinke, that the wi-*
cked are in vaine in this world, and that God
worketh not good from them: for euery bad man
therefore liueth, that he may either repent, or
that by him the godly and vertuous may be exer-
ciſed. Thus in this ſenſe God is ſaid to vſe
and apply the wicked to the benefit and
health of the vertuous. Againe the greatnes of Gods goodnes and mercy touching
the wicked in this life, mightily ſhineth
ſince he beſtoweth on them ſo many benefits and gifts, and inuiteth them with ſuch
a wonderfull longanimity & patience, that
they may be only partakers of heauenly felicity. To conclude, the ſeuerity of his diuine iuſtice appeareth in them after this life
by taking a moſt iuſt reuēge of their ſinnes;
and withall from hence we may gather,
how great the malignity of ſinne is, which
deſerueth ſo dreadfull a caſtigation and puniſhment, and laſtly there is miniſtred hereby to the Elect a iuſt occaſion of praiſing
and

and thanking Gods holy name, that they are deliuered frō thefe punifhments, Therfore, although the wicked do not arriue to the principall end of their creation (in which refpeɾt they may be faid to be borne in vayne) yet this cannot be abfolutly pronounced fo of them, becaufe they attaine the fecond end, whereunto they were ordained vnder condition (as it were) to wit, if through their vicious lyues they made themfelues vnworthy and incapable of the firft and chiefeft end. Now if the Soule of man fhould perifh with his body, none of thefe conueniences or profits could haue any place, but in lieu thereof it would clearly follow (as it fhewed aboue) that both man and the whole world fhould be created to no auailable purpofe or end.

THE XVI. REASON.

CHAP. XVII.

THE beauty of the world, and of all the things contained with in the vaft circumference thereof, is made by the authour of the world, to the end that it may be feene, knowne and efteemed; to wit that we behoulding the wonderfull magnificence of fuch a worke, may admire,

praife

praiſe and ioue the workeman of it . So the
pulchritude and goodly ſtructure & artifice of Churches , pallaces, pictures,& other
humane workes is framed , that it may be
looked vpon , and worthily prized. For if
it be not ſeene by any, it is houlden altogether as vnproſitable: for to what conduceth fayrenes , & due proportion in pour-
trature, remaining only in darkenes ? For
as ſmels , ſapours , and pleaſing ſounds are
but ſuperfluous and needles , if there be
no ſenſes of ſmelling, taſting , and hearing;
Euen ſo al beauty and ſplendour of things,
all ſubtility and perfection of art is but redundant and in vayne , if there be no eye
either of body or mynd , which canſee,ap-
prehend , and obſerue it . But if the Soule
doth periſh frō the body , the beauty of the
world , and of all things in it, remayne vnknowne,vnapprehended, and buryed (as
it were) in eternall darkenes. For in this
life we hardly attaine the thouſand part of
what is to be knowne , and this but confu-
ſedly and imperfectly; like a man of bad
ſight behoulding pictures a far off . For we
wholy reſt in the externall and outward
grayne of things , neuer penetrating into
the internall and ſecret eſſences of thē. And
yet there (I meane in the eſſence) is ſhut
vp all the beauty and truth of things, there
iſ

is the natiue and *speciall forme* ; & there lyes
all the artifice, and wit of that *great mind &*
supreme intelligece, which with its wisedome
hath inuented and framed all things ; there
are cōtained the re..sōs of al things; briefly,
so great is the beauty of things in their essence, and so admirable is the excellency
of the diuine art therein , as that it may be
boldly auerred that to behold clearly the
nature of a flie, or such like small creature ,
(as the Angels do see) is more to be desired,
then to obtaine the empire of the whole
world . For the Soule and mind would
doubtlesly draw more true pleasure from
this intellectuall light and contemplation ,
then from all corporall delights & honours
whatsoeuer. Such will easily belieue, what
I say, who haue at any tyme tasted the plea-
asure of truth, which lyeth hidden in these
small things . And the ancyent Philosophers do conspire with me herein , who
were so rapt and (as it were) drunke with
the fairenes of truth and wisedome , as that
for their better leasure therein, they contēned all riches and delights of the body. Seing then it is imcompatible with reasō, that
the beauty of the world, and of all other
things , and the inward art discouerable
therein , should be ordayned but in vayne ,
or but to continue euen in darkenes ; it is

not

not to be queſtioned, but that the ſoule of man ſuruiueth the graue, and ſhall after this life attaine to the perfect knowledge of all things. For then all hidden truths & the countenance of nature her ſelte (which now is latent) ſhall appeare in light, & thē ſhall the ſoule admire and praiſe the artificer of all, who hath impreſſed a peculiar forme in euery body, and hath ſo framed and diſpoſed it through his infinite wiſedome.

Some men may here ſay, that ſpirituall ſubſtances (ſuch as we call Angels) do perfectly know the ſtructure of the world, and of all other things therein; Therfore though man neuer haue any full knowledge therof, the world was not in vayne made.

I anſwere hereto, and deny the inference; for the ſtructure of the world ought to be knowne of him, for whoſe cauſe it was made, that by ſuch his knowledge, he may giue thanks to his Creatour. Now it was framed for the vſe and benefit of man, not of Angels (who haue no need of a corporeal world:) Therefore man is to haue knowledge of it, ſince to man it is made ſeruiceable, and that in a double reſpect; to wit, with it profits and fruites conducing to the leading of a corporeall life, & with it ſplendour and pulchritude, for the exerciſe of

wiſdome

wisdome and contemplation ; that so from the worke he may know the workeman, & in knowing him, that he may admyre , honour and reuerence him, and carefully obey & keepe his lawes.

THE XVII. REASON.

CHAP. XVIII.

THAT sentence & opinion, which banisheth away all vertue , and introduceth all impurity and vice , cannot possibly be holden , as agreable to truth : For *Truth and VVisdome* do auert men from al turpitude and vncleanes of conuersation , and incite them to the loue of honesty and vertue. For the vertue , which is in the vnderstanding , is the cause of all vertue , which is in the affection and will; and this from the other proceedeth no otherwise , then the beauty of any worke riseth from the art which is in the workemans mynd. Furthermore light cannot occasion darkenes ; But truth is light, and the square of what is right; and vice is darkenes, a lye , and a deuiation or declining away from the path & rule of truth. Now this opinion, which teacheth the Soule to be mortall & corruptible, doth

Y 4   subuert

subuert and ouerthrow the foundation of al
probity and vertue, and giueth the raynes
to all licentiousnes and sensuality. For who
would walke in the cragged way of vertue
refraine his desires, tame his lusts, abstayne
from doing wrong, and worship a diuine
power, if he did expect no reward for such
his deportment and carriage, nor fruite of
this his labour? Wherefore we find euen by
experience; that such as maintaine the Souls
mortality, are of a most licentious and prophane life & conuersation; for as in a commonwealth it cannot be brought to passe,
that externall iustice and politicall honesty
be obserued, and violence and iniury be restrained, except rewards and punishments
be ordayned by force of established lawes;
Euen so vertue in mankind cannot be pra-
ctized, & vice prohibited, where there is no
expectation of reward and commination of
chastisement set downe by the decree and
ordinance of God: The which remunerati-
ons and recompensations, seeing they are
not euer payed in this life, it followeth, that
they are to be reserued for the life to come;
since otherwise it might be said (which
were a heynous offence to auerre) that a cō-
monwealth is more wisely and prudently
ordayned and gouerned by man, then mankind is by God.

The

The Wifeman in the fecond chapter excellently defcribeth the improbity of fuch as deny the foules Immortality in thefe words : *Exiguum & cum tædio &c. Our life is short and tedious, and in the death of a man there is no recouery; neyther was any knowne, that hath returned from the graue. For we are borne at all aduenture, and we shall be hereafter, as though we neuer had been &c. Come therfore let vs enioy the pleasures, that are present, and let vs cheerfully vse the creatures, as in youth &c. Let vs leaue some token of our pleasure in euery place, for this is our portion, and this is our lot.* Thus we fee how thefe men do place their chiefe felicity in the pleafures of the body. Now after this, *Salomon* proceedeth further, fhewing how fuch men beare themfelues to the vertuous, how they fpoyle them, afflict them, & kill them, making their owne power and might the law of iuftice, fo holding that for lawfull, which they can and will execute; then the which nothing can be reputed more iniurious: for thus he bringeth in them faying: *Fortitudo nostra &c. Let our strength be the law of our vnrighteousnes, for the thing, that is feeble is reproued as vnprofitable.*

To conclude, the Wifeman endeth thus in his owne perfon: *Hæc cogitauerunt &c. Such things do they imagine, & go astray, for their owne wickednes hath blinded them; and they doe*

Y 5   *not*

not vnderstand the mysteries of God, neither hope for the reward of righteousnes, nor can discerne the honour of the soules, that are faultlesse: For God created man without corruption, & made him after the image of his owne likenes. In which words he giueth a reason, why man according to his Soule is inexterminable, without end, and incorruptible; to wit, becaufe he is like to God, as being his image: For in refpect of his mind and foule, man is capable of diuinity, as alfo of euery truth, and goodnes: Therefore feing this perfwafion ot the death and mortality of the foule is fo pernicious to all vertue, morality and conuerfation, we may infallibly conclude, that it is moft falfe, as being not warranted with any iuft fhew of truth.

Againe, that fentence, which is the fource and welfpring of all iuftice, piety & vertue, cannot be falfe; for as light cannot proceed out of darkenes; fo the fhining fplédour of truth cannot rife from the obfcurity of errours. And certainly, it is abfurd in it felfe, that the errour of iudgment and a falfe perfwafion of mynd, fhould become the fountaine of all iuftice and probity. But this article, which teacheth the foules immortality, and that after this life it is to be rewarded or punifhed, is the ground-worke of all iuftice and probity; fince through this expectation

pectation man is deterred from vice and impelled and perſwaded to vertue. Whereupon it hath been euer obſerued, that ſuch men, as euer grew eminent through the prayſe of vertue, were incited to the practiſe of it through the perſwaſion of the ſoules immortality: from thence then it followeth, that this ſentence muſt be moſt true; ſince it is *is* incredible, that the nature of the mynd or ſoule ſhould be ſo ordained, as that the true & perfect knowledge of it ſelfe ſhould be the cauſe of all improbity and lewdnes, and an erroneous perſwaſion the occaſion of vertue. For ſo it would follow, that nothing would be more neceſſary, and conuenient for the Soule, then to be ignorant of its owne nature; and nothing more dangerous, then to haue a true knowledge of it ſelfe, which paradox is moſt incongruous and abſurd; ſince all wiſemen eſteemed this ſentence: γνῶθι σιαυτὸν, *Noſce teipſum*, as an Oracle; in ſo much that *Plato in Charmide* witneſſeth that theſe words were inſcribed in the front of the temple of *Apollo* at *Delphos*, to the end (no doubt) that all ſhould take notice, that the obſeruing of this ſentence is the only way to true felicity, reuealed to man by a ſupernaturall power. Whereupon *Iuuenal* thus writeth: *E cælo deſcendit*, γνῶθι σιαυτὸν: that is, this ſentence, *Know thy ſelfe*, *deſcended from heauen*.   Per-

Perhaps thou maift heere fay, that vertue is a reward to it felfe, and vice its owne punifhment; therefore though the Soule be mortall, and that it is not to expect after this life either reward, or to feare punifhment; yet by this meanes it is fufficiently incyted and ftirred vp to imbrace vertue and flie vice.

I anfwere hereto and fay, that this Stoicall imagination is but weake, and of fmall force to gouerne the affections of men; (though at the firft appearance it beareth fome fhew of probability) and this for feuerall reafons. Firft, becaufe the beauty of vertue and deformity of vice, is a very fecret & hidden thing, and apprehended but by few, wherupon it rifeth, that it cannot efficacioufly mooue the mynds of men: fince nothing, which is vnknowne, ftirreth the affection.

Secondly, becaufe this reafon is little preuailing, euen in thofe minds, which make fhew to admit the force of it; for who is he, which flieth pleafure only by reafon of its inward turpitude, & as it is aduerfe to the law of reafon; and imbraceth the way of vertue, only becaufe the vertue is in it felfe fayre; and agreable to reafon, not being induced thereto through any other motiues? For the Stoicks themfelues (who firft did

Marginal note: Whether vertue be a reward of it felf.

did vendicate and teach this doctrine) were
not perſwaded to liue anſwerably hereto,
as mooued only through the force of vertue
and vice, but rather through honour or cō-
tumely and diſgrace; as thoſe which were
famous among the Romans and Grecians
were accuſtomed to do. This Tully witneſſeth in many places : *Trahimur omnes &c.*
VVe are all drowne with the deſire of praiſe, and
euen the beſt are led with glory; yea thoſe very Pro Ar-
Philoſophers, who haue written of the contempt of chia.
glory, haue notwithſtanding ſubſcribed their Poeta.
names to their owne bookes; And thus in deſpiſing
of honour and reputation, they ſeeke after ho-
nour and reputation. For the incytements &
allurements of pleaſures (which are obuious and neere to the ſenſes) are far more
preuayling to draw men to pleaſures, then
their vglines and foulenes, (which is very
ſubtill and ſcarce conceyued in mynd) is of
force to reſtraine them; ſince things & obiects, which are accōmodated to the ſenſes
do vehemently and forcibly moue . In like
ſort the aſperity and vnpleaſing ſharpnes of
vertue (which is repugnant to the fleſh &
our innate deſires and affections) is more
powerfull to deter the mind (naturally e-
uer confederate with the fleſh) from the
practiſe of it, then the beauty of it is forcible to procure loue and admiration therto.
                                        Therefore,

Therefore, from hence it is moſt euidēt, that man ſtandeth in need of other more ſtrong incentyues, by the which his mind may be impelled to the ſtudy and purſuite of vertue, and to the profligation and driuing away of vice and impiety.

Thirdly, becauſe that Paradox of the Stoicks. *virtus ſibi iuſtum eſt præmium* : *Vertue is a ſufficient reward to it ſelfe* , is moſt falſe : for nothing worketh only to the end, that it may worke ; and that it may reſt, and be contented in the worth of its own operation; but it euer intendeth ſomthing further, which it may obtaine by ſuch its action, as is euident both in thoſe things, which are wrought and performed by nature; as alſo by Art : for the Heauens (for example) are not moued, as taking delight in ſuch their motion, but for the conueniency of the inferiour world, and the benefit of man .

In like ſort, the ſeminall vertue, which is in ſeads, plants, and liuing creatures, worketh not to the end, that it may pleaſe it ſelfe with ſuch its operation ; but that therby things may be formed, borne, grow, nouriſhed, and bring forth fruyte : neither do liuing Creatures worke for the worke it ſelfe, but that therby they may procure & get ſuch things, as be profitable to thē, and auoyd, what is dangerous & hurtfull.

After

After the same manner Artificers do ayme
at some things beyond the practise of their
arte, for the which they worke. The like
may be said of the operarions of vertues
which are not performed by reason of that
good and beauty, which is in them; but are
finally directed to some one thing, which
is most good, and which is chiefly to be desired. And although seuerall vertues do not
extend themselues in their actions beyond
the peculiar and formall reason of what is
good, which is set downe to euery one of
them; yet the mynd, which possesseth thē
and vseth them, as it instruments, is not
satisfied with that good, but expecteth some
further end thereby; whether it be honour
and glory, or the ioy of future felicity,
which is to be giuen by God after this life.
And hence it proceedeth, that those, who
are either ignorant, or do not thinke of the
reward of the future life, haue in all their
famous and most celebrious actions bene
moued with the desire of glory. And hereupon we find *Tully* thus to wryte : *Ex
omnibus præmijs &c. Among all the rewards of
vertue, glory is the most ample reward, by the
which the shortnes of mans life is comforted with
the memory of posterity. As also in* another place
*(2) Nullam virtus &c. Vertue desireth no other
reward for her labour and paines, then this of*
glory :

*Pro Milo-
ne.*

*(2) Pro
Archia
Poeta.*

glory ; *of which if we should be depriued, to what purpose should we undergoe so great paines, and labours in this so short a course if mans life?* This was Tullies opinion, becaufe he was ignorant of greater rewards. So the ancient Romans, who were wont to make a fpecious and fayre fhew of vertue in their actions , were for the moft part led therto through the defire of praife , as *S. Auguftine* (3) fheweth. So euident it is , that mans nature in performing the works of vertue, doth defire and expect fomewhat more , then the beauty, & goodnes , which is in thefe actions. And this which is further expected ought to be fuch , as that it may more powerfully draw and impel mans wil to vertuous operations, then the pulchritude and inward fayrenes of it is able to do. Which point is made more euident by this confideration following .

(3) *l.5. de Ciuit dei c.* **12.**

God (the authour of nature) hath mixed thofe functions, which belong either to defend life , or to propagate and continue the kind of any Creature(to wit taking of meat and procreation of offpring).with great pleafures; leaft otherwife (perhaps) liuing Creatures, as being weary of the labours & troubles accompayning the fame , fhould neglect thofe functions ; or at leaft fhould not performe them fo diligently, as were
neceflary

neceſſary for the conſeruation of the particular or continuance of the *ſpecies* and kind. But with the moſt operations of vertue, either no pleaſure or very ſmall is adioyned, but for the moſt part great labours, ſolicitude and trouble. For the way of vertue is hard, and is not paſſed ouer without toyle or moleſtation.

It is hard for men to bridle the paſſions, to curbe the affections of the mynd, to moderate deſires, to extinguiſh malice & enuy, and to encompaſſe all motions within the circle of reaſon. It is a labourſome thing to ſuffer iniuryes, to reſtraine hate and anger, to relieue the needy with their goods, and duly to pay debts. Therefore ſeing in the exerciſe of vertue, there is either none or very ſmall allurements; but on the other ſide, many aſperities diuerting the mind frō thence, it was requiſite that (beſides the force of vertue) there ſhould be ſome other cauſes, which muſt forcibly impell the mind therto, and deter it from vice, to wit rewards & puniſhmēts without the which no man would enter into the thorny path of vertue, or being entred would go forward therein, or would contemne the inuitements of ſenſuality: for if the *Prouidence of God* hath much ſweetned theſe loweſt functions, cōſiſting in the preſeruing

Z

of

of life, and perpetuating of posterity, least otherwise they might be pretermited and neglected; who then can be perswaded, that the chietest operations of the soule of Man (by the which we are made like to God) should be so little respected by the said Prouidence, as that we shonld want al incytements for our greater encouragemēt therein? Certainly this care of Prouidence were most preposterous . For although vertue be sharpe and aduerse to the flesh, & vyces gratefull and pleasing; notwithstanding the consideratiō of the reward, which is adioyned to vertue(wherin is contained an eternall and inestimable pleasure) doth so temper and gentle the bitternes thereof, as that it maketh it to seeme sweet and to be desired; and on the contrary part, an inward and serious reflexion and meditation of the most seuere punishments prepared hereafter for vyce and wickednes, causeth the pleasure of it to seeme bitter and loathsome.

Now, what is hertofore spoken of the operations of vertue(to wit , that it selfe should not be a sufficient remuneration for it selfe) is to be vnderstood of those actions of vertue, which can be performed in this life . For we do not deny, but after this life there is an action of vertue, which is a reward

ward of it felfe, and of all other precedent
operations of vertue . And this is the cleare
vifion of God , and the loue and ioy flowing
from thence : for thefe functions or actions
of vertue are chiefly to be defired for théfelues , fo as no other further commodity is
to be expected therein ; feing in this vifion
our fupreme felicity, *formalis beatitudo* (as the
Schoolemen fpeake) confifteth. Now that
thefe operations make vs happy , this rifeth
not frō thence , that they are the operations
or functions of any vertues, but in that they
conioyne and vnyte the Soule with God ,
who is *fummum verum* , *fūmum pulchrum* , *&*
fummum bonum : our chiefeft truth, chiefeft
beauty , and good . Wherefore from hence
we may obferue, that we do not place in
thefe actions our happines , as the Stoicks
did in vertue : for they repofed their fupreme happines in vertue it felfe , and in a
refolution of the mynd fubiect to reafon, &
not in the Obiect , to the which vertue
tyeth our mynd ; thus they made vertue it
felfe to be both the *formall* & *obiectiue* beatitude ; that is, the fubiect from whence this
beatitude rifeth, and the formal caufe, why
in thefe functions of vertue confifteth mās
beatitude . But we place not this our felicity principally in thefe operations of vertue
but in the Obiect, to the which thefe ope-

rations do vnyte our foule and mind ; fo as
thefe operations cannot be called our felicity, but with reference, as they are a certaine perfect vnion and vitall coniunction
with our *fummum bonum,* or fupreme happines. Befides the Stoicks taught, the operation of vertue to be in our power, flowing
(at our owne pleafure) from the freedome
of our will ; wheras we maintayne that
bleffed function not to be in our owne power ; but to be a celeftiall, conftant immutable, and fempiternall guift, diuinely infufed.

But it may be heere obiected, that *glory*
and *praife* is a fufficient incytement to the
ftudy of vertue, and confequently, that
there is no need of rewards or paynes after
this life. And of this opinion *Tully* may
feeme to be, who wonderfully magnifyeth
this reward in thefe words following.
Nulla merces à virtute &c. No other reward is
to be expected for vertue, then this of honour &
glory.

Of all the rewards of vertue, glory is the moft
ample and large: which comforteth the shortnes of
life with the memory of posterity: which maketh
that being abfent we are prefent, and being dead
we do liue; by which degrees of honour, men may
be thought to afcend to heauen. In like fort in
another place he thus wryteth; *Non vita hae*
&c.

&c. This is not to be tearmed life, which consisteth
of the body and the soule or mind ; but that, euen
that is truly life, which flourisheth in the memory
of all ages, which posterity nourisheth, and which
eternity it selfe euer beholdeth.

I answere hereto and say, that glory &
humane praise is no sufficient reward for
vertue, and this for diuerse reasons. First,
because the desire of glory corrupteth the
good & perfectiõ of vertue, leauing therof
only an outward shew, and a mere repre-
sentation : for *vertue*(as *Aristotle* and al Philosophers defyne it*) is a loue of that, which is* **2.** *Ethic. c.*
good, or honest, only in that respect, that it is good; **4.**
Therefore if one do a vertuous worke, not
through any loue of vertue, but through
the hope either of profit, pleasure, or praise,
it is not the worke of true vertue, but only
an external pretext thereof; for the inward
life, and (as it were) the soule of vertue is
absent heere; for as a liuing creature consisteth of soule & body, so a perfect worke
of vertue is grounded vpon an inward liking of what is good, & an outward worke.
And as when the soule leaueth the body
there remaineth only a dead Carcas; euen
so the desire and affection of what is good
and vertuous being extinguished, nothing
is left, but only an empty shew or image of
vertue.

Z 3   So

So far ſhort then is glory and praiſe from being a ſufficient and efficacious incytemēt of vertue, as that true vertue is euen corrupted and depraued therby; no otherwiſe, then certaine hoat poiſons do ſo ſtir vp & awaken the ſleeping ſpirits of a man, as that they do vtterly diſſolue, diſſipate, and extinguiſh them.

Secondly, Glory is not ſufficient hereto, becauſe the ſcope and End of glory is preuailing only in certaine few externall actions, which are performed vpon the open ſtage of the world; for (as it is aboue ſhewed) it doth not excite and perſwade a man to the inward affection and loue of vertue, but only to the outward action; & this not to euery action, but to ſuch as may be moſt conſpicuous and markable in the eyes of many. For the humour of glory & praiſe is fully ſatisfyed, if a man ſeeme externally vertuous, honeſt and valorous, though in the ſecret cloſet of his ſoule he is found to be wicked, and cowardly. Therfore this deſire of praiſe (which is but an idle diuerberation or empty ſound of ayre) rather engendreth Hypocrites, then true followers of vertue.

Thirdly, becauſe the reward of vertue ought to be a certaine ſolid and intrinſecal good, which may affect the ſoule it ſelfe,

and

& which is more noble then vertue; since
the End ought euer to be more excellent
then the meanes. But humane glory is a
thing merely extrinsecall, resting only in Why are
the perswasion and iudgement of men; but men so
bringing no perfection or worth to the desirous
mynd. For what can the opinion of a cō- of prayse
pany of poore mortall men aduantage me?
Or what can their speeches and words a-
uaile me? Thou maist heere reply, from
whence then procedeth it, that almost all *Valerius*
men are ouerruled with the desire of praise *Max c. 8.*
and glory? For as one saith. *There is no such*
humility of mynd, which cannot be molifyed with
the sweetnes of glory. Which saying is so true,
as that this affection of *Philotimy*, and loue of
honour & reputation hath suddenly crept
into the mynds of most holy and deuoute
men.

I answere, that there are three causes
hereof. First, because there is in all men an
innate appetite and desire of excellency,
which mightily ruleth and swayeth in the
mynd : for there is nothing more to be desired in that, which is good, (whether it
be vertue, power or nobility) then to excell others in the same good. Now honour
is the testimony of this excellency; glory a
knowledge and opinion of the same excellency, and praise a diuulging and dilating

of

of the fame. Whereupon when thefe are afcribed and giuen to any one, there rifeth in him an apprehenfion of his owne excellency, with the which he is wonderfully delighted. Euen as (on the contrary) by conuicious fpeaches and reproach there is ftirred vp a cogitation of ones vility and bafenes, which is difpleafing and diftafting to euery one. Therefore all men loue praife and glory, becaufe thefe are fignes of excellency; and hate, contumely & difgrace, as markes and badges of abiection and vnworthines of mynd.

Secondly, all men couet honour; becaufe as the mynd greatly defireth to be eminent and excelling; fo it defireth to be fo reputed in the iudgements of others; for the foule or mynd of man deemeth this to belong to it, as a certaine new effence, or as a new *intelligible life* (as I may call it) vnder the glorious fhew and forme whereof, it being knowne, it feemeth to liue in the mynds of men. For as the Philofophers do fay *Intelligere, eft quoddam rei intelligibilis effe*: to vnderftand and know a thing, giueth a certaine effence and being to the thing fo knowne.

This point Tully may be wel thought to infinuate in the words aboue recyted: *Ea eft vita &c. That is the life, which flourisheth in*
the

the memory of all ages which posterity nourisheth,
and through the which we being absent, are pre-
sent, and being dead, do liue. Therefore this memory, this estimation, & eternizing of ones
fame is a certaine life of the soule, and her
endowments ; which is not discerned by
the eye, but vnderstood by the mynd ; consisteth not by nature, but by the iudgments
and censures of mynds ; doth not intrinse-
cally inhere to the soule, but is extrinsecal-
ly possessed ; by which meanes the soule
may be said to liue in the mynds of men, &
to haue so many liues, as there are men, in
whose hearts it is highly magnified and va-
lewed. This life is so much esteemed sometimes by the soule, as that it is content oftentimes to contemne corporall life for the
preseruing of it, and to expose the body to
most certaine death, before it will suffer the
least blemish & losse of reputation & name,
so holding it more worthy to liue by memory in the mynds of others, then in his
owne person and body by nature. Which is
an euident argument, that glory (although
it be but an imaginary and empty thing) is
more worthy and preciable then riches or
pleasures. For such is the excellency of the
mynd, as that it preferreth the least goods
properly belonging to it, before the greatest
corporall goods.

Thirdly

Thirdly, All do seeke after glory, because glory is conducing and profitable to many things; for it retayneth and keepeth man in his duty, withdrawing him from all turpitude, sloth, and improbity, leaſt otherwiſe he ſhould looſe his good name; for want of ſhame, and an vtter contempt of what honeſt men do thinke of one, is a point moſt dangerous. Furthermore, Glory maketh, that men may with pleaſure, grace, & credit negotiate with others in publicke & in the eye of the world, where baſe and degenerous perſons dare not appeare. Againe it procureth, that men are aduanced to magiſtracy and publike gouerment; ſince the gates of honours and dignityes are ſhut to the infamous, and ſuch as are abiect. Laſtly, it cauſeth, that we conuerſe among men with fruite; for whether it be in a courſe of doctrine and learning, or in the adminiſtration of iuſtice, neither of them can be performed without the reputation of a good name; and therefore the *VViſeman* truly ſaid: *Melius eſt &c. A good name is to be choſen aboue great riches: as alſo* in another place; *Curam habe &c. haue regard to thy good name, for that ſhall be prized with thee, aboue a thouſand treaſures of gold.*

Prouerb.
22.
Eccleſ .4.
1.

THE

THE XVIII. REASON.

CHAP. XIX.

AGAINE, if the Soule dyeth with the body, then (befydes all the former inconueniences aboue alleadged) thefe two do follow. Firft, that *iniuries* and wrongs fhould remayne *vnreuenged*, and that any wickednes whatfoeuer in mankind fhould be committed with all impunity, & without any fuffering on the delinquents fide. Secondly, that there fhould be no *reward allotted* for *vertue* & piety, nor no fruite thereof. That in this life oftentimes there is no reuenge or compenfation taken for wrongs, is manifeft : for we fee daily many moft wicked and impious men, and oppreffours of the innocent to flourifh greatly in this life, and to abound with all kinds of temporall goods, as riches, honours, and delights ; but the iuft and vertuous to be ftill entangled with diuers calamities, and to paffe their whole time in afliction; as if Profperity fhould be the reward of Impiety, and calamity of iuftice and piety. Therefore of there be no retribution of thefe matters after this life, then in this ἀτκξία. or perturbation of order it is moft euident;to wit that

all

all heynous offences and crimes ſhould be vnpuniſhed , vertue vnrewarded, Iuſtice troden vnder foote through contempt, and iniquity erected. For wrongs and flagitious ſinnes are ſuppoſed to continue, and to pollute this Common wealth of the whole *Vniuerſe* , till they be reuenged, and become expiated by due puniſhments , as is euident from the common iudgment of all men.

It alſo farther might be inferred, that if there be no chaſtiſement of vice , nor remuneration for vertue , there were no *diuine power or prouidence* , vndertaking the care of mens affaires; but that all things are carryed with temerity & raſhnes, & that euery mas will & power becomes a law to himſelfe : for nothing can be more aduerſe &repugnát to the nature of Prouidence , then this kind of licence & impunity. For as we may truly ſay, that, that Kingdome orState(if any ſuch were) eyther wanted a gouernour, or that the gouernour were iniuſt, & a defender of wicked men ; if therein there were decreed no reuenge for notorious & publicke tranſgreſſours; Euen ſo if in this Kingdome (as it were) of all mankind, all actions ſhould proceed freely without any expectation either of rewards, or feare of puniſhments, we might well collect, that there were no prouidence, nidence, nor any fupreme moderatour, by whome humane affaires are gouerned, or if there were any, yet that he is vniuft. This is confirmed, in that the firft office of a gouernour is, that Lawes may be obferued with due diftribution of rewards and punifhments, according to mens different coportment and carriage: for thus all actions are brought to the ballance of iuftice, then the which nothing is more defired in this world.

Now where this is wanting, it is certaine, that prouidence and true gouerment is alfo wanting. The fame point is alfo further made euident, becaufe it chiefly belongeth to Prouidence, to giue to euery one, what is his owne; this being the inuiolable law of iuftice, which in gouerment & true adminiftration of things is moft religioufly to be obferued : whereupon *Diuine Prouidence* obferueth this moft precifely in all things created (according to their different capacities) giuing to euery one what is agreable to their nature and condition. Now if this order be kept in the loweft and meaneft creatures, then with much more reafon ought it to be obferued in the worthyeft thing of the world, which is mans Soule, which only is capable of Iuftice and iniury, right and due. Certainly, it is abfurd that all
things

things agreable to their natures should exactly be measured and giuen by the *Prouidence of God* to myce, gnats, worms, and the like (who are not capable of iustice or wrong)& yet those things should not be giuen to the soule of man, which are due, and best sort to it; and which the soule it selfe through her good or bad actions deserueth. We cannot but thinke, that the care of diuine Prodence is about small matters very preposterous, if it be wanting in the greatest things. For from this then would fall out not much vnlike, as if a Prince should carefully prouide of al things necessary for horses, mules, and dogs, and yet should absolutly neglect his owne family, without setting downe any recompensations to his most trusty seruants, or chastisement to malefactours. The the which proceeding what can be imagined more exorbitant, or lesse agreable with reason? For by how much any thing is more worthy and more neere to God, by so much it requyreth a greater care of Prouidence, that it may attend its end. *A reasonable nature is the sole family and houshold of God*; since this nature only acknowledgeth God, and prosecuteth him with honour and reuerence. This also alone contemnet: and offendeth him; and therfore it alone deserueth reward and punishment.

Now

New from thefe premifes it is manifeftly conuinced, that there is no diuine power,
nor any Prouidence, if the foule be extinguifhed with the body : for if it be extinguifhed, then is there no retribution nor any
iuftice; but iniuryes and wrongs remayne
vnfatisfyed, vertue becomes difhonoured;
and finally there is found in the worthyeft
creature of the world, the greateft perturbation and inuerfion of order, that can be
imagined. All which inferences being granted, do euidently prooue the world to be
deftitute of a Rectour or Gouernour. And
hence it is, that this confideration chiefly
hath in al ages perplexed the minds of men,
and hath impelled them to deny diuine prouidence, and to fatisfy their owne affections
& defires. And the greateft motiue to withdraw men from this falfe opinion, was to
confider good or euill was prepared for man
after this life, as the Prophet moft excellently explicateth in the 72. Pfalme. Only the
mature ponderation of this, appeafeth the
mynd, and caufeth it to tread a vertuous &
refolued courfe in all aduerfities.

But it may be heere anfwered, that the
foules of the wicked are fufficiently punifhed for all their wrongs, iniuftice, & other
their tranfgreffions, in that they are extinct
with the death of their bodyes : but againft
this

this I ſay, that this periſhing and death of the ſoule (if any ſuch were) is ordained not as a puniſhment, but as a condition of nature; which no leſſe the vertuous and iuſt do vndergoe, then the wicked. Like as in a Commonwealth, if there were no other other puniſhments to be inflicted vpon delinquents, then the naturall death of body, which according to the courſe of meaſure is to fall to euery one; it might be truly ſaid, that no paine or chaſtiſement at all were abſolutly ſet downe for maletactours; but that all liberty and impunity preuailed therein; for puniſhment ought to be inflicted for the fault, as a iuſt recompenſation of the ſame. So as if there be no fault, then is there not any place for puniſhment. Now this ſuppoſed extinction of the ſoule (aboue vnderſtood) is not inflicted for any fault; ſeing the vertuous are no leſſe ſubiect to it, then the wicked.

THE XIX. REASON.

CHAP. XX.

THE world was created by God, to the end that the perfection of his Diuinity might ſhine, and appeare in it, as in his moſt beautifull and admirable worke: for
this

this manifestation is the last end of God, or
of the first agent in the framing of the world.
For nothing is more worthy then God ,
who worketh for his owne sake, and intendeth lastly his owne good, which good is
not intrinsecall to God (for this kind of
good is euer present vnto him, neither can
it be increased or diminished) but only extrinsecall, which is nothing els, then an open
declaration of his perfections in his Creatures, and by his creatures, in the which his
extrinsecall glory consisteth. And in this
sense the Philosophers are accustomed to
say, *Idem est primus agens, & vltimus finis. One &*
the same thing is the first agent, and the last end.
The reason hereof being, because the first a-
gent doth not necessarily intend in the last
place his owne good. Which point is war-
ranted out of the holy Scripture, *Omnia prop-* *Prouerb.*
ter semetipsum operatus &c. The Lord made all 16.
things for his owne sake ; yea euen the wicked for
the day of euill. God worketh all things, not
only by a positiue action in doing, but also
by a negatiue action, in suffering and permitting, for the word, *to worke*, is heere taken
in a large signification: God worketh *propter*
semetipsum, that is, for his owne glory, that
thereby the perfections of his excellency
may be manifested and knowne: *Impium*
quoque, yea euen the wicked &c. because he

A 2   suffereth

fuffereth a man to be wicked, and being wicked he ordaineth him to damnation and eternall punifhment, & all this, which God doth, tendeth to his glory. But if the foule be mortall, the diuine perfections in God are fo farre off from fhining in the fabricke & difpofition of the world, as that they may rather feeme to be obfcured: for it is no figne of the power of the Creatour, but rather of his weaknes, that he could not make the Soule of man (which is the Lord of things) immortall, feeing that condition is beft forting to the dignity of the foule. It is not a point of wifdome to make fuch things eternall, as are feruiceable, and (as it were) flaues to man, as the world (which is his houfe) and the like; and yet to fhut or confyne the Lord of all within a narrow compaffe of tyme, and that being once ended, himfelfe for euer to be extinguifhed and to refolue to nothing. It is not the office of goodneffe to bring all other things to that perfection, which is agreable to ech of the; and yet fo to neglect the Soule of man, as that he can neuer attaine vnto the hundreth part of that good, of which it is capable. It is no Prouidence to leaue the foule to its own appetites and defires, without fetting of any rewards, which may allure it to vertue, or punifhments, which may deterre it from
vice;

vice ; to leaue finne vnpunifhed, and iuftice violated, & to permit in the world fo great a diforder and confufion;the impious ruling and tyrannizing , and the iuft and vertuous remaining oppreffed, and this without any future hope of bettering of things , or of reducing them in any more conuenient order.

What fhould I heere fpeake of *Mercy* & *Iuftice* ? For what mercy is it , that man fhould liue fo fhort a tyme, and lead his corporall life afflicted with fo many miferies , without any expectation of happines for the time to come? Or what pleafure can this life afford , which is mixed with fuch ftore of wormewood, as that to a prudent man it feemeth moft bitter , except the fweetnes of a future expectancy doth téper it ? Or what equity & iuftice is it, that good men fhould be oppreffed, afflicted, & murthered by the wicked without any reuenge or recompenfation of fo great and infufferable wrongs : that there fhould be no rewards propofed for piety, iuftice & vertue ; nor punifhments for wickedneffe and iniuftice? that the wicked fhould abound withal the goods of this life (as riches, honours, pleafures, and domination or rule) & the godly & pious fhould liue plunged into all afflictions and calamities? Who confidering thefe things, will not

repute

repute them rather signes of cruelty and iniuftice, then of mercy and iuftice? And that
the *diuine power* is a fauourer of the wicked,
and an enemy to the vertuous, if there be
not after this life a iuft compensation & retaliation made to both thefe kinds of men?
And hence it is, that the Heathens, who
thought litle of any retribution after this
life, did often accufe the Gods of cruelty &
iniuftice. Of which point many examples
are extant in *Homer, Euripides, Athanaus,* and
others. Yea fuch a cogitation will enter into the minds of fome Chriftians, whiles
they do not caft their eye of things to come
after this life. And certainly if nothing were
to chance to the foule after its feparation frō
the body, it were not an eafy matter to vindicate and free God from the afperfion and
note of cruelty & iniuftice, as aboue is fhewed out of *Chryfoftome.* For who would ef-
teeme that King to be iuft & benigne, who
fhould fuffer in his Kingdome fo great a cō-
fufion, as that no reward fhould be propofed for vertue, nor punifhment for moft facinorous crimes; but that the wicked fhould
perpetrate any mifchiefes (though neuer fo
heinous) without any feare of law, or feeling of any due punifhment or caftigation?
But now acknowledging the foules immortality, all the former inconueniences do
ceafe,

ceafe, and all fecret murmuring and com-
plaints againft God are filent. For this forefaid confufion lafteth only for a fmall time;
which (being once paffed) fhall heereafter
be corrected in an eternall order, for to euery one after this life fhalbe allotted his place
ftate, and degree; and there fhalbe a iuft retribution for all actions whatfoeuer; there
no euil fhall remaine vnreuenged, nor good
irremunerated and vnrewarded. For as a
skilful painter is not ignorant in what place
he is to put each particular colour (as black,
white, & the reft:) fo God knoweth where
to range euery one in this whole *Vniuerfe*,
be he vertuous or wicked.

And as from that fitting diftribution of
colours rifeth the beauty of the picture,
euen fo from this difpofall of Soules, the
fplendour of the *Vniuerfe* proceedeth; which
Vniuerfe is (as it were) a certaine portrature
of Gods diuinity, wonderfully exhibiting
to vs his power, wifdome, goodneffe, Prouidence, mercy and iuftice. Therefore there
is no true reafon, why the iuft fhould complaine of the Prouidence of God for their
fuffering of calamities in this life; fince the
preffures and afflictions heere are but fhort,
and but fmall in a generous mind; but the
the fruite thereof moft great, magnificent, &
eternall. It being true which the Apoftle

ſaith (then whome no man perhaps in this world whome no man perhaps in this world hath ſuffered more) *Momentaneum & leue &c.* Our *affliction, which is but for a moment, worketh in vs a farre more excellent and eternall weight of glory.* Now that ought not to be accounted grieuous, which is recompenſed with ſo great & ineſtimable a reward. Beſides Tribulations are of force to fyle away the ruſt of the ſoule, and to cauſe an abſtertion and waſhing away of its dayly ſpots; for no man in this world is ſo pure, but ſome ſmall blemiſhes are dayly contracted in his ſoule, which by meanes of affliction are obliterated & remooued.

2. Cor. 4.

  In like ſort, there is no cauſe, why the vertuous ſhould ſtomacke the proſperity of the wicked, ſince this is ſhort, momentary and mixed with much bitternes; & is hereafter to be attended with euerlaſting complaint and lamentation. There is no man, which will enuy a draught of wyne to be giuen to a thieſe, or the enioying of ſolace for ſome few houres, which is already condemned to the wheele and death. And the Prophet ſaith, *Noli amulari &c. Fret not thy ſelfe, becauſe of the wicked men, neyther be enuious for the euill doers &c. for they ſhall wither, as the greene hearbe.* In like ſort the wiſeman thus teacheth: *Stuppa collecta &c. The Congregatiō of the wicked is like tow wrapped togeather; their*

Pſalm. 36.

Eccleſ. 21.

their end is like a flame of fire to destroy them.
The harueft will come, when all finners
like hurtful hearbs or chaffe fhaíbe gathered
togeather, and caft into the fire, as our Lord
himfelfe hath taught in that wonderfull parable of his, in *Matth. cap.* **13.**

THE XX. REASON.

CHAP. XXI.

IT is fo prouided by nature, that who
haue committed grieuous finnes, do fuffer a fecret fting, and *touch of Confcience,* with
the which they are fometimes fo tormented, as that they depriue themfelues of their
owne liues. For their confcience doth dayly accufe & condemne them, & pronounce
thē worthy of punifhment, & caufe them e-
uer to ftand in feare, as if fome dreadfull euil
were hanging ouer their heads. From hence
it proceedeth, that thefe men (that they may
the more diuert their myndes from thefe
thoughts, and free themfelues of all fuch
trouble) giue themfelues ouer to all fports,
recreations, bankettings, and to other externall focietyes; thus auoyding their inward
accufer and torturer, for nothing is more difpleafing to them, then to be folitary and a-
lone, and to enter into any fecret difcourfe

A a 4   with

with their owne foules. Now this horrour
of mynd & pricke of confcience is a prefage
of a future iudgment and reuenge, which
expecteth the foules of the wicked after this
life. Their finnes & offences are (as it were)
feedes of eminent punifhments; & therefore
this their trouble of mynd ryfeth euen by an
inftinct of nature from the remembrance of
their owne finnes. But now, we are not to
thinke, that the prefages and foretellings of
nature are but idle and needleffe inftincts;
for if nothing were to be feared after the bodyes death, and that no euill were to enfue
thereupon, then fhould in vaine this inftinct
be implanted in mans foule, and in vayne
fhould an euil confcience proiect & forecaft
any fuch dreadfull and dyrefull matters.

In like fort a confcience priuy to it felfe
of its wel doing, bringeth great folace to the
mynd, and therefore Tully faith : *Magna eft*
vis confcientiæ &c. The force of confcience both in
the good, and in the bad, is great ; that they who
committed no euill, do not feare, & thofe who haue
offended , may euer haue their punifhment before
their eyes. He alfo in another place thus writeth : *Si optimorum confiliorum &c. If our conf-*
cience be euer a witnes throughout our whole liues
of our good deliberations and actions, then fhall we
liue without feare in great integrity & honefty of
mind. And the reafon thereof is, becaufe the
foule

foule doth prefage that good and happynes,
which is referued after this life, for all true
worfhippers of vertue.

CHAP. XXII.

THE Immortality of the Soule is further euicted from the *returne backe of
Soules* after this life. For it is euident euen by
infinite examples, that the dead haue been
raifed vp, and that the Soules of the dead
haue returned from the places, wherein they
were, and haue appeared to the liuing. We
read in the firft booke of the *Kings* cap. 28.
and in *Ecclefiafticus* cap. 49. that the Soule of
Samuel (then dead) appeared to the Enchan-
treffe *Pithoniffa*, and to *Saul*, and did prophecy vnto him his deftruction. Againe the
foule of *Moyfes* (whether in his owne body
reftored vnto him at that tyme by diuine
power, or in a body affumed by him) togeather with *Elias* appeared in the mount *Tha-
bor* to *Chrift*, and to the three chiefe Apoftles
Peter, *Iames*, & *Iohn*, as is related in Mathew
cap. 17. and Luke cap. 9. The foules of *O-
nias* & *Ieremy* the Prophet exhibited themfelues to the fight of *Iudas Machabeus*, and
much encouraged him to the vanquifhing
of

of his Countries Enemies, as appeareth in the first of the *Machabees* c. 15. The Apostles *S. Peter* and *S. Paul* appeared in sleepe to Constantine the Emperour, and shewed him a meanes to cure his leprosy, as it is recorded in the seauenth Synod Act 2. and testifyed by many Historians. *S Iohn* (the Euangelist) and *S. Philip* the Apostle appeared to *Theodosius*, & promised him victory against *Eugenius*, which presently followed and not without great miracle. The same apparitio̅ was seene also by a certaine souldier at the same tyme, least otherwise it might be thought to be forged by the Emperour, as *Theodoret* wryteth, l. 5. histor. c. 24. The same Euangelist with the blessed virgin exhibited theselues to the sight of *Gregorius Thaumaturgus* then waking, and instructed him in the mistery of the Trinity. This point with the forme of the doctrine is recorded by *Gregorius Nissenus*, in the life of *Thaumaturgus*.

I omit many other apparitions of our blessed Lady recorded by *Gregory* the great and other more ancient authours. In like sort *Amborse* serm. 90. wryteth, that S. *Agnes* appeared to *Constantia* the daughter of *Constantine*, and cured her of a most dangerous impostume or swelling. *Eusebius* reporteth l. 6. histor. c. 5. how *S. Potamiena* (the

(the third day after her martirdome) appeared to her Executioner in the night, and told him, that she had obtained fauour frō God in his behalfe in recōpenfe of his gētle proceding with her; vpon which apparitiō the Executioner inſtātly became a Chriſtiā & after his conſtāt profeſſiō of the Chriſtiā faith, ſuffered a moſt glorious death, and martyrdome.

It were ouer laboursome to recount all the apparitiōs both of the holy and wicked ſoules, which are found in approued authours; all which to ſay to haue bene forged were ouer great impudence; ſince this were to take away the credit of al hiſtoryes and to caſt an aſperſion of falſhood and deceite (without any ſhew of reaſon) vpon many moſt holy, learned, and graue authours; for many both of the ancient Fathers, as alſo of hiſtoriographers(eſpecially Chriſtians) haue made frequent mentiō of this point;yea euen among the very heathens, it was a thing generally acknowledged, as appeareth out of *Homer,Virgil* & others.

Therefore ſeing it is a matter moſt euident by ſo many examples, that the Soules of the dead haue appeared to the liuing, we may demonſtratiuely conclude, that thoſe Soules did not dye with their bodyes; but

Homer .l. 11. & a- jibi virgil. 8. l Ænead. Ouid . l. 4. Metamorph.

do

do continue immortall, and haue their reward of glory or puniſhment, according to
their actions performed in this life.

This point of the Soules immortality is
in like ſort made cleare from the *raiſing of
the dead to life.* Now that the dead haue bene
recalled to life, is proued by many vnanſwerable examples. And firſt the Prophet
Elias reſtored to life the dead Sonne of the
widow *Sareptana,* as appeareth in the third
of the Kings c. 7. *Eliſeus* alſo raiſed the ſone
of *Sunamite,* as we read in the fourth of the
Kings c. 4. Yea *Eliſeus* (being himſelf dead)
only by the touch of his bones reſtored to
life one, that was dead, as we find in the 13.
chapter of the ſaid booke.

Chriſt (our Lord and Sauiour) beſides
others raiſed, to life *Lazarus* (being dead
foure dayes afore) and this was perfourmed
in the eye of all *Ieruſalem,* as *S. Iohn* relateth
c. 11. Finally to auoyde all prolixity, diuers were reſtored to life by the Apoſtles,
and other moſt holy men, as appeareth
from Eccleſiaſticall hiſtoryes, and other approued authours. Now the *reſurrection and
riſing of the dead,* is an euident ſigne, that the
ſoules are not vtterly extinct; but that they
remayne ſeparated after death, till through
a conueniēt diſpoſitiō of the body, they be
reunited to it. For ſo ſoone, as the whole
diſpoſition

disposition of the body (which is necessary
to this vnion) shalbe perfected, and that
the soule shall there exhibit it selfe inwardly present, then doth this vnion imedia-
tly and freely follow : partly like as fire
touching chips, or any other such combu-
stible matter, doth through a mutuall attraction, naturally cleaue thereunto. For the
body being made apt, and rightly disposed
doth couet through a naturall propension,
to be vnited with the soule ; as in like sort
the soule desireth to be conioyned to the
body, which propension or inclination is
reduced into Act, when the Soule and the
body (after the last disposition once finished) are mutually and inwardly present
together.

THE XXII. AND LAST REASON.

CHAP. XXIII.

TO conclude this point touching the
Soules immortality ; it may be further
alledged, that the Soules *Immortality* is the
foundation of all religion, Iustice, *Probity,
Innocency*, & *sanctity*. Now if this ground-
worke be false, then is the whole sacred
Scripture false and a meere fiction; then are
the Oracles of the Prophets false ; false also
is

is the doctrine and preaching of Christ; false
his miracles . Finally , false are all those
things , which are deliuered by the Euan-
gelists touching the resurrection of Christ,
his conuersing with the Apostles fourty
dayes after his resurrection , his ascension ,
and the descending of the Holy Ghost vpō
the Apostles, and other the faithfull. And
thus are all deceaued, who haue embraced
the religion of Christ ; And therefore in
vaine haue so many thousands Saints ta-
med , and brought vnder their flesh, practi-
zed iustice , innocency , temperance, & all
other vertues , with indefatigable and incessant paynes. In vayne are all the Sacra-
ments of the Church, all the institutions &
diuine laudes and praises, all Ecclesiasticall
Orders, all sacred assemblies , all labours
of prelates and Pastours , all doctrine of the
ancient Fathers , and all manner of liuing
among Christians .

For all these things are bootlesse , and of
no fruite or benefit , (as being grounded
vpon a false foundation)if the Soule be extinguished with the body. Finally all those
men , haue bene extremely deceaued, who
at any tyme haue bene excellent for sactity
of life, guift of prophecy, glory of miracles,
or heauenly wisedome ; & on the contrary
part, the truth of this poynt hath bene re-
uea90led

ꝛealed only to prophane, wicked and sē-
suall Epicures, all which things are most
repugnant euen to the light of Reason.

Thus far now (to draw towards an end)
haue we alledged reasons and arguments,
by the which, the *Immortality of the soule* is
established & confirmed, which if they be
seriously weighed, do so conuince the iudgement, as that they take away al ambigu-
ity and doubt of this point. Now to these
we will adioyne a testimony or two of a
heathen. Therefore *Seneca* in his 102. E-
pistle thus wryteth. *Magna & generosa res est
humanus animus &c.* The Soule of man is a great
and generous thing ; It suffereth it selfe to be limited with no bounds, but such as are common
with God. *Seneca* here meaneth, because the
Soule extēdeth it selfe to all place & tyme.
Now this authour further explicateth this
point in these words: *Primùm, humilem non
accipit patriam &c.* First the Soule admitteth
not to it selfe any obscure or meane Coūtry, whether it be *Ephesus* or *Alexandria*, or any other one
place, though more populous, & better furnished
with buildings and edifices: but its Country is all
that, which is contained within the compasse of
this vniuerse; yea all this conuexity, within the
which the Ayre, which diuideth all celestiall
things from humane and earthly, is comprehēded;
within which so many Numina or powers (still
ready

ready to performe their operations.) are included.
Now here the word *Numina*, *Seneca* vnder-
standeth the starres , and perhaps also the
Intelligences or spirits. And thus far of the
place or Country of the Soule. Next touching the age or tyme of it, he thus writeth,
Deinde arctam ætatem &c. Furthermore the
Soule suffereth not any small tyme to be allotted
to it, for it thus saith. All yeares are myne : No
age is excluded from high Wits , and each time
lyes open to my contemplation . When that shall
come , which shall dissolue this mixture of what is
diuine , and what humane , then will I leaue the
body , where I did find it ; and I will restore my
selfe to the Gods . Neither now am I altogether
estranged from them , though I be heere detained
with a heauy and earthly matter . By meanes of
these delayes of this mortall age , preparation is
made for a better , and longer life . Euen as our
mothers wombe , containeth vs nine monthes, and
prepareth vs , not for it selfe , but for that place ,
whither it sendeth vs ; that so we may be fit to
breath, and to liue here in sight: So by the helpe of
this tyme (which indureth from our infancy to
old age) we are made ripe and ready for another
birth . Another beginning expecteth vs, and another state of things . As yet we cannot enioy heauen , but (as it were) a far off ; therefore behold
that appointed day without feare or dismayednes;
since it is not the last to the Soule, but to the body.
                                                        What

VVhat thing foeuer doth here cōpaſſe vs, all is to be
eſteemed, but as an vnprofitable cariage or burdē
in an Inne ; for we are to depart. Nature leauing
this world, is depriued of all things, as well as
entring into it. It is not lawfull for thee to carry
more out of the world, then thou didſt bring in.
Yea a great part of that, which cōduced to our life,
is to be left off. The skin, wherwith thou art couered, as with thy next garment, ſhalbe takenaway,
the fleſh and blood ſhalbe taken away, the bones &
ſinews (which are the ſtrongthings of the weaker
parts) ſhalbe taken away. That day, which thou
feareſt as the laſt, is the birth day of Eternity. Caſt
of thy burden. Why delayeſt thou, as if thou hadſt
not afore come out of that body, wherein thou
dideſt lye? Thou now pawſeſt & ſtrugleſt againſt
it, and yet euen at the firſt thou was brought out,
with the like paines, and labour of thy mother.
Thou cryeſt and bewayleſt, and yet to cry is moſt
peculiar to a body newly borne And thē *Seneca*
thus further enlargeth himſelfe. Quid iſta ſic
diligis &c.

Why doſt thou ſo loue theſe terrene and
earthly things, as if they were thine owne? Thou
art couered & ouerwhelmed with theſe. The day
will come, which ſhall reueale or lay thee open, &
which ſhall free thee from the company of a filthy
& ſmelling belly. The ſecrets and miſteries of nature ſhalbe once made euidēt vnto thee, this darknes ſhalbe diſpelled, and thou ſhalt be encompaſſed

one

on each side with a shining light . Imagine , how great that fulgour shalbe, when so many starres do mingle their lights together . No shadow shal hinder this brightnes . Euery part of heauen shall equally shine. The day and night are but alternations and enterchanges of the lowest part of the ayre . Then shall thou say , that afore thou liuedst in darkenes , I meane , when thou shalt at once behold all the brightnes and splendour together , which thou now darkly seest by the narrow helpe of thy eyes ; and yet dost admire it being so farre of from thee: what shall that diuine light seeme to thee, whē thou shalt se it in its owne natiue place? This cogitation admitteth no base, vile , or inhumane thing in the mind . But in lieu thereof it saith , that the Gods are witnesses of all things ; it commandeth vs, that we seeke to be approued & accepted by the Gods ; and teacheth vs , that they prouide and prepare Eternity for vs. Thus farre Seneca of this point : in which discourse he hath deliuered many excellent things as concerning the Soule of man . First , that the Soule is like vnto God; since it extendeth it selfe to all places , and to Eternity. Secondly , that when it leaueth the body , it is ranged amongst *Gods* & *spirits.* Thirdly, that we heere stay vpon the earth, as but in the way of our iourney ; heauen it selfe being our Country. And that al things in this world, which are externall or independēt

of

of the foule, are to be reputed in that de_
gree, as burdens or prouifions are, which
ferue only the more conueniently to finifh
our iourneys. Fourthly, that as an Infant is
prepared in nyne months for to liue in this
wo rld ; fo ought we (during all the tyme
we liue here) to learne to difpofe our felues
for the entertaining of the immortal life of
the world to come. Fiftly, that the laft day
of our mortall life is the beginning of Eternity. Sixtly, that the Soule being departed
from the body, is then clearly to fee the mi-
fteries of nature, and a diuine light and
fplendour. Seauenthly and laftly, that E-
ternity is euer to be fet before eyes; as that
we may make our felues apt to enioy it, &
that we ought to lead our life in fuch fort
as it may be approued of God, who is the
beholder of al things. The like matter hereto we may find in *Plato*, *Plotinus*, *Cicero*, *E-
pictetus*, and other heathen wryters. But
now it next followeth in Methode, that
we produce fuch arguments (and after dif-
folue and anfwere them) as may feeme to
impugne the former verity of the Soules
Immortality.

THE ARGVMENTS, OBIECTED
against the Immortality of the Soule; and their
Solutions, or Anfweres.

C A A P. XXIV.

The 1.
Argumēt

THE firſt may be this . That Soule,
all whoſe operation and function depends vpon a corporal *Organ*, or inſtrument , cannot conſiſt ſeparated from the
body ; But the reaſonable Soule of man is
ſuch : Therefore the reaſonable ſoule cannot conſiſt ſeparated from the body . And
thus is this firſt argument contracted. I anſwere, and diſtinguiſh of the *Maior,* or firſt
Propoſition ·

Two wayes then may the operation of
the Soule depend of a corporall or bodily
organ or inſtrument . Firſt by it ſelfe & immediatly . Secondly accidentally and mediatly . Yf the operation and working of
the Soule depend of the body in the firſt
manner , then is it euident , that ſuch an o-
peration cannot be performed without the
helpe and aſſiſtance of the body ; and conſequently , that, that Soule (whoſe working dependeth after this ſort) cannot exiſt
ſeparated from the body . And ſuch is the
ſoule of beaſts. And ſo in this ſenſe the *Ma-*
ior

ter Proposition is true. But if the operation of the soule depend of a corporall instrument after the second maner, then is the foresaid Proposition false. And the reason hereof is, because what agreeth to another thing *per accidens* (as the phraze is) *& per aliud,* that is accidentally, casually, and in regard only of a third thing, may be taken away. Therefore, seing the function of the *vnderstanding* (which is an essentiall faculty of the reasonable soule) doth not depend of the body, by it selfe, necessarily and immediatly, but only accidentally & mediatly; there is no hinderance, but that it may be performed without the body. Now that the function or operation of the *vnderstanding* doth not depend of the body by it selfe and immediatly, may be proued by many reasons. And first, the function of the *vnderstanding* chiefly consisteth in iudging; but to iudge of a thing the *phantasy* (which is a corporeall internall sense) or any *Idea,* or image framed therein, is not in any sort furthering or coducing, but rather an impedimēt therto; as giuing an occasion oftentimes of erring. For the *vnderstanding* ought not to follow the imagination and conceit of the *phantasy,* neither ought it in iudging to be guided thereby; but rather it is to correct the *phantasy,* that it selfe may by this meanes arryue

vnto

vnto the truth . Now if the force of the *vn-derſtanding* be ſo great, that it is able to correct the errours and miſtakings of the *phantaſy* , and to attaine vnto the cleare truth of things (which tranſgreſſeth the nature or working of the *phantaſy*) then may we frō hence conclude, that the working of the *vnderſtanding* doth not immediatly, or in its owne nature depend of the *phantaſy*. Secōdly, the former point is further proued , becauſe we chiefly couet to know things ſpirituall ; of which things the *phantaſy* is in no ſort capable .

Thirdly, becauſe the knowledge of truth is not reckoned among the goods of the body , but of the mind only ; and therfore is to be deſired for the perfection only of the mind. Fourthly, becauſe deuout and holy men are ſomtimes eleuated in an *Ex-taſis* to that ſpirituall contemplation, which cannot be expreſſed in words ; and conſequently not to be repreſented by the imaginatiō or *phantaſy* ; as may be gathered out of the Apoſtle in his ſecond Epiſtle to the *Corinthians* c. 12. But becauſe I ſtryue to be ſhort, therefore, I omit heere to iterate diuers things aboue ſet downe, touching the force of vnderſtanding and deſiring .

But ſome here may demaund: How thē cometh it to paſſe , that we cannot vnderſtand

ftand any thing, except we forge a certaine image of it in the *phantaſy* ? And frō whēce procedeth this neceſſity ? To which I an-ſwere, that this procedeth from the preſent ſtate of the ſoule ; to wit, becauſe the ſoule is the forme of the body , actually infor-ming and giuing life to it . For as during al that tyme , that the ſoule remaineth in the body , it (after a certaine manner) putteth vpon the ſtate and nature of the body, and becometh in a ſort groſſe and dull , that thereby it may better accōmodatate it ſelfe to the body . So all things , which then it conceaueth , it conceaueth & apprehēdeth vnder a certaine corporal ſhew and forme. For it is an *axiome* in Philoſophy , *that the manner of working followeth the manner of ex-iſtence* . But when the ſoule ſhalbe ſepara-ted from the body , and ſhalbe gathered (as it were) into it ſelfe and ſubſiſt by it ſelſe ; then ſhall it enioy another degree or kind of vnderſtanding ; neither ſhall it haue any neceſſity of framing the *Idea's* & images of things in the *phantaſy* ; no otherwiſe then the Intelligences haue , which wee call Angels . To conclude, as long as the Soule is in the body , it cānot rightly exerciſe the *vnderſtanding* and reaſon, except it haue the externall ſenſes looſe , and it liberty ; as is euident euen from thoſe dreames , which

we

we haue in ſleepe . Now the cauſe hereof is not, that the function of the ſenſes do ad-uantage the function of the *vnderſtanding* , or that this doth depend of that other; but becauſe the faculty of the *vnderſtanding*, is the ſupreme and moſt excellent faculty of the ſoule . Wherupon it riſeth , that for the perfect exerciſe of the *vnderſtanding*, it is re-quiſite, that the ſoule be altogether free & vnbounded ; that ſo it may bend & beſtow all the force and power of its eſſence vpon ſuch an operation. And of this point a ſigne is , that when we vehemently apply our mind to vnderſtand , and apprehend any thing , we ſcarcely obſerue and note ſuch things , as do occurre our ſenſe ; the force of the ſoule buſiyng it ſelfe in its moſt ſu-preme and moſt noble action of all . Ad he-reto , that there is ſuch a connexiõ, aſſocia-tion , and ſympathy of the powers of the ſoule in the body , as that the ſoule cannot exerciſe the higheſt & moſt worthy of thē , if at the ſame preſent it doth alienate and eſtrange it ſelfe from the loweſt . Here I meane of the reciprocall affinity of theſe powers only , which belong to knowled-ge .

The 2
Argumēt

The ſecond argument. Yf the ſoule, af-ter, it is diſueſted of the body, be immortall, then ſhall it eyther continually remayne ſeparated

parated from the body, or els sometime be
restored to it. But it seemeth, that neither of
these can be warranted with reason. Not the
first, because it so should continue in a state,
which is violent and aduerse to nature; for
seing the soule of man is the lowest & mea-
nest of all spirituall substances; it requyreth
to be in the body, as the forme of it; & therefore it hath a naturall propension to be vnited with the body; therefore to be separated
from the body, and to exist and continue separatly, is cōtrary to its naturall inclination,
and in some sort violent. But *Violence & perpetuity are incompatible.* Not the later (I meane
that sometime after its separatiō the soule is
to be restored and reunited with the body)
because from hence it would follow, that
the resurrection of the body should be naturall, and due to the naturall course of things,
which point is not to be granted; both because it is a high mistery of Christian fayth,
as also in that all ancient Heathen Philosophers were vtterly ignorant of this doctrine
of the resurrection of bodyes.

I answere: first that *Origen* and the *Platonicks* vtterly denyed the reasonable soule
to be the forme of the body, who placed the
same in the body, not as a forme in its naturall subiect for the commodity, and benefit of the subiect; but as one, that is guilty.
and

and detained in prifon for a reuenge of its
former errours . Whereupon they taught ,
that one fubftance (to wit Man) was not
properly compounded of the foule and the
body ; but they auerred, that only the foule
was man, and the body the prifon ; & therfore they faid , that euery body was to be
auoyded. But for confutation of this errour
it is manifeft, that it is repugnant to reafon.
For if the foule be with-houldē in the body
as in a prifon, why then doth it fo much
feare and auoid death? Or why is it fo grieuous to the foule to be difioyned and feparated from the body ? Why is it not painful
to the foule to ftay in a body fo ftored with
filth and impurity ? As we fee it is moft difpleafing to a man of worth , & accuftomed
to places of note and regard , to be kept in
a fordid and obfcure dungeon . Why doth
it fo much affect the commodities and pleafures of the body, and is fo greatly delighted therewith? Why at the hurt and loffe
of the body , is it fo infinitly afflicted and
molefted , fince otherwife it hath iuft reafō
to reioyce at thefe corporal endomages, no
otherwife , then captiues and imprifoned
perfons, who are glad to fee their chaines
fall afunder, & their prifon laid leuell with
the ground? Therefore feing the reafona-
bie foule is no leffe fēfible of ioy or griefe,
                                    touching

touching the pleasures or aduersities of the body, then the soules of beasts are; it is euident, that the reasonable soule is the naturall forme of mans body, and that it doth affect and couet to be vnited with it. Yet because it is not so immersed in the body as that it ought to be extinguished with it, but is able (through the benefit of its owne subtilty and spirituall substance) to subsist by it selfe; Hence then it riseth, that it predominateth ouer the affections of the body, contemning them at its pleasure; so as it yealdeth (if it selfe will) neither to pleasure, nor griefe, nor death it selfe; which priuiledge is not found in irrationable creatures.

This opinion then being reiected, we affirme that the soule is not to continue separated, but sometimes to be reunited to the body; because it was not first ordained to be an entyre and complete substance (as an Angell is) but to be only a part of a substance, to wit the forme, and consequently an imperfect and incomplete substance. Whereupon it is needfull, that we admit the resurrection of bodies. And yet we cannot tearme this to be naturall, for although the forming of the body, and the vnion of the soule with the body be a naturall thing, and due to the naturall state & perfection

perfection of the ſoule; yet this cannot be accompliſhed by naturall cauſes, but only by diuine power; and therefore it is to be called *ſupernaturalis*; euen as giuing ſight to the blynd is ſo reputed, or reſtoring of decayed and feeble parts of the body, and the curing of incurable diſeaſes.

Neither ought it to ſeeme ſtrange, that the ſoule of man cannot obtaine for euer its naturall perfection, without the power of God, and his extraordinary aſſiſtance; the reaſon hereof being in that it is capable of a double, & (as it were) of a contrary nature; to wit ſpirituall and corporall, mortall and immortall. Therefore the Soule requireth the body (once loſt) to be reſtored to it; but to be reſtored ſo firmely & ſtrongly, as that it is neuer more to be loſt, is ſupernaturall, ſince otherwiſe there ought to be infinite tymes a reſurrection of bodyes.

The Philoſophers were ignorant of this reſurrection, either becauſe they thought the ſoule not to be the naturall forme of the body, but a complete ſubſtance, or els, in that they thought it leſſe inconuenyent to teach, that the ſoule remained after death perpetually ſeparated, then to introduce & bring in (as a new doctrine) the reſurrectiō of the body. For though it be naturall to the ſoule to be in the body, yet in that reſpect,

peƈt, only, as it is separated from it, it feeleth no griefe, but rather it is freed therby
from all the inconueniences and discōmo-
dities of this life, & obtaineth a more high
and more worthy degree, and becomes
more neere to diuine & celestial substances.
Wherefore I do not thinke, that the soule
(being separated) doth of it selfe much couet to be reunited with the body; though
by the force and weight of nature, it hath
a propension therto; And the reason herof
is, because those goods and priuiledges it
possesseth, as it is separated, are more to be
esteemed, then those are, which it enioyeth in the body.

Neither is it true, that this separation is
violent to the soule; for although the want
of this vnion be in some sort violent to it,
to wit by way of negation; as it is a priuati-
on of that, to which the very essence of the
soule doth efficaciously propend and in-
ciyne, yet that liberty, which it then enioyeth, and that vigour of the Soule & mā-
ner of vnderstanding is not in any sort violent, but most agreable to its nature, as it is
in state of separation.

The third Argument. The structure of The 3.
the body may seeme to intimate & imply Argumēt
the mortality of the soule; for it is almost
wholy framed for the temporal vses of this
                                    mortall

mortall life; to wit that the body may be
maintained and preferued, and nature propagated and continued.

Thus the teeth and ftomacke are ordained to chew and concoct meate; the inte-
ftines and bowels to auoyd the fuperfluous
and excrementall matter; the liuer to con-
fect bloud; the gall to receaue the fharper &
more bitter parts of the nutriment; the fplen
or milt to containe the more groffe bloud;
the reynes to part and diuyde the *ferafus*, &
wheifh matter of the nourifhment from the
bloud; the bladder to receaue and fend out
this wheifh matter; the inftruments of the
fexe to procreatiō. But after this life, there
fhalbe no need either of the vfe of meates or
of procreation : therfore there ought not to
be thefe members, which are ordayned to
thofe ends; and confequently there ought
not to be the foule, which requireth fuch
members, and a body fo framed and compacted. For thofe members are to be accounted in vayne & fuperfluous, of which there
neuer fhalbe any vfe.

I anfwere; This argument directly &
immediatly oppugneth the refurrection, &
fecundarily and by way of cōfequence, the
immortality of the foule. For the compofition and ftructure of mans body prooueth,
that in it felfe, and by its owne nature, it is
                                    mortall,

mortall; but it doth not prooue the soule to be in like sort mortall. But although the body be disolued and do perish, yet it is a facill & easy matter for God to frame it againe in its due tyme, & to reinfuse the soule into it, and so to cause, that the body shall neuer after be dissolued :(for as *Plato* in his *Timæo*, teacheth ; *Quod natura sua solubile est &c. VVhat in its owne nature stands subiect to dissolution, and obnoxious vnto death, the same by the commandement and will of God may be made immortall, so as it shall neuer dye.* Certainly those functions of the members, which belong to nourishment of the body, and to generation shall cease, notwithstanding it followeth not, that those members shalbe superfluous; because they shall serue to the naturall constitution of the body, as parts necessary to its perfection and beauty: for this is their chiefe and principall vse, to wit, to conduce to the making of a perfect and complete body, and such, as is fitting to the condition & state of the soule.

Now these functions are only a secondary end, because they are ordained only for the tyme, and serue only to repayre the ruines of mortall body, the naturall heat feeding vpon, and consuming the substance of the flesh: whereupon it followeth, that as the augmentation or increase of the bodyes

greatnesse

greatneſſe ceaſeth, when it once hath attai-
ned its iuſt ſtature; Euen ſo ſhall nutrition or
nouriſhment of the body ceaſe, and the functions belonging thereto, when the body
by a diuine hand and power ſhall become
immortall. For ſeeing theſe functions are of
the loweſt degree, as agreeing to the ſoule
according to its meaneſt faculty and parte,
wherein it participateth with plants, and is
heerein attended with much droſſe, filth, &
rottennes, it was not conuenient, that they
ſhould be perpetuall, but that in due tyme
they ſhould be taken away, God reducing
the body into a better forme; Notwithſtanding the function of the ſenſes, becauſe they
are made after a ſpirituall manner without
corruption, they ſhalbe perpetuall: In like
ſort the function of the voyce and ſpeach
ſhalbe perpetuall, to the which thoſe members ſhall after their manner either neerely
or remotely be ſeruiceable; and therefore in
this reſpect alſo they ſhall not be in vaine &
ſuperfluous.

The fourth argument may be taken frō
thoſe words, which *Pliny* in his ſeauenth
booke of his hiſtory, c. 55. ſetteth downe,
though they be of ſmall force and validity.
Firſt then he to this purpoſe ſaith, *Omnibus a
ſuprema die &c. The ſame happeneth to all things
after their laſt day, which was at their beginning.*
Neither

The Ar-
gument
of Pliny.

Neither after death is there more sense to the body
er soule, then there was before its birth. I answere
and say, that that is heere assumed, which is
first to be prooued, and therefore it is denyed with the same facility, wherwith it was
affirmed. And that this saying of his is false,
it is prooued from rhe whole schoole of the
Platonicks, and the *Pithagoreans.* For,there is
no necessity, why that, which once begun,
should sometimes cease, especialle if it be a
simple and vncompounded substance, as the
soule and euery spirituall nature is. But indeed it is otherwise of corporall things consisting of the Elements, of whome only that
sentence is verifyed; *Omne genitum potest cor-*
rumpi : Euery thing that is made, may be corrup-
ted. Certainly *materia prima* (because it is
simple and vncompounded) though it had
a beginning, yet can it not be corrupted.
The same also (according to the doctrine of
the *Platonicks*) is to be said of the celestiall
Orbs. Therefore although there was no
sense of the soule before its creatiõ, yet followeth it not, that therefore after death it
shall haue no sense. And the reason hereof
is, because though the birth (as it were) of
the soule be ioined with the birth of the body, and thereupon the soule did exist before
the birth of the body ; notwithstanding the
destruction of the soule doth not follow the

destruction

destruction of the body, for death is not a destruction or extinguishmét of them both, but only a separation of the body from the soule.

In the next place *Pliny* demandeth, *Cur corpus &c. why the body followeth and coueteth the soule?* I answere, that no body followeth the soule departing from hence, because the soule (as being a naked and simple substance) can consist without the body. Then saith he, *Vbi cogitatio illi ? From whence hath the soule separated its cogitation, or discourse ?* The soule being in state of separation, hath no need of a braine or a body, that it may thinke, imagine, and discourse, (euen as we grant that God & spirituall substances haue not those *Organs*) because the force of vnderstanding, by how much it is more remote & distant from the body, by so much it is more excellent. Next asketh Pliny ; *Quomodo visus & auditus ? From whence hath the soule separated seeing and hearing?* Whereto it is replyed, that the soule needeth not the function and operation of the outward senses seing, that it perceaueth all things in its mynd. For the the mynd then doth not only serue to cogitate, or thinke, or to know things abstractiuely; but also to behold and apprehend all things, which in this life we apprehend with our externall senses ; euen as Pliny himselfe speaketh of God ; *Quisquis est Deus & c. VVhosoeuer God is , he is all sense , all sight, all hearing , all soule , all vnderstanding, all himselfe.*

In like sort we say of the soule being separated, that it is all sense, all sight, all hearing, all vnderstanding, all vigour and life. Againe he questioneth; *Quid agit ? qui vsus eius ?* What doth the soule separated ? Or what vse is there of it? Of whom by retortiō I demand, *what do other spirits and incorporeall substances?* As if it were nothing to contemplate, praise, and loue God, and to enioy the fellowship of celestiall spirits. Certainly the cecity and blindnesse of this man is wonderfull, who may be thought not to haue acknowledged the being of any spirits. Therefore how much more wisely & deliberatly did the *Platonicks,* and the *Peripateticks* teach , who placed mās chiefe felicity in contēplating of the first beginning and cause of all things ? Pliny proceedeth yet further: *Quid sine sensibus bonum ? VVhat can be good , which is not to be apprehended by the senses ?* I say to acknowledge no good of the soule without the senses is incident to swyne and beasts, not to Philosophers : next, *Qua deinde sedes? VVhat seate or mansion for the soules seperated ?* The answere is expedite and ready; to wit the mansion for the

C c <u>2</u>　　　　　　pious

pious and vertuous foules is heauen, for the
wicked Hell. And this opinion all Antiquity euer did hold. Next he asketh: *Quan-*
ta multitudo &c. how great a multitude is there
of foules, as of shadowes for so many ages? To
which is to be anfwered, that the multitude of foules is as great, as there is number
of men, which haue liued from the beginning of the world vnto this day. For feeing
the world tooke a beginning, the number
of the foules is not infinite, but it is comprehended within a certaine number, and that
not exceedingly great : for it were not very difficult to fhew, that this number exceedeth not two or three Myriades of millions. Now the foules are ignorantly called
by Pliny *Vmbra, Shadowes*, feing that they
are like vnto light, and the body is to be re-
fembled rather to a fhadow, as the Platonicks were accuftomed to fay. After this
Pliny thus expoftulateth: *Qua dementia &c.*
VVhat folly is it to maintaine, that life is iterated,
and begun againe by meanes of death? But herein (as in all the reft) he is deceaued; for the
life of the foule is not iterated after the
death of the body; but the body dying, it
continueth and perfeuereth. After he further enquireth : *Qua genitis qui es &c. VVhat*
reft can euer be, if the fenfe & vigour of the foule
remaineth aloofe of in fo high a place? To which

is

is to be anfwered that not only reft, quyet and fredome from the troubles and miferies of this life belongeth to the foules feparated, but alfo wonderfull pleafures and ioy, if they haue here liued well; but mifery, if they haue fpent their tyme in wickednes without finall repentance. And this the Platonicks alfo acknowledge. In the next place he thus further difcourfeth, faying, that, *the feare of what is to fucceed after this life, doth leffen the pleafures of this life*. Thus we heere fee, that this is the chiefe reafon, why wicked men are loth to belieue the immortality of the foule, to wit, becaufe this their beliefe confoundeth all their pleafures, & woundeth their mynds with a continuall feare of what is after to come. For being confcious and guilty to themfelues of their owne impiety, and of what they iuftly do deferne, therefore they wifh that their foule might dy with their body, fince they cannot expect with reafó a greater benefit. For fo they fhould be free from mifery and torments, which hang ouer their heads. And becaufe they earneftly defire this, they are eafily induced to belieue it to come to paffe. Now the extinguifhing of the foule is not the chiefe good of nature, (as *Pliny* thinketh) but the chiefe euill rather of nature, fince euery thing

C c 3   chiefly

chieffly auoydeth its owne deſtruction, as
loſing al it goodnes in Nature thereby. For
how can that be accounted the chiefe good
of nature, by the which all iuſtice is ouerthrowne, all reward and remuneration is
taken away from vertue ; and all chaſtiſement from vyce ? For though it were for
the good of the wicked, that the ſoule were
mortall , yet it were moſt iniurious to the
vertuous , and hurtfull to the publick good
of the *vniuerſe*, no otherwiſe then it would
be inconuenient to the good of a temporal
commonwealth , if no rewards ſhould be
propounded ;for vertue , nor reuenge for
exorbitancy and tranſgreſſion of the lawes.
Certainly the cogitation of death , & the
ſoules immortality increaſeth the anxiety
and griefe of the wicked ; ſince they do not
only complaine for the death of the body
(which depriueth them of all pleaſure of
this life) but alſo (and this with far greater
vehemency) for the puniſhments, which
after the death of the body , they are perſwaded (through a ſecret feeling of nature)
their ſoules are to ſuffer . But now on the
contrary part , the former cogitation doth
increaſe the ioy and comfort of the vertuous; ſeing they not only reioyce at the death
of the body (by meanes whereof they are
diſcharged of al the afflictiõs of the world)
but

but alfo (and this in far greater meafure) at
the certaine expectation of that felicity and
happines, wherwith after their death they
fhalbe replenifhed.

Now from all this heretofore deliuered
& fet downe it is euident, that the obiecti-
ons and reafons of *Pliny* are moft weake &
friuolous; as proceding rather from an in-
ueterated hate and auerfion of the contrary
doctrine, then from any force and ground
of reafon.

But here one perhaps may reply & fay;
Be it fo, that the foule is immortall, not-
withftáding it may fo be, that after this life
it fhall fuffer no euill, but enioy great liberty, bufiyng it felfe in the contemplatió
of things. Or if it fhall fuffer any punifhmét,
yet this fufferance fhall not be perpetuall,
but longer or fhorter, according to the proportion & nature of its offences committed
in this world: and that greater finnes fhalbe
expiated with a more long punifhment, or
at leaft with a more grieuous; and lefler
with a fhorter or more gentle chaftifemét.
Indeed I grant the iudgement of the *Stoick*,
to haue bene, that the foule after this life
fuffered no euill, but that inftantly after
death, it returned to fome one 'appointed
ftarre or other; and there remayned either
vntill the generall exuftion and burning

The
vayne
iudgmēt
of the
Stoicks
touching
the
Soule.

of the world, if it were vertuous & wife; or els only for a short tyme, if it were wicked and foolish; which period being once ended the foule was to be turned into the Element, from whence it was taken. But these affertions are friuolous, and not warranted with any reafon; for granting that foules do liue after this life, what then is more eafy to be belieued, then that they receaue either rewards or paynes, according to their different comporttments in this world? Since otherwife where should the Prouidence of God be? Or where Iuftice? But of this point we haue abundantly difcourfed aboue. Furthermore, if Soules for a certayne tyme can fubfift without a body, why can they not for euer continue fo? For feing they are fimple and vncompounded fubftances, they cánot in proceffe of tyme grow old, or loofe their ftrength and vigour (as bodyes compounded of Elements do.) Now if they can (but for one inftant) exift and liue without a body, thē can they for all eternity perfeuer in that ftate, as being not fubiect to any extinguifhment or deftructiō, as the whole fchoole of the *Peripatetiks*, and *Ariftotle* himfelfe do teach. For there is nothing, which can deftroy or corrupt a fimple fubftance, fub-fifting by it felfo. And therefore it is houlden,

den, that *Materia* (as being a simple substance, and inhering in no other thing, as
in a subiect)is incorruptible, and inexterminable.

Now touching that, which is spoken of
the burning of soules, in that sense, as if
they could be dissolued and vanish away
into ayre, by meanes of fyer (as bodyes) is
no lesse absurd. For the soule is not a body,
or an oyle-substance, which can be set on
fire; but it is a spirit more thin, pure, and
light, then either ayre or fyer. But what
is dissolued with fyer, ought to be corporeall, and more grosse and corpulent then
the fyre it selfe, or that, into the which it
is dissolued. It may be further added hereto
that the foundation of the *Stoicks,* whereupō
they grounded theselues, that soules were
to suffer no euill after this life (notwithsta-
ding their great sinnes and enormities here
committed) was, because they were perswaded, that our soules were certaine particles or relicks of a *diuinity*. And this *diui-*
nity they did hold to be *anima mundi*, the
soule of the world, from which soule they
further taught (as being the common and
vniuersal soule of al things) that the particular soules of liuing Creatures, & chiefly
the soules of men, were decerpted & ta-
kē; the which being after freed of their cor-

Vid. Epi-
ctetus dif-
sert. 1. c.
14. Sene-
ca epist.
92. Cicero
Tusc. 5.

C c 5   poreall

poreal bonds and chaynes, were to returne
to that principle, from whence they are deryued; meaning to that *vniuerfall foule* of the
world, with the which they finally clofe
themfelues. All which affertiõs are in their
owne nature fo abfurd, as that they need
not any painfull refutatiõ. For if the foules
be parcels of God, how can they be diffolued with fyre? Or finally how cã they be
depraued with fo many facinorous crymes
and impieties? Yea it would from hence
follow, that *Diuinity* it felfe fhould confift
(as bodyes do) of parts, and fhould be obnoxious to all euils and inconueniences
whatfoeuer. Therefore this vayne imagi-
natiõ of the *Stoicks* is to be reiected, which
heretofore hath bene well refelled by *Tully*.

   Origen did indeed confeffe, that foules
were immortall, and that they were neuer
to lofe their owne proper kind and nature;
notwithftanding he taught, that the punifhments of them were not fempiternall, but
were to take an end after certaine ages.
The fame he in like fort affirmed of the
paynes & torments of the Diuels. But this
errour of *Origen* (which he borrowed of
the *Platonicks*) was further accõpanied with
many other errours.

   1.　Firft that all Soules, Diuels, & Angels

gels were of the fame nature, and confequently, that foules were as free from all
corporall commere , as Angels were .

2. That Soules, before they were adioyned to the body did finne, and for guilt
of fuch their finnes, were tyed to bodyes,
and inclofed in them as in prifons.

3. That foules were coupled with bodyes in a certayne prefcribed order ; As
firft with more fubtill bodyes;then if they
continued finning, with groffer bodyes; &
laftly with terrene and earthly bodyes: &
further *Origen* taught that thefe feueral degrees of thefe foules defcéding into bodyes
were reprefented by the ladder, which appeared to *Iacob* in his fleepe *Genefis* 24.

4. That all foules, as alfo the Diuels ,
fhould after certaine ages be fet at liberty,
and reftored to an Angelicall light & fplédour; to wit, when they had fully expiated their finnes with condigne punifhméts.

5. That this viciffitude and enterchàge
of felicity & mifery fhould be fempiternal,
& for euer in reafonable creatures:fo as the
fame foules fhould infinite tymes be both
bleffed and miferable ; for after they had
continued in heauen for many ages bleffed
and happy, then (as being againe fatiated
and cloyed with the fruition of diuyne
things) they fhould contaminate & defyle
themfelues

themselues with finne; for the which they were againe to be detruded into bodyes, in the which if they liued wickedly , they were to be caft into the paines of hel, which being for a tyme fuffered, they were to be reftored vnto Heauen . This condition & ftate Origen impofed vpon euery reafonable creature , by what name foeuer it was called , whether Angels, *Principalities*, *Powers*, *Dominations* , Diuels, or Soules. See of this poynt *S. Ierome* in his Epiftle ad *Pāmachium* againft the Errours of *Iohn of Ierufalē*, and *Auguftin l. de harefibus c.* 43.

But *Origen* extremely doteth in thefe things.

The Errours of Origen

1. As firft, in affirming, that all fpirituall fubftances are of one nature and condition.

2. That Soules are not the formes of their bodyes; but feparated fubftāces, which are inclofed in the bodyes, as in certaine prifons.

3. That all foules were created from the beginning of the world.

4. That bleffed fpirits could haue a faftidious & cloyed conceit of diuine contemplation, and that they could finne.

5. That for fuch their finnes they were fent into bodyes, there (for the tyme) to be detaynd, as in prifons.

6. That

6.   That the torments of the Diuels & of all soules are once to be expired and ended.

7.   That all the damned are at length to be saued.

8.   Finally, that this Circle, by the which the Soule goeth from saluation to sinne, from sinne into the body, from the body to damnation, from damnation to saluation, is perpetuall, and continueth for euer.

Al which dreames of *Origen* might be refuted by many conuincing and irrefragable reasons; but this is impertinent to our purpose, & would be ouer tedious to perform. Only it shall suffice at this present to demonstrate out of holy Scripture, that the paines of the wicked and damned are to be most grieuous, & neuer to receaue a cessation and end.

Of the Punishments of the life to come, out of the holy Scripture.

CHAP. XXV.

ALTHOVGH it be most sorting to naturall reason, that *Gods diuine Prouidence*, should allot after this life to euery one a iust retribution according to the different

rent comportment of each man in this world;Notwithſtanding what thisreward ſhalbe (whether it be conferred vpon the good or the bad) and of what continuance, neither can mans reaſon nor the diſquiſitiō and ſearch of the beſt Philoſophers giue any ſatisfying anſwere hereto. The cauſe of which inexplicable difficulty is, partly in that it dependeth of the meere free decree of God; and partly becauſe the nature of ſinne (and conſequently the puuiſhment due to it) is not made ſufficiently euident and perſpicuous by naturall reaſon. Therefore to the end we may haue ſome infallible certainty herein, we are to recurre to the diuine Oracles of Gods written word, in the which we are able to ſee what the holy Ghoſt by his Prophets & other pious men, haue pronounced of this point; and eſpecially of the paines of the wicked, whereof we now intreate.

　　1.　　The firſt teſtimony then may be taken out of *Deuteronomy* c. 23. in that moſt admirable and propheticall Canticle or ſong of Moyſes. *Ignis ſuccenſus eſt &c. Fire is kindled in my wrath, and ſhall burne vnto the bottome of hell, and ſhall conſume the earth with her encreaſe, and ſet on fire the foundation of the mountaines.* In which words fiue things are to be conſidered. Firſt, that the fire (with the

the which finners fhalbe punifhed)is already kindled ; both becaufe the fire of hell is
prepared from the beginning, as our Lord
infinuateth in Matth. 25. and the like is
in Efay 30. as alfo in that though that fire
with the which the world fhalbe confumed be not already enkindled, yet it now
exifteth in Gods moft certaine prefcience
and preordinance. For what is certaine to
come by the force of Gods decree, is faid
after a propheticall manner now to exift,
or to be done. Of this fire Dauid the Prophet fpeaketh *Pfalm.* 50. *Ignis in confpectu
&c. A fire fhall deuoure before him, and a mighty
tempeft fhalbe moued round about him : as alfo
Pfalme* 97. *Ignis ante ipfum &c. there fhall go
a fire before him, and burne vp his enemies round
about.* Both which places are interpreted of
the fire of the laft iudgment. Secondly in
the forefaid words of *Moyfes* we are to note,
that this fire is kindled in the wrath of God
that is, his will and firme refolution of pu-
nifhing the wicked : and this not after an
accuftomed fafhion, but after a horrible &
vnheard manner, and fuch as fury is wont
to fuggeft and inuent. For the anger and
wrath of God are not paffions in him, (as
they are in vs) but a peaceable and quyet
will in him gouerned with reafo, notwithftanding it is moft feuere, efficacious, and
moft

moſt powerfull inflicting eternall puniſhments. Seing then that the effect of God herein doth equall , and indeed tranſcend all fury , it may therefore moſt deſeruedly be called *fury* , *wrath*, and *indignation.* Thirdly , that this fire is to burne vnto the bottome of hell;meaning hereby,that that fire ſhall not only heere on earth burne the wicked,when God ſhall iudge the world,but alſo in hell , and this for all Eternity.Fourthly,that this fire ſhall conſume the earth (that is the whole ſuperficies of the earth) & what proceedeth from the earth,as trees wood,,hearbs , and all works of man now extant,as Houſes,Cittyes,the proud Palaces of Princes , Towers , Munitions, & all riches contained in them . All theſe things ſhalbe conſumed with that fire, and turned into aſhes,as *S. Peter* (whoſe teſtimony hereafter we will ſet downe) plainly witneſſeth .

Fiftly and laſtly , that the foreſaid fire (being the miniſter of Gods indignation & reuenge) ſhall not only waſt the vpper and exteriour parts of the earth, & what it ſhall find thereupon;but alſo ſhall penetrate vnto the bowels of the earth; ſo as it ſhall conſume the very bottome of the higheſt moũtaines . Whereupon it followeth that all mettals , pretious ſtones , and all other riches

ches of the earth (with the pryde whereof
the world now vaunteth and insulteth so
much) shalbe destroyed by the same fire;
Since all these for the most part lye in the
lowest part of the mountaines , and in the
bowels of the earth . Thus nothing shalbe
found of that solidity, as to be able to resist
the rage and fury of this fire . Yea all such
bodyes (compounded of Elements) which
by a generall name are called by the Philosophers *Mixta,* shall in a short tyme be dissolued with the force of the said fire , and
shalbe reduced to their first principles .
This is insinuated in the 97. Psalm. which
intreateth of the Iudgement to come ,
though in a propheticall manner, it speaketh of things , as though they were already performed; for thus the Prophet there
saith : *Montes sicut cera &c. The mountaines
melted like waxe , at the presence of the Lord of
the whole earth.* And in *Iudith* likewise c. 16.
we thus read. *Montes à fundamentis &c. The
mountaines leape vp from their foundations &c.
The rockes melt at thy presence like waxe.* We
know by experience , that through vehemency of heat stones are dissolued, & rúne
through the plaines of the fields , like to a
fiery torrent. Now all these effects, which
are wrought by this fire , are showes and
forerunners of the horrible & interminable

D d   punishment

puniſhment of the wicked.

2.   The ſecond teſtimony is taken out
of *Indith* 16. *Dabit ignem &c.* *The Lord ſhal
ſēd fire & wormes vpon their fleſh, that they may
feele, and be burnt for euer.* In which words
we fynd expreſly, that the puniſhments of
the wicked ſhalbe for Eternity. The like
place hereto is that of *Eccleſiaſticus c. 7. Me-
mento ira &c. Remember that vengeance wil not
ſlacke. Humble thy mind greatly; for the vengeance of the wicked is fire and wormes.* But to returne to the former text of *Iudith*, *The Lord
ſhall ſend fire vpon their fleſh.* This is ſaid, becauſe the very bodyes of the wicked ſhall
inſtantly after the reſurrection be puniſhed
with fire, and ſhall ſo burne like wood, as
that they ſhall not need any externall matter to nouriſh the ſame although this alſo ſhall not be wanting; both which two
things ſhall hereafter be explicated out of
other paſſages of Scripture. But to proceed
to the words following of the foreſaid text
And wormes &c. I do not thinke that theſe
wormes ſhalbe corporall, ſo as they ſhall
hurt the fleſh of the dāned with their teeth
(though ſome graue Authors may ſeeme
to hold the contrary) for to what end ſhall
it be needfull to make ſuch baſe and vile
creatures immortall by force of a new miracle, and to liue in a moſt raging fire, for
the

the punithing of men, seeing the bytings of any beast whatsoeuer in comparison of the paines of that fire, are to be estemed, but as sports and of no moment? I here omit, that the damned by reason of their fury and impatiency shall wound with their teeth both themselues, and their fellowes. Therefore by the name of *wormes* in this place may be vnderstood those very small sparkes and flames of fyre, which in a thousand places breake out of the flesh of the damned like vnto little wormes; or els the *worme of Conscience* may be signifyed thereby, whose most bitter byting & gnawing doth in hel afflict euen the body. And that this construction may the rather be admitted, it is to be knowne, that two seuerall cogitatiōs do daily present themselues to the minds of the damned; to wit, not only that through their sinnes they are depriued of eternall glory, the which they might with small labour and paines haue purchased; but also that they are mancipated and bound to euerlasting torments, which easily(whiles they liued)they might haue auoyded. Now from hence is engendred a double griefe, which with extreme bitternes gnaweth & byteth(like a worme)the heart of those miserable soules.

The worme of Conscience.

And these former cogitations & afflicti-

ons

ons of ſpirit are moſt ſtinging wormes, whoſe bytings are the chiefeſt torments of the damned. For the apprehenſion of ſo incomprehenſible a good loſt, and ſo infinite and inſufferable a puniſhment to be endured (and both theſe for all eternity) more afflicteth the wicked, then the only paine of hell fire doth.

This point may be confirmed in that our Lord in the Ghoſpeli, & the Prophet Eſay in his booke, do expreſſe the torments of the wicked by fire, & by the word *worme*. If then the foreſaid double cogitation, and the double griefe proceeding from thence be not vnderſtood, thereby, the the chiefe torment of the damned may ſeeme to be omitted, and not ſpoken of by eyther of the.

Mark. 9.
Eſay .66.

3. The third is in *Iob. 21. Interrogate quemlibet &c. Aske them that goe by the way &c. For the wicked is kept vnto the day of deſtruction, and he shalbe brought forth to the day of wrath.* In theſe words holy *Iob* inſinuateth, that the doctrine concerning the puniſhment of the wicked after this life, was generally knowne and made vulgar to others, beſides the nation of the Iewes, euē in his owne tyme, that is, long before the dayes of *Moyſes*; for *Iob* is ſuppoſed to be more ancyent then *Moyſes*. In like ſort *Iob* c. 20. thus further ſaith. *Luet quæ fecit &c.*

He

He shall pay for all things he hath done, and yet he shall not be consumed; he shall suffer according to the multitude of his inuentions . In which words is signifyed the eternity of the torments of the wicked ; for the damned person shall so suffer, that he shall neuer be consumed and wasted away, but euer shal remaine whole to suffer fresh torments . Againe in the same Chapter we read . *Omnes tenebræ &c. All darknes shall be hid in his secret places ; the fire which is not blowne* (to wit by más endeauour) *shall deuoure him; that which remaineth in his tabernacles shalbe destroyed* .

4. The fourth. *Psalm.* 11. *Dominus interrogat &c.* The Lord *will aske* (that is he wil try) *the iust and wicked; but the wicked, and him that loueth iniquity, doth his soule hate. Vpon the wicked he shall rayne snares, fire , and brimstome, and stormy tempests; this is the portiō of their cup.* For the more full explication of this text it is first to be obserued, that a sinner (whiles he loueth sinne) hateth his owne soule (as here is said) because he procureth to it an euerlasting euill ; for what hate can be greater then that , which purchaseth to the hater so great a calamity ? Therefore euery sinner while he seemeth most to loue himselfe, (in doing all things which are gratefull to his lust, affections, and ambition) doth then most hate himself,

to wit, by falling into the greateſt euil that is, through an inordinate and intemperate loue of himſelfe.

Vpon the wicked he shall raine ſnares. Theſe ſnares or nets are inextricable and indiſſoluble links of miſery and euill; for all future puniſhments ſhall become ſnares, becauſe they ſhall ſo firmely cleaue to the wicked, as that by no art, or meanes poſſible ſhall they be of force to free themſelues of them for the ſhorteſt tyme. By the word *shal raine* two things are inſinuated. Firſt, that theſe euils ſhall come from a height, to wit from the decree & ſentence of a heauenly iudge, as raine deſcendeth from heauen. Secõdly, that with great force and wonderfull abũdance they ſhall precipitatly ruſh and fall vpon them: *fire, and brinſtone, and ſtormy tẽpeſts* &c. to wit; their hereditary portion which for euer they ſhall enioy: *Fire*, with which their bodyes ſhal burne ; *Brimſtone* with which they on each ſide ſhalbe encõpaſſed; *And ſtormy tempeſts*, with the which the fire of hell, and the brimſtone ſhalbe blowne. In the greek text it is κνεῦμα καται-γίδος, that is; the ſpirit or force of a whirle wind. In which words it may ſeeme to be ĩmplyed, that a moſt rugged wind ſhalbe ſtirred vp by diuine power, by meanes wherof the fire & thoſe ſulphureous lakes ſhall

with

with a horrible noise cōtinually be blown .
This kind of fragour and found is somtimes
heard for the space of many dayes in burning moūtaines , when they sed out fire &
such burning & sulphureous matter . Some
Deuines do vnderstād by the former phraze
stormy tempests, a *diuine Power*, by the which
hell fire shalbe enkindled and continued.

5.   The sift is in *Psalm.* 2 1. *Pones eos &c.*
Thou shalt make them like a fiery Ouen, in time
of thine anger . The Lord shall destroy them in his
wrath , and the fire shall deuoure them . The
meaning of which place is , that at that
tyme when the Lord shall shew his anger,
(that is, when he shall iudge the world) he
ouerwhelme his enemies with a mighty
fire ; so as they shall burne, as if they were
in an Ouen; and then after he shall detrude
them in his wrath into hell, where they
shalbe tormented with euerlasting fire. S.
Ierome translateth the foresaid words, *præci-*
pitabit eos: he shall cast them downe headlong ,
because after the fire hath once encōpassed
them (the earth gaping wyde) they shalbe
precipitated and cast into the gulfe of *Hell.*
In the Hebrew , it is , *deglutiet eos,* because
the earth shall swallow sinners vp.

The fire shall deuoure them . Yet not so , as
their bodies shall perish and decay ; but that
they shalbe on euery side so encompassed
with

with fire, as that they may ſeeme to be abſorpt and deuoured with it.

6.   The ſixt. *Pſalm.* 140. *Cadent ſuper eos
carbones &c. Let coales fal vpon them, let him caſt
them into the fire, and into deepe pits, that they
riſe not againe.* In which words is ſignifyed,
that not any momentary flame, but a ſolid
permanēt fire (ſuch as is of burning coales)
ſhall fall vpon ſinners, from the high com-
mandemēt of the ſupreme iudge. This ſhall
promiſcuouſly happē to all them at the laſt
iudgement, when through Gods appoint-
ment the fire, wherewith the world ſhall
burne, ſhall torment ſinners. *Let him caſt the
into the fire,* that is, firſt they ſhall here be puniſhed with fire, and then after they ſhalbe
caſt into another fire, to wit, into Hell.
Thoſe words, *& into deepe pits, that they riſe
not againe,* ſignify according to the Hebrew
reading, That after the wicked are heere
puniſhed with fire, they ſhalbe caſt into
that fire, which is in the loweſt ditches, to
wit, into the infernall gulfe, out of which
they ſhall neuer be able to ryſe.

7.   The ſeauenth. *Pſalm.* 49. *Laborabit in
æternum &c. He ſhall labour for euer &c.* that
is, the ſinner ſhalbe puniſhed for euer, and
ſhall neuer be extinguiſhed, and conſumed
away. Againe in the ſame pſalme we thus
read: *Sicut Oues &c. Like ſheepe they lye in hel,*
                                                    death

death deuoureth them : that is , finners by heards and flocks fhalbe fhut vp in the infernall foldes , like weake fheepe , which cannot help themfelues , and death fhalbe their fheepheard, who fhall feed them with all bitternes , for fo the word, *feed,* is to be taken , as appeareth out of the Hebrew & Greeke text. For in the Greeke it is, θανατος ποιμανει αυτης, that is , *death shall gouerne them , as a shepheard* . And the Hebrew fignifyeth the like. Behold here the fheepheard and Prince which gouerneth the damned. By the name of *death,* is vnderftood either the Diuell (the authour of death) or els it is a *Profopopeia,* or forging and affigning of a perfon vnto death : And deferuedly fhall they haue *death* there , for their fheepheard, who here refufed *life* for their fheepheard , which was *Chrift* . In the forefaid pfalme, we alfo thus read . *Introibit &c. He shall enter into the generation of his fathers, & he shall not liue for euer. And Pfalm* 92. *Quam magnificata &c. O Lord how glorious are thy workes , and thy thoughts are very deepe. An vnwife man knoweth it not, and a foole doth not vnderftad it. VVhen the wicked grow as the graffe, and all the workers of wickednes do flourish, then they shalbe deftroyed for euer . But thou O Lord art moft high for euermore. For loe, thine enemies, O Lord , for loe thine enemies shall perish: all the*

workers

workers of iniquity shalbe beſtroyed &c. Thus farre in this place ; and certainly the booke of the Pſalmes is full of ſuch comminations and threats of puniſhments after this life, & of moſt ſeuere ſentences of future retributiõ and recompenſation according to euery mans works and merits.

8.   The eight. In the booke of *Eccleſi-aſticus c. 2 1. Stuppa colleſta &c. The congregatiõ of the wicked is like to tow wrapped together , their end is a flame of fire to deſtroy them . The way of ſinners is made plaine with ſtones , but all the end thereof is hell , darknes, and paines .* The ſenſe of the firſter verſe, is, that the whole multitude of the wicked ſhalbe gathered together in one bundle , and ſhalbe like to tow , folded together , the which being thus made ſhall burne eternally . For as a bundle of tow quickly taketh flame, ſo the multitude of ſinners being gathered toge-ther ſhall with ſmall labour be ſet on fire. This ſhalbe effected in that terrible & great day of the generall iudgment, in the which all the chaffe ſhalbe heaped together to burne , and the wheat gathered , to be laid vp in our Lords garner , euen as Chriſt himſelfe hath foretold . *Their end &c.* in the greeke, it is ϲυντϵλϵιϵ that is , the laſt con-ſummation & end, which the wicked ſhall haue ; after the which nothing is further to

Math. 13.

be

be expected, becaufe they fhall thus continue without end. Thus in this word it is
infinuated, that the whole multitude of the
wicked fhalbe fit for nothing els then eternally to burne. The other verfe (to wit,
The way of finners is made plaine &c.) fignifi-
eth, that the way and courfe of wicked 'mē
feemes eafy, cōmodious, fweet, and like to
a way fairely paued; but it endeth in a precipitious and fteepe-downe place, from
whence who falleth, falleth fuddenly into
hel!; where there is nothing, but darkenes
and eternall punifhments.

9. The ninth is out of the booke of *Wif-*
dome c. 5. Where the lamentation of the dāned is defcrybed, the which they vfe in hel,
when they fee the iuft trāflated into glory,
and themfelues caft into fuch infufferable
miferies. Their complaint is this: *Nos infen-*
fati &c. We fooles thought their liues madnes, &
their ends without honour. How are they accoū-
ted among the children of God, and their portion
is among the Saintes? Therefore we haue erred
from the way of truth, & the light of righteoufnes
hath not shined vnto vs, and the funne of vnderftanding rofe not vpon vs &c.

10. The tenth, in *Efay* c. 30. *Praparata*
eft ab heri Topheth &c. Topheth is prepared of
ould; it is euen prepared by the King: he hath
made it deepe and large. The burning thereof is
$\qquad$ *fire*

fire and much wood. The breath of the Lord(like *a riuer of brimſtone*) doth kindle it. This text is interpreted by *S. Ierome,* and ſome other ancient fathers of the place of *Hell,* which long ſince was prepared by God (the ſupreme King and iudge) for the Diuels and his adherents: which place is *deepe,* as being in the loweſt bowels of the earth; and *large,* that it may be capable of all bodyes. The burning of it is *fire,* meaning ſulphureous fire, and *much wood,* that is the bodies of the damned, which ſhall burne like to dry wood. The ſinners are tearmed in the Scripture, *dry wood,* & the iuſt, *greene wood;* according to thoſe words of *S. Luke. If theſe things happen in the greene wood, what ſhall become of the dry wood ?* The ſame ſignificatiõ of *wood* is in like ſort gathered out of that paſſage of *Eccleſiaſtes c.* 11. *If the tree do fall towards the South, or towards the North, in the place, that the tree falleth, there ſhall it be.*

Now if it be demanded by what force Hel fire is kindled, the Prophet anſwereth in the former place. *The breath of the Lord like a riuer of burning brimſtone doth kindle it.* And here by the words, *The breath of the Lord,* is vnderſtood a ſtormy blaſt, there cauſed by Gods power: Or els a diuine and ſupernaturall force of God, by the which that fire ſhall continually burne without
consuming

consuming or wasting away . And this
breath shall so kindle the fire in hell , as if a
torrent of burning sulphur were powred
therein. Now what can the mynd conceaue
more horrible and dreadfull then this?

11. The Eleuenth, is also in *Esay c.* 33.
*Contriti sunt &c. The sinners in Sion are a-
fraid ; a feare is come vpon the Hypocrites : who
among vs shall dwell with deuouring fire ? VVho
among vs shall dwell with euerlasting burnings?*
Which passage of Scripture is expounded
by many of the Auncient authours , of the
paynes and torments of *Hell* .

12. The twelfth, in *Esay.* 50. *Ecce vos omnes &c . Behold , all you kindle a fire , and are
compassed about with sparkles ; walke in the light
of your fire , and in the sparkles , that you haue
kindled . This shall you haue at my hand; you shal
lye downe in sorrow .* This place of Scripture
is not only vnderstood of that fire , wherewith the *Romanes* vanquished the Iewes, &
which through their sinnes they deserued;
but also of *Hell* fire, which all sinners haue
kindled to themselues , as *S. Ierome* and o-
ther Fathers do interprete : for Sinnes are
(as it were) certaine fiery seedes , containing within them , a secret flame, which
in its due tyme breaketh forth into an open
fire. Therfore how many sinnes ech Man
hath, so many hoat ashes of fire, & so many
seedes

Sinne
the seed
of Hell
fyre.

feedes of flames he hath, as being inuiſibly
encōpaſſed with ſo many flames. Againe,
Sinnes in the holy Scripture are compared
to a matter eaſy to be ſet on fire, as *dry wood,*
hay, chaff, ſtraw, and *thornes*. Who therefore
encreaſeth the number of his ſinnes, gathe-
reth together a combuſtible matter, with
the which he ſhalbe eternally burned. But
to returne more particularly to the former
text : *Walke in the light of your fire,* that is, cō-
tinue in your ſinnes, and increaſe flames,
which you begin to kindle . *This ſhall you*
haue at my hand. Thoſe are the words of
Chriſt, through whoſe iudgment & ſentence the Iewes were deſtroyed by fire ; &
all ſinners (not repenting) ſhall hereafter
be tormented with the ſame.

13.   The 13. *Eſay* 60. *Et egredientur*
&c. And they ſhall goe forth , and looke vpon the
carkaſes of men, that haue trangreſſed againſt me.
Their worme ſhall not dye, neither ſhall their fire
be quenched , and they ſhalbe an abhorring of all
fleſh. The Prophet here calleth. *Carkaſes,* the
bodyes of al the wicked, both becauſe they
ſhalbe like to dead carkaſſes for their filth
& ſtench ; as alſo in that they ſhalbe hurled
and caſt vpon the earth; and finally, by reaſon they ſhal in *Hell* (like carkaſſes)lye vpō
heapes, therefore the ſenſe of this place is
this: Euen as the inhabitants of the heauēly

Ieruſalem

Eſay. 30.
Malach.
4. *Mark.*
25.

Ierusalem shall enioy peace, and see themselues abounding with all goods ; so shall they go forth in consideration and contemplation , and shall behold sinners subiect both in body & in soule to most cruell torments. *Their worme shall not dye,* because inwardly in their soule, they shalbe continually afflicted with the griefe of so great a good lost , & so infinite an euill contracted through their sinnes . *Neither shall their fire be quenched ;* because they shall burne for all eternity , and these paynes they shall suffer in the sight of the Elect .

14. The 14. is in *Daniel c.* 12. *Multi de his &c. Many of them, that sleepe in the dust of the earth , shall awake ; some to euerlasting life, and some to shame and perpetuall contempt.* That is, the iust shall rise againe , that they may enioy eternall saluation ; & sinners, that they may suffer and sustaine endles reproach.

15. The 15. in *Malachy c.* 4. *Ecce dies venit &c. Behold the day commeth , that shall burne as an Ouen ; and all the proud, yea and all that shall do wickedly, shalbe stuble; & the day , that cometh shall burne them vp (saith the Lord of hostes) and shall leaue them neither roote nor branch.* The reason hereof being, because sinners shall vtterly be' rooted out of the earth , so as no remembrance of the shalbe left ; for heere the Prophet speaketh of the
day

day of iudgment.

16. Now we will deſcend to the new
teſtament. And the 16. authority may be
taken from the teſtimony of *S. Iohn Baptiſt* ,
who in Matthew 3. in one ſhort admonition doth thrice inſinuate the paynes of the
life to come. And firſt, when he ſpeaketh
to the Phariſies : *Genimina viperarum &c. O
generation of vipers, who hath forewarned you
to flie from the anger to come?* meaning frō that
eternall reuenge, which hangeth ouerthe
heads of ſinners. Secondly, where he ſaith:
*Omnis ergo arbor &c. Therfore euery tree, which
bringeth not forth good fruite, is hewē downe , &
caſt into the fire.* Thirdly, in theſe words :
Cuius ventilabrum &c. Who *hath his fanne in his
hand, and will make cleane his flowre , & gather
his wheate into his garner; but will burne vp the
chaffe with vnquenchable fire.* For as the huſ-
bandmā with his fanne ſeuereth the chaffe
from the corne; ſo Chriſt by his iudging power ſhall ſeparate the good from the euill,
aſſigning to them their fitting place, lot, or
portion.

17. The 17. is in Marke c. 9. *Si ſcanda-
lizauerit &c. If thy hand cauſe thee to offend ,
cut it off ; It is better for thee to enter into life
may med, then hauing two hands, to goe into Hel,
into the fire that neuer ſhalbe quenched ; where
the worme dyeth not , & the fire neuer goeth out.*

The

The like he faith , touching the wanting
of a foote and an eye. In which words he
inftructeth vs , that all things which giue
occafion of finning, (though they be as
profitable to vs, as the hand, the foot, and
the eye are) are to be forfaken; fince it is
farre more fecure to want temporall benefits and folaces, then to be caft into eternall
fire. And heare we are to obferue, that this
fentence is three tymes repeated by our
Lord, & Sauiour, therby to infinuate both
the certainty of it; as alfo that by the often
iteration of it, it might be firmly imprinted
in the minds of al Chriftians . Heere alfo
we are to note, that it was not fufficiét for
Chrift to fay , *To go into hell into fire that ne-*
uer shalbe quenched , but ingeminating and
doubling the fame, he addeth: *VVhere the*
worme dyeth not , *and the fire neuer goeth out* ;
thus fuggefting to vs twice in one fentence
the eternity of this fire . He further addeth
in the end : *Euery man shalbe falted with fire* ,
and euery facrifice shalbe falted with falt : in
which words he infinuateth the reafó, why
finners are to be burned with fire : for as e-
uery facrifice, which according to the pre-
fcript law was offered to God , was accuftomed to be fpinkled with falt, (according
to that faying of *Leuiticus* 2. *All thy oblations*
thou shalt feafon with falt) fo all finners, feing

E e   hereafter

hereafter they are to become as certaine o-
blations to be sacrificed to the Iustice of
God, are to be seasoned (as it were) with
fire, as with salt; for here sinners are compared to a sacrifice, and fire to salt. And indeed we fynd, that the holy Scripture in
many places calleth the punishment of the
wicked a sacrifice or oblatiō; as in *Esay* 34.
*Victima domini &c. The Lord hath a great sacri-
fice in Bosra, and a great slaughter in the land
of Edom.* And *Ieremy* 46. *The Lord God of hostes hath a sacrifice in the North country by the riuer Euphrates.* And finally in *Ezechiel* 39.
*Assemble your selues, and come, gather your sel-
ues on euery side to my sacrifice, for I do sacrifice
a great sacrifice for you vpon the mountaines of I-
sraell.*

For as beasts were killed in honour of
God to expiate sinnes, and to appease the
wrath of God so the whole multitude of
the wicked shalbe slaine in the last night,
& (after a sort) shalbe sacrificed vnto God,
that their punishment may in some sort satisfy for the sinnes, and so Gods indignatiō
(as being appeased therewith) may ceafe.
Furthermore *fire* is rightly compared to *salt*
for as salt burneth and conserueth the bodyes, wherupon it is sprinkled; so fire burneth the bodyes of the damned; yet in that
sort, as it neuer consumeth them, but euer
keepeth

keepeth them entyre and whole for further torments.

18. The 18. in *Matthew* 10. *Nolite timere &c. Feare you not them, which kill the body , but are not able to kill the soule; but rather feare him, who is able to destroy both soule and body in hell .* And likewise in *Luke* 32. *Dico autem vobis &c.* I say vnto you (my friends) *Be not afraid of them , that kill the body , & after that , are not able to do any more . But I will forewarne you , whome you shall feare: feare him, who after he hath killed , hath power to cast into hell; yea I say vnto you, him feare.* Here S. *Matthew* sheweth that only God is to be feared , and that all Euils of this life are not of any moment or importance , if they be compared with the euils of the life to come , which God can afflict .

19. The 19. *Matthew* 13. where he expresseth the paines of *Hell* in two parables. The first is of the *tares* growing amõg the corne in those words: *ficut colliguntur zizania &c. As the tares are gathered and burned in the fire , so shall it be in the end of the world The sonne of man shall send forth his Angels, & they shall gather out of his kingdome al things, that do offend , and them which do iniquity ; & shall cast them into a furnace of fire . There shalbe wailing and gnashing of teeth . Then shall the iust men shyne (as the sunne) in the kingdome of the Fa*

ther,

ther. Heere by the words, *All that do offend*;
are vnderſtood all thoſe, that either in gouernment, doctrine, counſell or example do
prouoke others to ſinne; ſuch are tyrants,
hereticks, wicked counſellers, and publick
offenders. But thoſe other words: *And the*
which do iniquity, do ſignify other ſinners,
which are the cauſe of their owne iniquities only, withoꝛut giuing occaſiõ to otheꝛs
to ſinne: & all theſe are as hurtfull hearbs,
which being gathered into a bundel ſhalbe
caſt into an euerlaſting fire.

The ſecond Parable is of the Fiſhers-
Net in theſe words: *Sic erit in cõſummatione*
ſæculi: exibunt Angeli &c.. So ſhall it be in the
end of the world. The Angels ſhall goe forth, and
ſeuer the bad from among the luſt. And ſhall caſt
them into a furnace of fyar: there ſhalbe way-
ling, and gnaſhing of teeth.

20. The 20. is taken from the 25. Chap. of
Matthew, where our Lord by diuers parables laboreth firmely to imprint & plant
this doctrine of future rewards and puniſhments in our minds. As firſt, from the parable of the ten Virgins. Secondly from
the parable of the Lord of the family going
from home, and diſtributing to his ſeruáts
his talents, wherewith they were to negotiate. Thirdly, from the ſimilitude of the
ſheepheard, ſeuering the ſheepe from the
goates:

goates : for there we thus read : *Cùm vene-rit filius hominis in Maieſtate ſua, & omnes angeli eius, tum ſedebit ſuper ſedem Maieſtatis ſuæ.*

And then he ſhall ſay to thoſe of his left hand : *Diſcedite a me maledicti in ignem æternū. &c.* *Depart from me, you curſed into euerlaſting fire:* but touching the iuſt, it is thē ſaid. *Come vnto me yee bleſſed of my Father &c.* Heere we ſee the forme of this iudgment , the ſentéce of the iudge, and the eternity of puniſhmēt and reward is moſt clearly and euidently deſcribed by the iudge himſelfe. To con-clude , nothing is more frequently propo-ſed and inculcated, both in Parables , and in other moſt graue ſétences by Chriſt him-ſelfe , then puniſhment and rewards after this life .

21. The 21. The Apoſtle in the ſecōd to the Romans thus ſaith : *Secundum duritié tuam, & impœnitens cor &c.* After thy hardnes &c. thou heapeſt vnto thy ſelfe wrath againſt the day of wrath &c. Heere the multitude of ſinnes are to be accounted as the treaſury of puniſhments; and ech ſinne as a ſeed of e-ternall fire, which except it be waſhed a-way in this life with the teares of true re-pentance, it will hereafter cauſe an vnquē-chable fire.

22. The 22. in the ſecond to the Co-rinthiās 6. 5. *Omnes nos manifeſtari oportet ante*

tribunal

tribunal &c. VVee muſt all appeare before the
iudgment ſeate of *Chriſt,* that euery man may receaue the things, which are done in his body , *ac-*
cording to that , which the hath done , either
good or euill. The like he repeateth in many
other places .

23.   The 23. in the 2. to the *Theſſaloni-*
ans c. 1. *Qui pœnas dabunt &c.* The wicked ſhall
be punished *&c.* Here the Apoſtle ſpeaketh
of all ſinners, who belieue not the Goſpel;
who being depriued of al the goods, which
here they enioyed, ſhall eternally be puniſhed, euen by the iudgment, ſentence and
power of our Lord; and theſe paines they
ſhall endure in the ſight of God himſelfe &
all his Saints; and this ſhall happen to all
them, when our Lord ſhall come , that he
may remunerate his ſeruants with eternall
glory , and transfer them into his moſt glorious kingdome .

24.   The 24. in the ſecõd of *Peter* c. 3 *Cali*
qui nunc ſunt &c. And after he ſaith: *Adueniet*
autem dies domini &c. Laſtly S. *Peter* thus
there addeth . *Cum igitur hæc omnia &c.* to al
which places for greater breuity I referre
the ſtudious Reader; they cõtaynig in thé-
ſelues a moſt dreadful & feareful deſcriptiõ
of the day of iudgment, and of the puniſhment reſerued for the wicked .

25.   The 25. is in the *Apocalyps* c. 14. Si
                                                    qui

quis adorauerit beſtiam &c. Et ſi quis Antichriſto consenserit &c. And c. 20. *Qui non eſt inuētus in libro vita &c.* And c. 21. *Timidis autem & incredulis &c* Heere he calleth thoſe fearful, who throgh teare of death or loſſe of goods depart from the true faith of Chriſt; & thoſe *blinded*, who liue according to the manner of Idolaters; and finally *lyars*, who perniciouſly and dangerouſly do lye; as all periurious and calumnious men doe. All which men (without finall repentance)ſhal burne (as the text ſaith) *in ſtagno ardente igne & ſulphure, quod eſt mors ſecūda: in the lake which burneth with fire and brimſtone , which is the ſecond death.* I here omit many other teſtimonies of ſacred Scripture, by the which the laſt dreadful iudgment, and a remuneratiō after this life is moſt euidently cōfirmed & warranted : for there is no ſentence or article of faith , which is more eſtabliſhed and grounded in Gods holy word , then this is, it being the foundation of all vertue and Iuſtice; Since it more perſwadingly inuiteth man to piety and more vehemētly deterreth him from vice,then any other motiue or cogitation whatſoeuer. Whereupon the wiſeman in the 7. of *Eccleſiaſticus* deſeruedly ſaid. *In omnibus operibus tuis memorare &c. In all thy works remember the end , and thou shalt neuer do amiſſe.*

Ee 4   Neither

Neither is there any iuſt cauſe to ſuſpect that this doctrine of future retribution was firſt excogitated and forged only for policy, & the more eaſily to retaine people in obedience and obſeruation of the lawes; ſince a thing, which is a mere fiction and forgery cannot be ſo powerfull, as to beget probity, innocency, and iuſtice (as aboue we haue ſhewed.) Furthermore, ſuch men as moſt laboured in the diuulging of this doctrine, regarded nothing leſſe then external policy, and temporal domination or gouerment. For they did not only in their owne perſons contemne al worldly matters, as honours, dignities, and all terrene principality; but alſo in their books and writings they taught the ſame to be contēned. It is vſuall to flatterers, and ſuch as gape after the fauour of Princes, to inuent ſuch proiects, which may beſt ſerue for policy, and cauſe the ſtates of thoſe princes to become more illuſtrious, and more permament; with which kind of Sycophants the world at this preſent ſwarmes. To cōclude we may ad hereto, that al thoſe, who were the moſt reſolute maintainers of the foreſaid aſſertion, were indued with wonderfull ſanctity and wiſedome, infuſed euen from heauen; as alſo moſt of them became admirable & moſt eminent for working

king of miracles, & the spirit of Prophecy; so as there is no shew or colour, why we should now call in question the irrefragable truth of the former doctrine.

THE CONCLVSION.

CHAP. XXVI.

QVo ibo a spiritu tuo, & quo a facie tua fugiam? Si ascendero in cælum &c. Whither shall I goe from thy spirit? Or whither shall I flie from thy presence? If I ascend into heauen, thou art there: If I lye downe in Hell, thou art there. Let me take the wings of the morning, and dwell in the vttermost parts of the sea, yet thither shall thy hand lead me, and thy right hand hould me. Woe be to the mynds of mortal men, blinded through their owne malice; woe to the hearts of the foolish encompassed on each side with the darknes of their owne sinnes. Thou (*O most mighty powerfull, and most wise God*) fillest the heauens and the earth, and yet thou art not acknowled God of many; thou art most intimately and inwardly present to al things, & yet art not knowne. Thou createst, informest, nourishest, perfectest, supporst, & gouernest all things, and yet they deny thee to be fountaine & authour of all these things; thou giuest the

Psalm. 138.

being

being to all things, and yet they belieue,
thou haſt no being. Thou manifeſteſt by
infinite meanes & wayes thy power, wiſedome, goodnes, mercy and iuſtice to the
eye of al; and yet diuers of theſe eyes (as being blind) do not perceaue this thy mani-
feſtatiõ. The nature of all things do preach
and proclayne thee, and yet they are deafe
to ſuch a lowd and notorious a proclama-
tion. *The Heauens declare the glory of God, &
the firmament sheweth the works of his hands*.
All things do confeſſe, ſaying, *Ipſe fecit nos
&c*. *He made vs, & not we our ſelues;* neither
are we thus become through any caſuall
concourſe of *Atomies*. It is he, that by his
owne omnipotécy euen out of the darknes
of nothing, brought vs forth into this light.
It is he, who thus hath framed vs, & hath
imprinted in euery one of vs this our ſeuerall pulchritude, ſplendour, and beauty
through the infinitenes of his owne wiſedome. Finally it is he, who through his
goodnes conſerueth, and through his prouidence gouerneth, & directeth ech thing
to its peculiar end. This is the voyce and
language of euery creature in the world;
neither can any one be ignorát hereof, who
is not poſſeſſed with a deafe Diuel. For frõ
whence proced the moſt ſwift reuoluti-
ons of the heauens, but from his *power* and
wiſedome?

Pſal. 18.

Pſal. 99.

wisedome? From whence is that most established and certaine harmony of those celestiall motions, which neuer are intermitted, neuer broke any wauering vncertainty, but euer indeclinable continue in one and the same tenour? From whence are the structures of so many liuing Creatures, & their multiplicious and wonderful formes? From whence those innumerable & most fit and Symmetriall proportiōs both of the parts among themselues, as also of the parts with reference to the whole? Frō whence that different internall temperature of euery part of a naturall body, and that externall most congruent fabrick and conformation of them to their proper function & operations? From whence that stupendious force in seedes, by the which the bodyes of all things, & of all smallest parcels of those bodyes are disposed, framed, and made apt & sorting to their ends? Nothing of these cā be made by it self, since nothing of these is for it selfe. No one of these is an end to it selfe, and therefore no one of thē is a beginning to it selfe. Neither can they receaue their being from *fortune*, or *chance*, for nothing that is firme, constant, regular, and consisting of most due and precise proportions proceed frō these; all their effects being (indeed) changeable, vncertaine, &
full

full of diforder, and confufion.

Therefore it is moft neceffary, that all thefe things do take their beginning from fome *mind* which through its *wifedome* was able to excogitate and inuent fo many wōderful & infinite things, through its *power*, to performe them, & through its *Prouidēce*, to gouerne them. And this *mind* or *intelligēce* we call Thee, being our *Lord* and *God*. Therefore thou art the Origin and fourfe of all things, the efficient caufe of all, the forme of all, the end of all, the fupporter, foundation and conferuation of all. In thee all things do pre-exift, and this not confufedly, but moft ordinately; yet after a fimple and abftracted manner, and in a moft pure effence or being; like as the worke of the artificer lyeth inwardly hid in his vnderftanding, and refteth knowne to him alone, before it becometh an externall and fenfible worke. All things are *in thee, from thee, by thee, for thee, and thou art aboue all things.* For thou art more diffufed & large, then any magnitude; more ancyent, then all eternity; more ftrong then all power; more radiant & fhining then all light; more faire then all beauty; more fweet then all pleafure; more worthy and eleuated then all honour; more intrinficall and inward then any fecret; more high, thē al height;

and

and more low , then any depth. Thou art
moſt ſupreme , and yet beſt; moſt ſtable, &
yet incomprehenſible , moſt powerfull, &
yet moſt benigne ; moſt mercifull, and yet
moſt iuſt ; moſt ſecret, and yet moſt preſent
and inward; moſt faire and yet moſt ſtrong.
Thou art immutable , and yet changeſt all
things ; neuer new , neuer old ; thou rene-
weſt all things, & yet bringeſt the proud
man to decrepit old age. Thou art euer
working, and yet euer quyet , creating,
nouriſhing, and perfecting all things ; ſupporting, filling and protecting all things .
Thou art aboue all, and vnderneath al ; internall with all, and externall to all; aboue
all in gouerning of things , vnderneath in
ſupporting and ſuſtentating of them; internall by penetration, externall by compre-
hending all things within thy large circū-
ference. O how wonderfully and bounti-
fully dealeſt thou with vs, moſt dreadful &
infinite maieſty! *Tu ſolem tuum &c. Thou ma-
keſt the Sunne to ariſe on the euill, and the good;
thou ſendeſt rayne on the iuſt , & the inuſt.* **Mat⸳5⸳**
Thou moſt copiouſly powreſt out the trea-
ſures of thy goodnes vpon thy enemyes ,
which betrample thy law, blaſpheme thy
holy name, deny thy prouidence, and impugne thy Church; enriching them with
all the temporall goods of this life, & inuiting

ting them to a contrite repentance ; that ſo they may be made partakers of thy eternall goods . Thou ſeekeſt vs, yet wanteſt nothing ; thou loueſt, yet art free from heat of deſire ; art angry, yet remaineſt quyet ; repenteſt, yet grieues not; chágeſt thy works, and yet not changeſt thy determinations . Thou art not poore, and yet thou reioyceſt at gaines; not couetous, yet expecteſt vſury; thou repayeſt debts, owing nothing; thou forgiueſt debts, looſing nothing . What more ſhall I ſay, *My God*, *my life*, *Light*, *and ſweetnes of my heart*? What can we ſay, when we ſpeake of thee who aboue all ſpeach art ineffable, and aboue all vnderſtanding incóprehenſible ? Only this we may ſecurely pronounce of thee, that thou art more excellent, then either words can deliuer, or mind conceaue. Woe then be to all thoſe , that are ignorát of thee, *woe*, *woe*, to al ſuch who knowing thee, do not ſerue thee, but contemne thy lawes & commandements. Woe, *woe*, *woe*, to all them, which do either oppugne or reiect (as Atheiſts do) thy wholſome doctrine, which thou haſt reuealed by thy ſonne *Ieſus Chriſt our Lord & Redeemer*, and haſt propoſed to vs by thy ſpouſe the *Church*. Thou, who art the fountaine of al good, ſuffer the beames of thy infinite mercy to ſhyne vpon the miſerable ſoules

of

of all such, that they may acknowledge
their owne cecity, blindnes, and errours;
that they may see the danger of their owne
eternall damnation; that they may imbrace
the certainty of thy doctrine; the which
thou propoundest to all by the Church; and
finally, that they being thus illuminated,
may acknowledge, feare, loue, praise and
reuerence thy Maiesty and prouidéce, both
here during the tyme of this temporall life,
and hereafter for all Eternity. *Amen.*

FINIS.

Gentle Reader,

Pag. 207 . lin. 17 . for ἰγγασρέμυθοι, read
ἰγγαστρέμυθοι.

And if any the like verball faults haue in other
places escaped ; it is desired, thou wouldst be
pleased to correct them , by thy owne iudici-
ous reading